CW00663475

Hesitant Co

Hesitant Comrades

The Irish Revolution and the British Labour Movement

Geoffrey Bell

PLUTO PRESS

First published 2016 by Pluto Press
345 Archway Road, London N6 5AA

www.plutobooks.com

Copyright © Geoffrey Bell 2016

The right of Geoffrey Bell to be identified as the author of this work has been
asserted by him in accordance with the Copyright, Designs and Patents Act 1988.

British Library Cataloguing in Publication Data
A catalogue record for this book is available from the British Library

ISBN   978 0 7453 3665 7   Hardback
ISBN   978 0 7453 3660 2   Paperback
ISBN   978 1 7837 1740 8   PDF eBook
ISBN   978 1 7837 1742 2   Kindle eBook
ISBN   978 1 7837 1741 5   EPUB eBook

Typeset by Stanford DTP Services, Northampton, England

Contents

Acknowledgements

This book began life as a PhD thesis. Thanks to my supervisor Kevin Theakston for guiding me through this and to my external examiner David Howell for his comments. Before all of that, at Trinity College Dublin as an undergraduate, I was fortunate to have David Thornley as my tutor on two specialist courses, European Working Class Movements and Ireland 1913–39. As our tutor group sipped sherry, and occasionally something very Irish and much stronger, my interest in these subjects was nurtured and encouraged. My fellow students who were part of that included Brian Walker, Roger Cole, David Haire, John and Shelia Healy, and Shelia Deedy.

This book is also a product of many conversations and discussions over many years, all of which added to my understanding of political ideas and their application. In Belfast, I would thank my parents, Herbert and Mary Bell, James McBeigh and Liam Barbour. In Derry, there was Eamonn McCann, Dermie McClenaghan and Kitty O'Kane. In Dublin there was Bill Moran, Greg Murphy, Mick and Katherine Ford and Breedge Docherty. In London, Mick Sullivan, Nadine Finch, Tariq Ali, Aly Renwick, Davy Jones, Steve Potter, Hilda Kean, Valerie Coultas and Piers Mostyn. Special thanks to the staff and librarians of the British Library, including the Newspaper Library at and after Colindale, the National Archive, the London School of Economics, the Labour Party Archive, the TUC Archive, the Marx Memorial Library and the National Library of Ireland. Thanks as well to all at Pluto Press for their professionalism and support.

This book is for Mary Margaret McHugh, our daughters Lauren and Iona, and our son Sean. It is they who have taught me most.

Abbreviations

ASLEF	Associated Society of Locomotive Engineers and Firemen
BSP	British Socialist Party
CPGB	Communist Party of Great Britain
ILP	Independent Labour Party
ILPTUC	Irish Labour Party and Trades Union Congress [which succeeded the ITUCLP]
IRA	Irish Republican Army
ISDL	Irish Self-determination League
ITGWU	Irish Transport and General Workers Union
ITUCLP	Irish Trades Union Congress and Labour Party
LRC	Labour Representation Committee
MP	Member of Parliament
NAC	National Administrative Council, ILP
NEC	National Executive Committee, Labour Party
NUR	National Union of Railwaymen
PLP	Parliamentary Labour Party
SLP	Socialist Labour Party
TUC	Trades Union Congress
UVF	Ulster Volunteer Force
WSF	Workers' Suffrage Federation (from 1918, the Workers' Socialist Federation)

Prologue

Afterwards, it was called 'Bloody Sunday'. The blood came from those protesting about British government policy in Ireland. Their march had been declared illegal. Their deaths were at the hands of the police and the British army. It is Sunday, 13 November 1887, Trafalgar Square, London. The demonstration had been organised by the Metropolitan Radical Federation, a socialist, anarchist and labour movement alliance, and the Irish National League, whose activities in Ireland were being increasingly targeted by the Conservative government's Crimes Act. A particular focus of the protest was the 'Mitchelstown Massacre' of September 1887, when police had fired on a crowd of Irish demonstrators in Mitchelstown, County Cork, demanding land reform and fair rent. The police had killed three and wounded two. The outcome of the London demonstration was similar: two dead, 200 demonstrators hospitalised. Next day the *Pall Mall Gazette*, not the most subversive newspaper, gave its version of Bloody Sunday.

AT THE POINT OF A BAYONET

It was a strange grim sight that a hundred thousand Londoners witnessed yesterday ... The Government in the name of the QUEEN, decided to forbid a real, *bona fide* political meeting summoned long before to condemn of the incidents of their coercive policy in Ireland. Therefore London was delivered up to the terrorism of the soldiery and police ... Ruffians in uniform were despatched to ride down and bludgeon law-abiding citizens who were marching in procession towards the rendezvous. Savage scenes of brutality are reported from Westminster from Shaftsbury-avenue and from the Haymarket. The right to procession ... was rudely trampled underfoot ... It is a new experience for Englishmen to see peaceful citizens ridden down at the gallop by police cavalry ... Our Tory Government prefer to rely on the bludgeon, on the bayonet and on buckshot. As a result, Ireland has been brought to the verge of rebellion, and London, if it is persisted upon, will become ungovernable.[1]

It was nearly 30 years later before Ireland passed from the verge to actual rebellion, and London never did become ungovernable. Nevertheless, Trafalgar Square's Bloody Sunday has an historical relevance beyond the drama of the day itself. Those present were both reflecting and passing on a notable inheritance, the nature of which is suggested in some of those who marched that day. They included John Burns, to become a leader of the 1889 London Dock Strike; Eleanor Marx, a socialist and feminist militant and daughter of Karl; William Morris, artist and writer; (Henry) H. M. Hyndman, a leader of the left wing Social Democratic Federation; George Bernard Shaw, the Irish playwright who was already a pamphleteer for the influential left wing Fabian Society; and Ramsey MacDonald, to become the first Labour Prime Minister. They represented an impressive range of radical and socialist activism. They were also representing a legacy.

Long before that particular Bloody Sunday, there is a significant history of British radicalism identifying with the cause of Ireland, whether that was self-rule, land reform, Catholic emancipation or opposition to coercion. Only the outlines need be sketched here, but this stretches back at least as far as the Levellers and other radicals of the seventeenth-century English revolution, who made public their objection to Cromwell's military expeditions against the Irish.[2] This tradition was carried on by some English Jacobins in the late eighteenth century, notably the London Corresponding Society, 'the first political association in Britain which largely consisted of working class people'.[3] In January 1798 the London Corresponding Society published the *Address to the Irish Nation*, which protested against British government coercion in Ireland.

During the early nineteenth century radical individuals, organisations and newspapers who expressed sympathy with the Irish national cause included William Sherwin in his weekly *Political Register* (1817), Richard Carlile in *Gauntlet* (1833), the *Cap of Liberty*, (1819) and Henry Hunt in *Address from the People of Great Britain to the People of Ireland* (1820). There was also the National Union of the Working Class which, in 1832, fused with the London-based Irish Anti-Union Association and added repeal of the union between Britain and Ireland to its aim of radical parliamentary reform.[4] This latter goal was most spectacularly pursued in the first half of the nineteenth century by the Chartists in whose ranks there developed the most sustained attempt to coalesce British radicalism with Irish nationalism. To the fore was Irish Member of Parliament (MP)

Fergus O'Connor, one of the leaders of the Chartists, and he and those who thought like him were successful in securing repeal of the union in the second petition of the Chartists in 1842.

There is an alternative tradition. As Irish immigration into Britain grew in the eighteenth and nineteenth centuries, there were frequent physical clashes between the Irish in Britain and the rural and industrial proletariat. The background to these events varied – native xenophobia, religious differences and the use of the Irish as cheap labour or strike-breakers – but they broke out often enough and in enough different areas to suggest that those who sought to establish an identity of interests between the native and Irish common peoples did not always do so in the most conducive of atmospheres. For example, there were anti-Irish riots in Liverpool in 1819 and 1835, Preston in 1837, Penrith in 1846, Stockport in 1852, London in 1858, Birmingham in 1867 and various towns in Lancashire in 1868.[5]

Whatever the social tensions or political affiliations, by the closing decades of the nineteenth century, the issue of Ireland had become difficult to ignore. The rise of the Irish Home Rule movement under the leadership of Charles Parnell and the accompanying land agitation thrust themselves to the centre of the British political stage. Indeed, British parliamentary politics and general elections were dominated on occasions by the politics of Ireland and in particular the Irish policies of Gladstone. There was also action on the streets. In the 1870s and 1880s there was agitation in England and Scotland in support of the Irish Land League, with a demonstration in London in 1879, protesting against the imprisonment of its leaders, attracting 100,000 people according to the *Irish Times*. Similarly, a Hyde Park protest against an Irish coercion bill in April 1887 was attended by between 100,000 and 150,000.[6] These protests would have attracted Irish immigrants who, following the Great Hunger of 1846–47, had come to Britain as never before. According to census figures, Irish residents in Britain increased from 419,256 in 1841 to 806,000 in 1861, although that probably underestimated the real numbers. It seems safe to assume that some of these were bitter or angry enough about British government policies in Ireland to find their way to Hyde Park or Trafalgar Square to demonstrate against them. But even with that consideration, the tradition of English native involvement in protest against their government's policies in Ireland remained very alive, at least until the end of the 1880s. In short, the Bloody Sunday protest was not an isolated example. Indeed when one of these demonstrators, Hyndman, founded the Democratic Federation in 1881, the forerunner of the Social Democratic Federation, one of its chief preoccupations was Ireland.[7] Yet even Hyndman could, on occasion, acknowledge that it was not always the case of proletarian hands eagerly stretching across the Irish Sea. In February 1884 his newspaper *Justice* insisted that the 'real allies' of 'English workers' were the Irish, but admitted 'little as they [the English workers] realise it.'[8]

The defeat of Gladstone's Home Rule bills in 1886 and 1893, the fall of Parnell over a divorce scandal, splits in his party, his death and the attempt of a Conservative government to 'kill Home Rule by kindness' meant that from the early 1890s the Irish issue lost its prominence in British politics. It re-emerged after the 1910 election when a Liberal government became dependent on trying to secure a measure of Irish Home Rule for its own parliamentary survival. By then though, and certainly in the years leading up to the outbreak of the Great War, the nature of the 'Irish Question' was evolving and those who wished to try and answer the question needed to revise their understanding of it. Nevertheless, at least those on the left could look to their own history for guidance. Or, to put it another way, they had a tradition of solidarity to remember.

I

Easter 1916

The British labour movement and James Connolly were well acquainted. ✳
Connolly, born in Edinburgh in 1868 of Irish parents, had from his youth
immersed himself in socialism and trade unionism. In Scotland, Ireland
and the United States he became a workers' leader, agitator and Marxist
writer. He met, worked with or argued against many of the famous British
socialists of his generation, including H. M. Hyndman, Eleanor Marx
and Keir Hardie. Then, in Dublin, Easter 1916, he led his Irish Citizen
Army to fight side by side with combatants from another, but particularly
Irish, tradition: that of Irish Republicanism or Fenianism. At first glance
this seemed a peculiar alliance; a socialist whose theory insisted it was
class allegiance that mattered joining with those who stressed national
identity. Connolly realised there were those who would ask questions.
Within days of the defeat of the alliance he had been executed, but just
before his death he asked his daughter, Nora, if she had read the socialist
papers. He said, 'They will never understand why I am here'. He added,
'They will all forget that I am an Irishman'. That was never going to be
a sufficient explanation.

Guns in Dublin and Beyond

The Irish Republican Brotherhood and, as a junior partner, the Irish
Citizen Army seized Dublin's main post office on Easter Monday 1916
and declared the establishment of the Irish Republic. So began Ireland's
Easter Rising, an insurrection against British rule. The 'rebellion', as
British politicians preferred to call it, lasted less than a week and ended
in surrender. The dead included 450 Irish and 100 British soldiers. In the
immediate aftermath 14 leaders of the Rising were shot by the British
military authorities. One hundred and sixty others were charged and
imprisoned for offences connected to the Rising, and 1,862 men and five
women were deported to England and interned without trial. Many of
these had no involvement in the Rising.

Before the Rising, the political leadership in Ireland was held by the Irish Parliamentary Party – or Nationalists – led by John Redmond, which advocated devolution or Home Rule but supported the maintenance of the constitutional link with Britain. After Easter 1916 the leadership passed to Sinn Féin who, following the example of the Rising, sought the establishment of an independent Irish Republic. The contest for that Republic, against the British government and minority opinion in Ireland, mainly in the northeast, dominated the politics of Ireland for the next five and a half years. It also became an issue of contention within Britain itself and attracted significant international attention. These were revolutionary times when, at their end, one existing political system and state formation was replaced by another. That was signposted with the signing of the Articles of Agreement for a Treaty Between Great Britain and Ireland (or Anglo–Irish Treaty) in December 1921.

The verdict of the vast majority of historians of these years, Irish and British, is that the British overreacted to the Rising, creating martyrs and giving the impression that they were no longer interested in 'Justice for Ireland', to recall the mission of William Gladstone who a generation before had tried to enact Irish Home Rule. In the aftermath of the Rising different emotions held sway. When the British government's Chief Secretary for Ireland and Liberal Member of Parliament, Augustine Birrell, did the decent thing and stood down because the Rising was on his watch, he referred to it in his resignation speech to the House of Commons as, 'this great evil'.[1] The passing of a few years did not always calm emotions. Also in the Commons, more than four and a half years after the event, another Chief Secretary and Liberal MP, Sir Hamar Greenwood, told the Commons, 'I always think that the rebellion of 1916 was the greatest crime in modern history.'[2]

What fuelled such overreaction was not just the traditional emotionalism to which British politicians have often been prone when Irish disaffection is concerned but also, in this instance, the fact that in 1916 the United Kingdom and the British Empire were at war. Thus not only would the British define the Rising as a rebellion in normal circumstances, it was especially traitorous because the rest of the 'nation' was involved in a life and death struggle for what was, many assumed, its very existence.

The Great War had commenced in August 1914 and, although it had not done so with unanimous support in Britain and Ireland, certainly there was majority backing, especially after war had been declared. Two examples, relevant to what follows, can be given. The first is Redmond. The war's outbreak had been accompanied by what was, for him, a dream realised, the promise of Home Rule. While the application of the relevant legislation was postponed until the end of the war or for two years, whichever came later, and while the legislation itself had included a proposed partition of Ireland, temporary or longer it was not clear, nevertheless the pledge was there. With this in his pocket Redmond declared his Irish Volunteers, a private militia originally raised to ensure previous promises of Home Rule were kept, would now become an army of defence against any German invasion. He took this to its logical conclusion telling his soldiers to 'account yourselves as men, not only in Ireland but wherever the firing line extends'. He thus became a recruiter for the British war effort and its army. As many as 50,000 Irishmen enlisted in the first six months, 140,000 in all. Redmond's encouragement was only one of many reasons for this, but undoubtedly one it was.[3]

The second relevant example of the pro-war sentiment is the British labour movement. That is defined here and throughout as the Labour Party, its political affiliates, most notably the Independent Labour Party (ILP) and Fabian Society, the trade unions as represented by the Trades Union Congress (TUC) and those left-wing socialist parties or groups outside the Labour Party, such as the British Socialist Party (BSP). Not all of these supported participation in the war. Indeed, on the eve of the conflict, there was the following:

Hold vast demonstrations against war in every industrial centre ... There is no time to lose ... Workers, stand together therefore for peace! Combine and conquer the militarist enemy and the self-seeking Imperialists to-day, once and for all. ... Down with class rule. Down with the rule of brute force. Down with war. Up with the peaceful rule of the people.

(Signed on behalf of the British Section of the International Socialist Bureau.)
August 1 1914
J. Keir Hardie
Arthur Henderson

Hardie and Henderson were leaders of the Labour Party, the International Socialist Bureau was the organising body of the Second International or Socialist International to which Labour, the ILP, the Fabians and the BSP were affiliated. The International had warned of capitalist war and declared resistance to it in numerous conference resolutions and speeches from the 1890s onwards. They turned out to be mere words. Only the major socialist parties in Russia, Serbia and Ireland opposed the war. One of the signatories of the above, Arthur Henderson, was soon putting his name to another document, issued by leaders of British trade unions, supporting participation in the war and declaring that the reason for the conflict was that Germany was 'seeking to become the dominant power in Europe, with the Kaiser the dictator over all.' The other signatory of the previous statement, Keir Hardie, the first ever Labour MP and first Labour Party leader, continued to oppose the war as did the ILP both on largely pacifist grounds. Hardie died a broken man the following year.

In the month the war began, the TUC and the Labour Party leaderships declared an industrial truce for the duration of the conflict. The same month, the Labour Party declared an electoral truce. Arthur Henderson became leader of the Parliamentary Labour Party (PLP), succeeding Ramsay MacDonald who had opposed the war. Henderson became a member of the coalition government in May 1915, an enrolment overwhelmingly endorsed at the TUC conference in September 1915 and the Labour Party conference in January 1916. The leadership of the trade unions agreed to the Treasury Agreements of March 1915 and the Munitions of War Act of July 1915 which outlawed strikes and imposed compulsory arbitration. In early 1916, when the government introduced conscription, although the Labour Party and trade union leaderships opposed the bill when it was tabled, a special party conference decided to offer no further opposition. In pursuit of victory in the war all other political matters which had preoccupied minds prior to August 1914 were put aside by most leading protagonists, be it the suffragettes campaigning for votes for women, Irish Home Rulers and those resisting them, or the leaders of the growing tide of industrial militancy. Even the left-wing BSP supported the war. As MacDonald declared, 'when this war broke out organised Labour in this country lost the initiative. It became a mere echo of the old governing classes' opinion.'[4]

The British Left and Ireland, 1916

The Labour Party was established in 1906, its precursor, the Labour Representation Committee (LRC) in 1900. By the second general election of 1910 it had secured 42 seats in the House of Commons – all but one of which were in constituencies where the Liberals did not stand, the consequence of early Liberal and Labour cooperation. By 1916 Labour had a membership of 2,220,000, but these were in trade unions and political organisations that affiliated to the party en masse; Labour did not have individual membership until 1918. The early motivation for the party sprang from the desire to increase working class representation in parliament and to reverse anti-trade union legislation. Many of the early prominent figures in the party reflected such concerns. For example, Henderson had started his political life as a Liberal, and while he became a trade union leader in the North of England he was a negotiator rather than a strike caller, someone who favoured employers and unions coming together to resolve difference rather than confronting each other. His non-conformist preaching and temperance advocacy underlined his actual and political sobriety.[5]

What ideology Labour had in these early years tended to be supplied by its two major political affiliates, the ILP and the Fabian Society. The ILP had been formed in 1893 and while it was more explicitly political than the pre-1918 Labour Party its largely working class membership ranged from Lib/Lab to Marxist, although subjectively, 'most rank and file members of the ILP and certainly all of its activists saw themselves as socialist crusaders.'[6] The ILP's membership at the outbreak of war was between 20,000 and 30,000 and it was to rise considerably during the war, which suggests the pro-war consensus was not as all-embracing as might appear.[7] The Fabian Society took no position on the war, although the majority of its membership supported it.[8] The Fabians had been established in 1884 and while during its first 30 years its members never exceed several thousand, its influence through its essays, tracts, leaflets and policy blueprints was much greater than this suggests. Its politics were eclectic: they were in favour of reform, not revolution; they were practical rather than theoretical; they were progressive, often claimed to be socialist, but of the gradualist variety. Thus they fitted in well with the early Labour Party and were by 1918, its leading historian has concluded, more influential in the party than the ILP.[9] The first significant ideological statement of the party, *Labour and the New Social Order*, was written in 1918 by the prominent Fabian Sidney Webb.

Larger than the Fabian and way to its left was the BSP, the successor to the Social Democratic Federation, still led in 1914, by H. M. Hyndman. Its membership then at 13,875 had fallen to 7,335 in 1916.[10] Many who left disagreed with Hyndman's support for the war, as did many who stayed. Accordingly, the BSP's Easter 1916 also had its drama. It was then, at the party's annual conference, that the pro-war position of the leadership was defeated and replaced by a call for an end to hostilities and peace by negotiation. The other major decision taken by the 1916 conference was to affiliate to the Labour Party.

Of those political organisations outside and to the left of the Labour Party, and anti-war, the most significant were the Socialist Labour Party (SLP) and the Workers' Suffrage Federation (WSF). Both were, by and large, confined to specific geographical areas. For the SLP this was Scotland, particularly Glasgow, while the WSF's base was in the East End of London and, to a lesser extent, in South Wales. Neither had a membership in four figures. It is worth emphasising that the SLP was by no means the most influential or largest working class political organisation in Glasgow. That role was filled by the Glasgow ILP, which since 1906 had been well-served by the weekly newspaper *Forward*, which, although independent, was dominated by the ILP and, by the outbreak of the war, was the most widely-read socialist newspaper in Glasgow.[11]

The WSF was under the leadership of Sylvia Pankhurst, and had emerged from the suffragette movement led by her mother Emmeline through the Women's Social and Political Union. The two had fallen out in 1913 with Sylvia forming the East London Federation of Suffragettes the following year. Significantly, one of the reasons for the split was Sylvia's appearance on a platform supporting the workers of the Dublin Lock-out, which was seen by Emmeline and another of her daughters Christabel as compromising the independence of the Women's Social and Political Union. The Workers' Suffrage Federation evolved from the East London Federation of Suffragettes and the Women's Suffrage Federation.

Such, briefly, was the British labour world in the second decade of the twentieth century. One further part of that world, relevant here, can be noted, that of Irish ethnicity. Labour MPs Jack Jones and James Parker were from Irish Catholic families, as was another Labour MP, James O'Grady, who spent 15 years as a union organiser in Belfast. Others prominent in the Labour Party in this period with Irish connections included J. R. Clynes, the son of an evicted Irish peasant, Ramsay MacDonald, who was an election agent in a Belfast by-election in 1905, Bruce Glasier, who had visited Ireland on behalf of the Fabians in 1899, and Keir Hardie himself who had worked with the leader of the Irish Land League Michael Davitt and, in 1898, had given a loan of £50 for the newspaper *Workers Republic* to James Connolly.[12] There were also the Irish connections of those who went on to establish the Communist Party in 1920. When the party was founded it included 'a large number of Irishmen', according to one historian,[13] and the party's first chairman, Arthur MacManus, was the son of a Fenian. McManus was schooled in the SLP, and other sons of the Irish and important SLP protagonists included Willie Gallagher and J. T. Murphy. Most notable of all perhaps was that the SLP's first national organiser in 1903 had been James Connolly. Others in the British labour movement with Irish birth included George Bernard Shaw and the left wing miners' leader Robert Smillie. There were also those who became well acquainted with the politics of Ireland through living side by side with Irish communities in Britain. In 1914 George Lansbury, a future leader of the Labour Party, was editor of the independent left-wing *Daily Herald,* and then of the weekly *Herald* for the duration of the war. In his autobiography, written in 1928, he relates his early childhood in Bethnal Green, East London, in the late 1860s:

> The Irish boys at our school were all 'Fenians'. Consequently, when the walls of Clerkenwell Prison were blown apart [the Clerkenwell Explosions] and the Irish martyrs were executed in Manchester [Manchester Martyrs] very great excitement prevailed. The teachers tried to make us understand how wicked the Irishmen were, but my friends would have none of it and when a few months later T. D. Sullivan's song *God Save Ireland* came out, we boys were shouting it at the top of our voices every playtime.[14]

Lansbury also tells of how in 1887 he organised a delegation of East London workers to visit Ireland 'and see what crimes were being committed in their name' by the British;[15] and then how he supported the Dublin workers in the 1913 Lock-out.[16] The newspaper also had the left-wing Irishman W. P. Ryan on its staff.

Obviously, it took more than a scattering of Irish people in the British labour movement to comprehend what was to occur in Dublin in 1916. It also needed an understanding of the politics of Ireland gained through discussion and policy formulation. How well equipped was British labour in that respect? To give a one word answer, poorly. The LRC never formulated a policy on Ireland, and it was not until 1918 that the first debate on the issue took place at a Labour Party conference. As has been indicated, this was not surprising because the Labour Party was generally light on policy on many issues before 1918. Moreover, the lack of collective discussion did not necessarily mean there were no opinions. In May 1907 the deputy leader of the Labour Party, David Shackleton, told the House of Commons that Labour MPs were 'strong Home Rulers before we were ever constituted as a separate party',[17] and in 1912 James Parker made a similar, although exaggerated, point when he said 'I have known most of the members of the [Parliamentary] Labour Party for ten to twenty years, and I believe there is not a man amongst them who has not been an advocate of Home Rule for years before he came to this House.'[18] The following year the Labour Party did adopt an Irish policy, although almost by accident. This was when the 1913 conference voted to endorse the Parliamentary Report and Presidential Address given by Labour MP George Roberts. By so doing, the party ratified those sections of both reports that referred to the support given by the PLP to the Government of Ireland Bill of 1912. Under its terms Ireland was to be given Home Rule, which in this case consisted of a parliament for internal affairs, with limited powers. The Westminster parliament would retain control of defence, relations with the crown, customs and excise, and, initially, the police. In explaining the support given to this bill, the Parliamentary Report of 1913 spoke of 'definite promises made to the constituencies',[19] and indeed just under two-thirds of the election addresses of Labour candidates in the first 1910 general election had included support for some form of Irish Home Rule.[20] This suggests that at that time support for Home Rule was almost an assumed part of Labour Party policy, even though it had not been endorsed by the authoritative body of party conference. Why such a policy was adopted was explained by James Parker when he told the House of Commons during the debate on the Government of Ireland Bill, 'We stand for Home Rule because we believe the mass of working people have the right to decide what form of government they shall have'.[21] Abiding by the wishes of the Irish people also meant, for the party at that time, abiding by the wishes of the Irish Nationalist Party in the House of Commons. When, in 1913, the Irish Trades Union Congress and Labour Party (ITUCLP) objected to this practice saying the Labour Party should, as a priority, refer to them on Irish matters, Labour's leaders defended themselves by saying that as the Nationalists were the political representatives of the majority of the Irish it was only right they, the Labour party, should take their counsel.[22] There was certainly a democratic logic in such reasoning, and at the time it was unlikely that anyone paused to consider what Labour's attitude would be if an Irish majority opted for an alternative political leadership.

The lack of formal discussion in the Labour Party was repeated elsewhere. Ireland was not mentioned in the programme of the ILP when it was established in 1893 and, as with the LRC/Labour Party, was not formally discussed in conference until 1918. This lack of a national policy allowed local branches, if they bothered to take up the issue, to say anything they wanted, and although ILP branches generally favoured Home Rule, especially in Scotland,[23] there were exceptions. In 1895 an ILP by-election candidate in Bristol East opposed Home Rule, and in the same year a candidate in Preston avoided the issue.[24] In 1912 Liverpool ILP sympathetically reported an Orange demonstration in the city against Home Rule, in an attempt to find favour with the local Protestant working class.[25]

Even the BSP did not discuss Ireland in conference, from its founding annual conference in 1912 until 1918. As for the Fabian Society, it did have a policy of sorts, as set out in a pamphlet in 1900, *Local Government in Ireland*, which preferred effective local councils to Home Rule, and which showed little sympathy to Irish self-government.[26] Of other organisations, the SLP needs particular mention. This is because it has been suggested that it was 'involved in the preliminaries to the Easter Rising'.[27] The only evidence to substantiate this claim is that when James Connolly's *Irish Worker* was suppressed in 1915, the SLP printed it in Glasgow and Arthur MacManus took copies to Dublin.[28] It is rather stretching the facts to suggest that this amounted to involvement in the Rising, especially, as will be seen shortly, because the SLP's reaction to it was the most circumspect of all on the British left.

The limited discussion outlined here would have been entirely understandable if the issue of Ireland had been a political side show in Britain. But it certainly had not been in the years 1912–14 when the Liberal government had sought to implement Home Rule and roused enormous controversy for so doing. The outlines of that settlement in the Government of Ireland Bill has already been noted, but limited although the proposed self-government aroused enormous hostility, especially from Ulster Unionists and the British upper class. The former organised a private army, the Ulster Volunteer Force (UVF), to oppose Home Rule; the leadership of the Conservatives supported this resistance. Sections of the British Army also supported it when a group of officers stationed at the Curragh camp in Ireland threatened mutiny if ordered to enforce Home Rule. King George V also showed pro-Unionist sympathies. On the nationalist side, following the lead of the UVF, the Irish Volunteers had been organised. It was only the outbreak of the Great War which froze this accelerating crisis.[29] One summation of existing research into these affairs has concluded that they represent 'the most dangerous conflict in British and Irish politics since the seventeenth century'.[30] Another has suggested that while it would be 'stacking the evidence' to say the British government joined the war to avoid the Irish issue, nevertheless 'it is inconceivable that it had no influence.'[31] Certainly, there were those in the socialist world outside Britain who attached great significance to these developments. The comment from one Vladimir Ilyich Lenin on the Curragh mutiny and the support it received from Conservatives was that it was, 'an epoch-making turning point, the day when the noble landowners of Britain tore the British constitution to shreds.' He concluded, 'this lesson will not be lost upon the British labour movement, the working class will now quickly proceed to shake off its philistine faith in the scrap of paper called the British law and constitution.'[32] This may be an example of misplaced revolutionary optimism if ever there was one; however, as will be illustrated shortly, some of the lessons of these years were referred to on the British left when discussions on the Rising occurred.

Reactions

Like many in Britain the Easter Rising took the British labour movement by surprise. Take the example of J. H. (John Henry) Thomas, former train driver, prominent Labour MP and General Secretary of the National Union of Railwaymen (NUR). He had had run-ins with James Connolly and his Irish friends before. Most notably in 1913, when he had successfully prevented his trade union members from taking solidarity action in support of other trade unionists led by James Larkin and Connolly in the Dublin Lock-out. 'A double-eyed traitor to his class', was how the rarely forgiving Larkin described him.[33] Nevertheless, Thomas knew his own world well and was a reliable witness when he wrote in May 1916 of the 'sorrow and amazement' with which Labour's leaders reacted to the Rising. He also maintained, 'there was no Labour leader in this country who did not deplore the recent rebellion in Ireland'.[34] Others, including some to the left of Thomas, were indeed condemnatory. It was nearly 50 years since George Lansbury had sung *God Save Ireland* in his London playground, but Easter 1916 did not see a repeat performance. The initial comment on the Rising of his *Herald*, then the most popular and anti-war independent left-wing journal in England, was, 'No lover of peace can do anything but deplore the outbreak in Dublin.' The editorial went on to maintain that the Rising was 'fighting between men of the same nation', although there was an acknowledgment that 'extreme nationalists ... have always claimed separation'. Nevertheless the conclusion was robust: 'that, we repeat, cannot prevent us from deploring that they have sought to gain separation by bloodshed.'[35]

These remarks were located within a pacifist framework. The front-page article in the same issue of *Herald* declared, 'we are against all wars – civil wars no less than wars between nations', and a similar starting point for assessing the Rising was adopted by the ILP. Its weekly newspaper, *Labour Leader*, proclaimed, 'we are opposed to armed force, whether it be under the control of the government or a Labour organisation.[36] Its next issue went on to 'condemn as strongly as anyone those who were immediately responsible for revolt.'[37] *Socialist Review*, the theoretical journal the ILP, then under the editorship of John Bruce Glasier, repeated these themes:

> In no degree do we approve of the Sinn Féin rebellion. We do not approve of armed rebellion at all, any more than any other form of militarism or war. Nor do we plead the rebels' cause ... Nor complain against the government (and the rebels themselves do not complain) for having opposed and suppressed armed Rebellion by force.[38]

However, in the same issue *Socialist Review* did publish an article by Eva Gore-Booth, the poet and sister of Countess Markievicz who, as a member of the Irish Citizen Army, played a leading part in the Rising. Although the editorial in *Socialist Review* distanced itself from this article, *The Sinn Féin Rebellion*, and although it was not an unqualified justification for the Rising, it did attempt to explain why it had occurred, arguing that 'desperation' had 'found an outlet in the rebellion.' A similar approach was shared by the *Call*. This was the weekly newspaper of the anti-war wing of the BSP and was to become the official voice of the party on 1 June 1916. So while formally its initial comments on the Rising were not made with official party approval, the BSP's Easter 1916 conference made it clear that the *Call* did generally reflect majority opinion in the party. Its first comment on the events in Dublin was:

> In the absence of more reliable information concerning the Irish rebellion ... we refrain from making any exhaustive comment on this latest phase of the war for liberation. We have no hesitation, however, in fixing full responsibility for the antecedents of the affair on the shoulders of successive British governments.[39]

Two weeks later, the opinion was:

> To rise as the men in Dublin rose, with inadequate force, in order to measure their strength with those whom they regarded as foes was foolish, and like every such rising was doomed. We ... can understand this effort of the Irish people to throw off the alien yoke. Might we not have believed that when England is abroad fighting for smaller nations, she would exercise clemency for those beneath her rule, who, rightly or wrongly, feel the Irish nation should be as free as the Belgium people or the Serbs?[40]

The organisation which was most sympathetic to the Rising was the Women's Suffrage Federation, soon to become the Workers' Suffrage Federation. In this organisation's *Woman's Dreadnought*, the initial reaction of editor Sylvia Pankhurst was, 'Justice can make but one reply to the Irish Rebellion and that is the demand that Ireland should be allowed to govern itself.'[41] Pankhurst went on to describe the Rising as 'reckless', but added 'their desperate venture was undoubtedly animated by high ideals'.[42] She concluded, 'We understand why rebellion breaks out in Ireland and we share the sorrow of those who are weeping today for the Rebels whom the government has shot.'[43] This was a different 'sorrow' than the one Thomas had spoken of, being engendered by the executions of the leaders of the Rising which followed its defeat. The following issue of *Woman's Dreadnought* (18 May) had what was, journalistically, the most vivid coverage of the immediate aftermath of the Rising in the British left press and indeed arguably in any section of the British press. This was headlined 'SCENES FROM THE REBELLION' and was written by a young Irishwomen, Patricia Lynch, then living in London and a political associate of Pankhurst who had gone to Dublin to compile her eyewitness report. It contained interviews with British soldiers, working class Dubliners, mainly women, and relatives of those who fought. 'I saw that in Ireland the attitude towards the rebels taken by many, even those who condemn the rising, is one of esteem, admiration and even love', wrote Lynch, adding, 'If not one leader had been shot, if clemency, toleration had been the order, the rebellion would indeed have been at an end.' Lynch, in later life, was to become one of Ireland's greatest writers of fiction for children.

Others in the labour movement were also critical of the executions. *Labour Leader*, while still insisting that the rebellion was a 'crime', expressed its 'horror and shame' when they occurred.[44] A similar attitude was adopted by the *New Statesman*, the unofficial voice of the Fabians. It condemned the Rising as 'madness', but even this initial response included advising the government to 'avoid conferring the martyr's crown upon the ring leaders of this non-popular revolt.'[45] When this recommendation was ignored and the first three executions were carried out there was alarm:

Nothing, it seems to us, is more to be regretted in connection with the Dublin tragedy than the hasty decision to execute the ringleaders. We question not the justice of this decision – as human justice is generally reckoned – but its wisdom ... A week ago these three men were recognised as foolish firebrands who had imperilled the welfare of their country, and as such were execrated by the great mass of their fellow citizens But now ... in the heart of every Irishman their names are added to the long list of heroes and martyrs who have died at English hands for the sake of Ireland's freedom.[46]

If this was a somewhat pragmatic view, albeit a perceptive one, Fabian Bernard Shaw, argued against the executions on more principled grounds. In doing so he was one of the first public figures to protest when he wrote a letter to the *Daily News*. First he said, 'the men who were shot in cold blood ... were prisoners of war and therefore it was entirely incorrect to shoot them.' Then he said, 'an Irishman resorting to arms to achieve the independence of his country is only doing what an Englishman would do if it be their misfortune to be invaded and conquered by the Germans in the course of the present war.'[47] *Socialist Review* also said the participants in the Rising should have been treated as prisoners of war when it condemned the government's 'needless harshness and excess' and 'above all the shooting of the men in cold blood after the rebellion was suppressed.'[48] A similar comment was made in *The Call*,[49] but others were more equivocal. The *Herald* wavered from its pacifism when it did not condemn the executions outright. Instead, Lansbury singled out James Connolly with a special pleading: 'We all hope the executions will have been stayed before his turn comes'.[50]

The one Labour politician to speak in Parliament on the Rising in its immediate aftermath was Will Thorne, MP for West Ham. Thorne was also a union leader and a war enthusiast, joining the 1st Volunteer battalion of the Essex Regiment at the start of the conflict and becoming a lieutenant colonel. He had also some knowledge of Ireland having visited there on union business many times. On one such occasion, he was to recall in his autobiography, at a meeting in Wexford he noticed members of the Royal Irish Constabulary taking notes of what he was saying at a public meeting. This, he wrote 'was a new experience to me' and when he asked the police what they were doing he was told to 'mind my own business'.[51] That brush with British law and order in Ireland did not noticeably prejudice him when it came to the Rising. His reaction to the executions when the first three were announced was, if not exactly to demand more, then certainly to travel along that path. On 3 May in the House of Commons, he asked, 'Can the Prime Minister state when the man, Sir Roger Casement, is going to be tried? He was the forerunner of this movement.'[52] Casement was involved in the Rising through his largely unsuccessful efforts to obtain German practical support for it. Although Prime Minister Asquith assured Thorne that Casement would indeed be put on trial, five days later Thorne returned to the theme this time asking the Attorney General, 'when [will] the military authorities propose to proceed with the trial?'[53] Thorne eventually got his wish when Casement was tried in late June and then executed.

More ambiguous was the reaction of Arthur Henderson, then a member of the War Cabinet. He was reported by *Forward* as cheering when the first three executions were announced in the Commons, something which he always disputed.[54] James Connolly's execution came after these first three and Henderson's first biographer, the very friendly Mary Agnes Hamilton, says he tried to prevent this, but no evidence for this was produced in the biography or has surfaced subsequently. When Henderson himself was later forced to comment on his role he said, 'Connolly was executed before I knew anything about it'.[55] This assertion does at least square with the government handing over responsibility for such matters to the military authorities in Dublin, under the control of General Maxwell.

Forward itself was one of the most critical of both the Rising and Connolly's role in it, even though Connolly had often written for the newspaper. His participation in the Rising was, for *Forward*'s editor, Tom Johnston 'mysterious and astounding', and the Rising itself he described as, 'not only a futile insurrection but one in which the insurrectionists were apparently being used as pawns and tools by the German government.'[56] Elsewhere the same issue of *Forward* added a few more insults and repeated the mistaken assumption that it was all a German plot:

> Call it madness or badness or both, it is impossible for an ordinary person to see what good the rebels hoped for even if they were successful ... The most reasonable explanation yet given is that the outbreak was part of a general scheme now on foot whereby Germany hopes to shatter British nerves and send us all to our beds.

Like others, *Forward* was critical of the executions, but tactically rather than ideologically. 'Nothing could be more likely to give a fresh lease of life to these rebellious elements' was the argument, but one which was prefaced with a renewed denunciation of the 'rebels ... absolute folly, folly military, political and moral'.[57]

Such opinions were a reflection of those held generally. British public opinion appears to have approved of the executions[58] and, according to John Redmond, 'the mass of the Irish people reacted to the Rising with detestation and horror'.[59] The extent to which this is true remains disputed[60] and there is some indication that the Dublin working class was not as hostile as previously been suggested.[61] Certainly though, the influential in Ireland were in no doubt. The *Freeman's Journal*, a supporter of the Nationalists and Ireland's most popular newspaper, said the Rising was, 'an armed assault against the will and decisions of the Irish nation'.[62] The Unionist *Irish Times* insisted, 'The rapine bloodshed of the past week must be punished with a severity that will make impossible any repetition of them for years to come'.[63] The *Irish Independent*, whose proprietor William Martin Murphy was the primary opponent of Connolly and Larkin in the Dublin Lock-out denounced the, 'insane and criminal rising'[64] and, when there was a lull in the executions and Connolly remained alive, called for them to be continued.[65] The Rising was also fiercely criticised by the *Cork Examiner*, *The Irish Catholic* and the leaders of the Protestant and Catholic Churches in Ireland.[66] This hostility was shared by the leading newspaper for the Irish in Britain, the *Catholic Herald*, which denounced the Rising's leaders as 'crazy fanatics'[67] and went on to support the executions.[68] As for the Irish labour movement, it sought to distance itself from the Rising. The ITUCLP, which Connolly had done much to establish, decided, in the words of the presidential address at its conference in August 1916, 'this is not the place to enter into a discussion as to the right or wrong, wisdom or folly of the revolt.'[69] Socialists outside Britain and Ireland were also, in general, unsympathetic. Some European ones dismissed the Rising as a *putsch*, especially the Russian notables Plekhanov and Trotsky.[70] Connolly's former party in the United States of America, the Socialist Labor Party, was also critical of his participation.[71] There were exceptions. From the pen of Lenin in July 1916 came what was to become the classic Marxist defence:

> Whoever calls such a rebellion a 'putsch' is either a hardened reactionary or a doctrinaire, hopelessly incapable of envisaging a social revolution as a living phenomenon. To imagine that social revolution is conceivable without revolts by small nations in the colonies and Europe, without revolutionary outbursts by a section of the petty bourgeoisie with all its prejudices, without a movement of the politically non-conscious proletarian and semi-proletarian against oppression by landowners, the church and the monarch, against national oppression, etc – to imagine all this is to repudiate social revolution.[72]

Explanations

Lenin did not view the Rising as a socialist one, as indeed it was not, but there is an important difference between his remarks, as well as those of the more critical on the European left such as Trotsky, and those of prominent left critics in the British labour movement, in particular the ILP and the *Herald*. The European revolutionaries placed their analysis within a socialist or Marxist framework, the ILP and the *Herald* derived theirs from pacifism. As such, they were not socialist critiques of the Rising but were reactions from individuals who happened to consider themselves socialist. However, there are examples of the British socialist press trying to offer a more ideological view and place the Rising in its historical context. The most frequent reference was to pre-war Ireland and, specifically, to the Ulster Unionists, under the leadership of Sir Edward Carson, and their threats to resist Home Rule by force. *Labour Leader* argued that the participants in the Rising were, 'only following the example set by Sir Edward Carson and his Ulster Army'.[73] The *Herald* made the same point when it said Carson and the UVF, 'set an example which they can scarcely blame others for following',[74] and *Forward* spoke of Carson's, 'share in the responsibility for the recent lamentable business in Dublin.'[75] The *New Statesman* also insisted, 'the chain of events goes back to the revival of a few years ago of the physical force idea in Irish politics. This, as everyone knows, began in Ulster.'[76] Another who employed this argument was Harold Laski who was later to play a not insignificant role in the development of twentieth century British socialist thought. He said:

> The rebels ... were mistaken, and I do not urge justification. But explanation there is, and responsibility it is possible to apportion. The guilt of this massacre is upon Sir Edward Carson's hands, and in a lesser degree, Mr Asquith, who shrank when the time called for action, must share with him the blame. The thing has been done and men who have dreamed, if in error, yet greatly, have gone to their death. Surely, for the first time England can try and understand.[77]

Despite the sympathy and tolerance displayed here by Laski, it can be asked how much did he and others who sought to pin the blame on the physical force precedent set by the UVF themselves 'understand' what lay behind the Rising. For while it is true that Irish nationalist forces only began to arm themselves after the UVF did, it is still too simplistic to conclude that Carson's actions provided the motivation for Easter 1916. A detailed examination of the reasons why Pearse, Connolly and others staged the Rising is beyond the scope of this analysis, although Connolly's motivation will be considered throughout, but the general observation can be made that they did so – in part, not so much to follow Carson's example, but to protest at the appeasement of him. More crucially, those guilty of this, in the minds of the leaders of the Rising, were not just Asquith and the British government but also the parliamentary nationalists under the leadership of Redmond. When they agreed to the 'temporary' partition of Ireland, Connolly wrote of the 'depths of betrayal to which the so-called Nationalist leaders are willing to sink' and prophesied, 'a carnival of reaction both North and South' if partition was realised.[78] Pearse also hurled insults at Redmond and his party. 'The men who have led Ireland', he wrote in his allegorical play *Ghosts*, 'have done evil things.'[79] Much as they disagreed with Carson for Pearse and Connolly neither Carson nor his Tory supporters were the principle villains, as they were for Laski and others; the principle villains were the British government and the Irish Nationalists.

A rather different analysis was offered by some on the British left. *Forward*, while accepting that 'If Great Britain had the good sense to adopt Home Rule in 1885 or 1893' the Rising 'would not have happened', added:

> On the other hand since Ireland has been able to express herself freely in the democratic way by a powerful party in the British Parliament her course was clear. 'Convince your fellow citizens' – that is the democratic way and duty. Great Britain has been convinced of the justice and wisdom of Home Rule and ... the end was in sight.[80]

The issue here was to dominate British/Irish politics over the next five and a half years, and indeed is what had occupied the minds of many of the Rising's participants. Namely whether the Home Rule solution was adequate, and whether the parliamentarianism and the methodology of negotiation and compromise adopted by the Nationalists could be relied upon. There were some British socialists who thought not. *Call* said, recalling Redmond's support for the war and his agreement to postpone Home Rule:

> Nor is the parliamentary Nationalist Party without responsibility. Mr Redmond may fervently disclaim the rebels and their actions, but no patriotic manifestos can efface the memory of his own treacherous acquiescence in the piece of disgraceful trickery which, in 1914, sacrificed the demand of self-government to the exigencies of party politics.[81]

The readiness of the BSP to indict Redmond may suggest the party was already appreciating that the crucial issue within the politics of Ireland over the next couple of years would be the contest between separatism and the Home Rule. However, it is also possible that the BSP's attack on Redmond was not solely motivated by events in Ireland. What was being expressed was a general political attitude, that is a distrust of the parliamentarianism of which Redmond just happened to be one variant. Similarly, it is not surprising that *Forward*, as an evolutionary socialist newspaper, was willing to publically defend 'Redmondism' and insist that the parliamentary method of securing an Irish settlement would have borne fruit. Indeed for many in the British labour movement the Irish Nationalists and their methodology of orientating towards the British parliament offered a model to those who advocated a separate political organisation for the working class, and some of Labour's early pioneers cited the Nationalists' impact on parliament as a reason why separate labour representation could be effective.[82]

There were, of course, those on the British left who distrusted parliamentarianism and looked to workers organising themselves on the factory floor or through direct action to secure victories. One was the SLP, an organisation where the Rising might have been expected to receive a more sympathetic hearing, because, as already noted, it had a strong personal link with the Dublin insurgents in James Connolly. It is rather remarkable therefore that the SLP monthly newspaper, the *Socialist*, made no comment whatsoever on the Rising or its aftermath. There was a sentence in the June issue which, in the course of a discussion on armies, said that the government's reaction to the Rising showed that 'armies are forces used by capitalist states to maintain their undisputed sway', but this was preceded by the remark 'leaving the merits or demerits of the revolt aside', which was exactly what the *Socialist* did. In the September 1916 issue it reprinted an article from an Irish magazine on the policies of General Maxwell, and in editorial comment on it said, 'in another column we state our position regarding Ireland', but there was no such column and indeed the newspaper made no further comment on Ireland for the rest of the year.

What is the most likely explanation for this silence? It was the case that the SLP was severely disrupted at the time of the Rising with the deportation from Glasgow of its central leaders, Arthur MacManus, John Muir and Thomas Clark. Also, taking a stand on the Rising would always have been difficult in a Glasgow which had seen much inter-worker religious sectarian strife in the nineteenth and early twentieth centuries.[83] Nevertheless, that the *Socialist* did not even carry an obituary for its former leader, Connolly, on his execution, is somewhat remarkable. The obituary was eventually carried three years later, but in the intervening period the *Socialist* had no coverage of substance on Ireland, which suggests that avoiding the issue in the aftermath of the Rising was not due to temporary dislocation. The most likely reason can be located in a review of a book on Connolly written eight years after his death. The writer is Arthur McManus, and he cites the words of Connolly quoted at the start of this chapter:

> Consequently, when he [Connolly], in his dying moments, complains that the 'Socialists ... will all forget that I am an Irishman,' he was speaking at a moment when the Socialist movement had not reached an understanding of the significance of struggling subjected nations. He was speaking at a moment when the leading International Socialists of the various countries could see no difference between Connolly fighting for, and defending, Ireland against Britain, and they themselves entering their several Cabinets to defend and participate in the prosecution of what Connolly termed a 'war of freebooters and thieves.'[84]

As has been shown, it was not the case that everyone in the 'socialist movement' or all 'the leading Internationalist Socialists' did not have at least a partial understanding of Connolly's involvement in the Rising. But if these phrases are replaced in the above by 'Socialist Labour Party' then it becomes clear why that organisation was silent on the Rising. Quite simply, for what it considered socialist reasons, it could not support it or Connolly's involvement, but, perhaps because Connolly had been such a prominent member of the SLP, or perhaps because there were differences within the organisation, it preferred to say nothing.

Either way, the SLP's reaction to the Rising, or rather the lack of it, is surprising. Most of the other views expressed in the working class movement were more predictable and can be contextualised within the general prevailing ideologies of that movement and its constituent parts. The leadership of the labour movement who had enlisted in Britain's war effort and had agreed to a national truce was always highly likely to react critically to those who they saw as taking up arms against that war effort and against that truce. Those who distanced themselves from the war on pacifist grounds would feel duty bound to employ the same standards when reacting to the Rising. Sympathy for the aims and methods of the Irish Nationalists in parliament would understandably prejudice opinions on the alternative agenda of the Rising's leaders. Those on the left who were themselves suspicious of parliamentarianism would always be likely to be the least horror-struck when reacting to Easter 1916. Finally, the lack of comprehension of or appreciation for the historical and contemporary circumstances which produced the Rising squares with the failure of the working class movement to collectively discuss the Irish question in the years preceding the Rising. Given all of this it is not surprising that the Rising was critically received by most of the British working class movement, and, after all, it was critically received by almost everybody else in Britain and Ireland and by many in the socialist world. There was the occasional exception. For example, Irishman Bernard Shaw and the *New Statesman* were among the first to realise that the executions of the leading insurgents could re-draw Ireland's political map. When that did occur it happened in such a way as to no longer allow those who took up the mantle of the Rising to be dismissed as a violent, unrepresentative few. And because during the same period the British labour movement was itself to undergo some far-reaching changes, then the outcome of the encounter between that movement and the Irish was liable to be less easy to foretell than it was at Easter 1916. Moreover, at least in the immediate aftermath of Easter 1916, three of the major topics that were to feature on the British left in its discussion and actions on Ireland in the years ahead had been introduced, namely the degree of separation Ireland should have from Britain; the Ulster question; and the relationship between socialism and nationalism. So too, but very much on the margins, had the question of what the British working class should do about events in Ireland, because just before Connolly's execution a lone voice in Wales had called for strike action from miners there to prevent the execution. That belonged to one Captain Jack White who had been born in Surrey in 1879 into an upper class Anglo-Irish family and had served with gallantry in the Boer War before turning to involvement in Ireland's revolutionary movement and, among things, commanding the Irish Citizen Army. By Easter 1916 he was no longer involved in that, but that was still where his sympathies lay. So it was, as he wrote, 'I am arrested in the South Wales coalfield for trying to get the Welsh miners out on strike. Why? To save Jim Connolly from being shot.' Not surprisingly, as White added, 'I failed'[85] and he was sentenced to three months in prison for his efforts.

If White was being somewhat optimistic, others showed a contrary inclination concerning the prospect of the re-birth and re-moulding of the Irish issue. One of those voices belonged to John Wheatley, the leading figure in the ILP in Glasgow, a city which, to repeat, had a record of worker class religious divisions. Wheatley was critical of both the Rising and of the government's reaction to it. For him 'there was only one way out of the situation', and that was 'by handing over the difficulty to the Irish people themselves and telling them to sort it out.' Because this hadn't happened, Wheatley feared the worst:

> Now we shall have the Irish problem and its resultant racial and sectarian bitterness with us for another generation. This is a distinct blow to the labour movement in Britain, which stands to gain by the disappearance from our public platforms of every political question that divides the working class.[86]

Apparently, there were difficulties ahead.

2

Interesting Times

In August 1919, Prime Minister David Lloyd George had a long discussion on Ireland with Harold Spender, a journalist and Liberal politician who had written a book about Home Rule and the following year was to publish a biography of Lloyd George. Spender was later to write to C. P. Scott, editor of the *Manchester Guardian*, relaying the conversation. Lloyd George, said Spender, had 'surrendered to the most anti-Irish hatred.' The following month Lloyd George's government had shown indications of such 'hatred, or, alternatively, took necessary measures. He 'suppressed' Sinn Féin, the Irish Volunteers, the Gaelic League and kindred organisations in Cork, southwest Ireland – a move soon to be extended to all of Ireland – and declared Dáil Éireann, the self-proclaimed Irish parliament, illegal. Yet, in his conversation with Spender, the Prime Minister seemed relaxed about Ireland. Spender reported to Scott, 'He said Ireland has always hated England and always would. He could easily govern Ireland with the sword: he was much more concerned about the Bolsheviks at home.'[1] This was to prove a questionable judgement.

The Irish Front

Lloyd George was Minister for Munitions in May 1916 when he was asked by Prime Minister Asquith to try and negotiate an Irish settlement. There was now a common acceptance that the pre-war Home Rule legislation was no longer fit for purpose. Lloyd George had been first elected a Liberal MP at a by-election in April 1890. He had not agreed with Gladstone's prioritising Irish Home Rule, but had remained with him when the Liberals split over the issue. According to one biographer, Roy Hattersley, David had been a 'British patriot' since his school days.[2] By the second decade of the twentieth century he also had radical credentials, established by his opposition to the Second Boer War and by his 'People's Budget' of 1909.

Success in negotiating an Irish settlement in 1916 proved elusive. As early as 1 June, John Dillon of the parliamentary Nationalists warned him that, thanks to government reaction to the Easter Rising, 'the temper of the country is extremely bad – and the temper of this city [Dublin] ferocious.'[3] The following month, his negotiations between the Unionists in Ireland, Unionists in Britain, the Nationalists and the government broke down. This time Dillon blamed Lloyd George: 'In his endeavour to be too artful, he over reached himself'.[4] In truth, the type of compromise Lloyd George had sought was now becoming out of reach of any British politician. As the Commissioner of the Dublin Metropolitan Police reported in December 1916, 'disaffection in this country would hardly be more widespread than it is',[5] a statement which turned out to err on the side of optimism. The same month, Lloyd George became Prime Minister in a Conservative and Unionist dominated cabinet.

In Ireland, the political new times were heralded in February 1917 when Count Plunkett, the father of one of the executed leaders of the Rising, defeated a Nationalist candidate in a Roscommon by-election. The following month, Philip Snowden of the British Labour Party and ILP predicted that, 'a general election now would show Sinn Féin triumphant all over Nationalist Ireland', and in this context spoke of 'the Irish Question' having 'taken a turn for the worse'.[6] Success for Sinn Féin over the Nationalists in by-elections in South Longford duly came in May and in East Clare in July. The victor at the latter was Eamon de Valera, the sole surviving commandant of the Rising. The Sinn Féin cause had been assisted in January 1917 when Lloyd George hinted at extending military conscription to Ireland. It was reinforced in July with the banning of Republican meetings and the prohibition of the wearing of uniform, aimed at the Irish Volunteers, as well as a new series of arrests. One of those arrested, Thomas Ashe, died in September following attempts to force feed him while on hunger strike. The search for a political solution was not abandoned by the government. In July 1917 there was the Irish Convention, an effort to involve interested parties in Ireland in securing a common political agreement. Neither Sinn Féin nor representatives of the Irish labour movement attended, and with disagreements between the Unionists and the Nationalists increasing by the day the Convention was never likely to succeed. Its demise was visible well before 9 April 1918 when its final report revealed irreconcilable differences. The following day, the Military Service Bill was introduced in the House of Commons.

The war was going badly and this, among other things, provided for the extension of conscription to Ireland, although the application of the principle was left hanging in the air. There was also a suggestion that Home Rule would accompany the application of conscription, but Home Rule was now seen by all parties in Ireland as a solution whose time had gone.

The conscription threat alone was enough to provoke an Irish national resistance, as indeed many in or close to the government had predicted.[7] The Irish Nationalists withdrew from the House of Commons, the Irish Catholic Hierarchy said conscription was 'a fatal, mistake surpassing the worst blunders of the last four years', adding significantly that it was 'an oppressive and inhuman law which the Irish people have the right to resist.'[8] The Irish labour movement took action, with a 24-hour general strike organised by the Irish Trade Union Congress on 23 April. The strike was successful in all areas except Belfast, where the majority Protestant proletariat remained, by and large, hostile to Irish nationalism of any variety. In the rest of Ireland, other forms of non-violent direct action were also being organised. With threatened food shortages, Sinn Féin in the west of Ireland seized large estates, cleared them of cattle, divided them up and leased them for tillage. There were, however, limits to this radicalism: the rents collected were handed over to the owners of the estates.

In May 1918, the government issued a proclamation, declaring that Sinn Féin was involved in a 'treasonable conspiracy' with Germany. It was an allegation based on the flimsiest of evidence and it seems likely that it was just an excuse to lock up the leadership of the anti-conscription movement which the government feared, incorrectly, was preparing for all-out war in Ireland.[9] There were sweeping arrests and deportations. These included de Valera, Count Plunkett, leading members of Sinn Féin such as Arthur Griffith and William Cosgrave, and the 1916 insurgent and Citizen Army veteran Countess Markievicz. Large areas of Ireland were placed under martial law in June, but the next month Sinn Féin demonstrated its continuing popular support with a victory in a by-election in East Cavan. Two weeks later it too was placed under martial law, or 'proclaimed', but with little effect. The results of the general election were announced on 28 December. The parliamentary Nationalists were reduced to six seats in the Commons; the Unionists won 26; Irish Labour had withdrawn from the contest, saying the national question was now predominant. *The Times* recorded, 'Sinn Féin swept the country'[10] winning 73 seats. Gorge Lansbury's *Herald* did not doubt the historical significance:

> The developing Sinn Féin victory is not a fact of yesterday. Ireland has been preparing for it for at least a quarter of a century ... Sinn Féin wants to bring a resourceful ardent, fraternal nation onto the country of nations ... Britain is represented in Irish towns and countrysides today as a tyranny monstrous and unabashed.[11]

The following week the same newspaper reported on the growing resistance to this 'tyranny': 'Advocacy of direct action instead of public demonstrations is universally urged; the general strike, stoppages of hunting, the boycott are instances.'[12]

Sinn Féin was pledged not to attend a British parliament. Instead, it unilaterally convened its own parliament, Dáil Éireann, which met on 21 January 1919 in Dublin. There, those successful Sinn Féin election candidates who were not in prison passed a 'Democratic Programme'. Although the original drafters of the programme, Labour leaders William O'Brien and Tom Johnson, intended it to be 'more democratic than it proved to be in its final form',[13] it was not without radical content. It ran,

> We declare that the nation's sovereignty extends not only to all men and women ... but to all its material possessions, the Nation's soil, all the wealth and all the wealth-producing processes within the Nation ... we reaffirm that all right to private property must be subordinated to the public right and welfare.

It ended with a promise of 'social and industrial legislation with a view to a general and lasting improvement in the conditions under which the working class live and labour.'

The same day as the Dáil met, the first shots were fired in what was to become the War of Independence when two policemen escorting gelignite were killed in an ambush by Irish Volunteers at Soleheadbeg, County Tipperary. The *Herald* assured its readers, 'Cold blooded murder not an Irish characteristic, a Sinn Féin characteristic least of all.'[14] Other forms of Irish resistance sprang up. After the death of two policemen in Limerick during an attempted rescue of an imprisoned Volunteer, Robert

Byrne, who was himself mortally injured in the fracas, martial law was declared. The Limerick trades council replied by calling a general strike for the city and established the 'Limerick Soviet', which lasted two weeks.

By the end of the year, 21 policemen had been killed by members of the Irish Volunteers, which was to evolve into the Irish Republican Army. In effect, 'Ireland in 1919 slipping into a state of war ... government policy, stumbling between ineffective repression and half-hearted attempts at conciliation, seemed to lack all direction.'[15]

In January 1920, Sinn Féin won 550 seats in municipal elections: the Irish Labour Party, which was Republican on the constitutional issue took 395 seats, the Unionists 238 and the Nationalists just 108. The following month, the government put forward its own solution with the introduction of the Government of Ireland Bill. This sought to establish two parliaments, one with jurisdiction over the six north-eastern counties, the other with authority in the remaining 26. A Council of Ireland, with no legislative or executive powers, was also envisaged for consultation on matters of common interest between the two parliaments. The powers of the two parliaments were to be limited. Defence, foreign relations, the police, even the Post Office were all to remain under the control of the sovereign British parliament.

With the little common ground between the government and the now popularly supported Republicans, an intensification of the War of Independence followed. Republicans were to claim in January that over 1000 raids were conducted by British forces with 220 arrests, and in February there were over 4,000 raids and 296 arrests.[16] In March, the government sent the 'Black and Tans' to Ireland, mainly ex-soldiers who served as police reinforcements. They were joined in September by the Royal Irish Constabulary's Auxiliary Division, an officer equivalent of the Black and Tans. By now, British forces were operating a policy of 'reprisals', a policy which became official in the autumn of 1920.[17]

Before then, the conflict between government and Republican forces increased and took different forms. In many areas the Republicans administered their own courts and quasi-governmental functions. In April 1920 the Irish Labour Party and Trades Union Congress called a general strike in support of 100 prisoners who had been held without trial, 60 of whom had started a hunger strike. After three days they were unconditionally released and the strike ended. In May 1920 in county council elections Sinn Féin was victorious in all but four counties. In many areas,

British governmental authority barely existed: the *Daily News* reported on 28 May 1920 that 'Sinn Féin effectively is taking over the Executive'.

The Restoration of Order in Ireland Act, introduced in August and providing for internment without trial and court martial, proved ineffective in living up to its title. The following month the *New Statesman* judged, 'the Irish situation is very obviously going from bad to worse.'[18] Roy Foster, the most lauded historian of his generation, has confirmed this contemporary judgement, saying that that British 'coercive reaction escalated from late 1920; draconian powers of search and arrest, occasional berserk sackings of Irish Republican Army (IRA) villages and towns, and an unrelieved demonstration on the part of the military.'[19] In October 1920 came the death of Terence MacSwiney. MacSwiney, an accountant, playwright and organiser of the Irish Volunteers, had been elected as a Sinn Féin candidate to the British parliament in 1918 and as Mayor of Cork in March 1920. He was seized while presiding over a meeting of Cork IRA and sent to Brixton prison. There, he went on hunger strike and died on 25 October. The *Daily Herald* commented, 'He has won immortality. His name will remain an inspiration to all that come after him.' The same article called the government 'liars' and 'brutes', with 'tyrannical ends ... the children's children will remember them with horror.'[20]

Then, on 'Bloody Sunday', 21 November 1920, the IRA killed 14 suspected secret service agents in Dublin; later that afternoon, auxiliary police opened fire on an Irish football crowd in Dublin. The British were to claim they had been fired on first, a version of events fiercely disputed in Dublin. Twelve died, all spectators. Later the same evening, the auxiliary police executed the commandant and vice-commandant of the Dublin IRA while in police custody. The ILP's *Labour Leader* commented: 'These events are the natural and inevitable outcome of government policy in Ireland. They put beyond doubt the failure of the British government to govern Ireland by methods of terrorism.'[21]

The pattern was repeated two weeks later in Cork when 18 Auxiliaries were killed in an IRA ambush and, in reprisal, Black and Tans and Auxiliaries looted and burnt parts of Cork city, causing £2.5 million of damage. The year's death toll for British security forces was 176 police fatalities and 54 soldiers. According to the partisan but well-informed Republican historian Dorothy Macardle, the number of unarmed persons killed by Crown Forces in Ireland during the twelve months of 1920 reached two hundred and three; these included six women and twelve children under 17 years of age. Sixty-nine persons were deliberately killed in the street; the rest were victims of indiscriminate fire.[22]

Whatever the precise details, there is little doubt that, in the words of Professor Richard English, who no one could accuse of being a Macardle acolyte, 'Not for the last time in British Ireland, military measures taken to repress IRA violence often led to increased rather than diminished Republican sympathy among the Catholic nationalist population.'[23]

On 23 December the Government of Ireland Act received the royal assent. Early in the new year elections took place for the two parliaments established by the legislation. In the north the Ulster Unionists won by a large majority; in the other 26 counties Sinn Féin was returned unopposed in all but the university seats. De Valera was by now the undisputed leader of Sinn Féin; James Craig became the northern Prime Minister. While clashes between the IRA and government forces continued in the south, in the north on 22 June the new parliament was opened by King George V with a speech urging conciliation. Two days later Lloyd George invited Craig and de Valera for talks in London, and two weeks after that a military truce was agreed between the British and the IRA. Negotiations continued in fits and starts until the Anglo-Irish Treaty, or Articles of Agreement, was signed by British and Irish negotiators on 6 December. Details of this will be given subsequently, but it can be summarised as confirming the division of Ireland as provided for in the Government of Ireland Act, but with the southern parliament receiving considerably greater autonomy than envisaged by that Act.

Various details of this chain of events will be explored subsequently. The point of this brief narrative is to outline the nature of the evolution of the Irish question in these years. Several themes can be highlighted. The first is the change in Irish public opinion from the previous support for Home Rule to one endorsing the Republicanism of the 1916 Rising, although what that Republicanism precisely constituted often remained undefined. Nevertheless, a change in political loyalty was evident, first in the by-election victories for Sinn Féin, its triumph at the 1918 general election and in subsequent local government elections. Approximately 70 per cent of the electorate consistently voted for Sinn Féin. Second, and flowing from the first, is the nature of the conflict that developed between Britain and the Irish majority. It no longer centred on whether 'Home Rule' would be conceded. All the major political parties in Britain agreed that, in one form or another, it should be; the issue now was Sinn Féin's demand for unconditional self-determination and Irish unity, and the British government's opposition to both. Third, it could be expected that various characteristics of the Irish independence struggle would attract the interests of socialists, especially socialists living with the impact of the Great War and the Russian revolution. These would include the eclipse of the parliamentarianism of the Nationalists by the 'direct action' of the Republicans, the radicalism or lack of the Democratic Programme, the use of the general strike against conscription and to secure the release of the prisoners, the Limerick 'Soviet', the appearance of dual power situations in the south and west of Ireland, the physical force aspect of the conflict and, from late 1918 or early 1919, the support of the Irish labour movement for total separation from Britain. That labour movement, it is also important to record, while intervening in the national struggle in these years was also fighting other battles. Evidence of this is the growth of trade unionism, with ITUC affiliated unions rising 50 per cent between 1916 and 1921, and the membership of the Irish Transport and General Workers Union (ITGWU), the legacy of Connolly and Larkin, growing from 12,000 in the autumn of 1917 to 68,000 by the end of 1918.[24]

All of which had more than a passing relevance to the issues, tactics and strategies the working class movement in Britain and internationally were debating in these years, and often debating so fiercely that splits in the movement occurred. The degree of relevance will become clearer when the parallel evolution of the British working class movement is summarised shortly, and the wider issues will subsequently be examined in depth. However, even at this point it is worth establishing some reference points. The most obvious is to enquire into the general judgements made at the time by representatives of British socialism on the pattern of events outlined above. For the *New Statesman*, by the time of the threats of conscription, the folly of the British government was apparent:

It was foreseeable and it was foreseen that the indefinite shelving of Home Rule would weaken Mr Redmond and lead to the growth of the view that Ireland had once more been 'sold' ... It was foreseeable and it was foreseen that the executions in cold blood [Easter 1916] ... would lead to their canonisation and enormously stimulate Sinn Féin. And it was above all evident that the whole of Nationalist Ireland would be solid against the endeavour of a British government to force Irishmen into the Army.[25]

As the war intensified, so too did British labour movement criticism of the British conduct of that war. The following from *Labour Leader* in October 1920 is typical:

Mr Lloyd George has no policy to suggest except the ruthless use of armed force to suppress the rebellion of the Irish people against British injustice and tyranny ... The British government in Ireland is an object of contempt and ridicule to the whole world.[26]

And:

What is the case of this terrible crisis? The Irish people, by the forms of the democracy conferred on them by Britain, have set up a national government. English law has ceased to operate over the greater area of Ireland and where native law has managed to secure free operation, peace, justice, content and morality reign ... Mr Lloyd George, instead of welcoming this happy assertion of democratic will resolves to smash the national government, and its works at all costs, and floods the country with soldiers, tanks, spics and armed hooligans.[27]

There was no ambiguity here: *Labour Leader* was very clear on whose side it was now on, or at least who it was against, that is Lloyd George and his armies. Similarly, there is the *Herald*, which became the *Daily Herald* in April 1919, and in November 1920 asserted:

However far back we go, whether we reckon in times of centuries or years or weeks, the record of England towards Ireland is the same. Ireland was conquered by the sword, and has been hold down by the sword ... now comes Mr Lloyd George ... letting loose a reign of terror which includes the wounding and maiming of women and little girls.[28]

The hesitancy, indeed criticism with which that newspaper and its editor, George Lansbury, had greeted the 1916 Rising was now if not exactly air-brushed from history then certainly given a revisionist covering: 'When Ireland broke out in Easter 1916, all our sympathy was with Jim Connolly and his comrades', wrote Lansbury in a signed article in March 1919. He continued, 'Not that we believed in their violence, but because we recognised the right of Irishmen to fight and die for liberty.'[29]

As is apparent, the *Daily Herald* did not disavow its pacifism, and certainly did not cheer-lead the Irish Volunteers/IRA. In October 1920 an editorial said the government's policy was one of 'blind and brutal outrage', but pleaded, 'Let Ireland leave them to their horror and shame. Let not the wickedness of the tyrants who have outraged Ireland be made an excuse for [IRA] reprisals. No good can come of violence'[30] Similarly, in the article mentioning Connolly quoted above, Lansbury also said, 'I cannot say often enough, we of the *Herald* believe that war is evil, whether it is "civil war" or any kind of war'. 'Civil war' was a repetition of a phrase used by the *Herald* after 1916, although the inverted commas were additional. But now, having lived through the entirety of a world war, circumstances had changed. The pacifist framework remained but was contextualised: 'Therefore we express our disapproval of force, but the government and those with intelligence who are responsible for the maiming and slaughter of untold millions cannot with any show of consistency denounce others who use the same methods to achieve their methods.'

The Great War was one context. Another was what had happened in Ireland and was still happening. Again, there is the pacifism; but again, there were deeper relevancies:

> Irishmen on their side murder British and policemen. We do not for one moment excuse or paliate these excesses. We have appealed over and over again to the Irish to hold their hands and abstain from violence. We condemn the violence unreservedly, but we affirm that the *ultimate* responsibility both for the slaughter of innocent Irish children and for the shooting of British soldiers rests squarely with the British government which will not do justice, but seeks to murder liberty.[31] [Original emphasis]

The *Herald* and *Labour Leader* were both on the left wing of the broader working class movement, albeit the social democratic left. The Labour Party was not. Certainly, Arthur Henderson was a far more centrist politician than George Lansbury ever was. Accordingly, it would hardly be surprising if the Labour Party and Henderson gave a more temperate interpretation of what was happening in late 1920 than the above. The opportunity to do so came when Henderson headed an official party commission to Ireland in December 1920. The PLP, the National Executive of the Labour Party and the TUC were represented on the commission and Tom Johnson of the Irish Labour Party and TUC was also a participant (The ITUCLP had become the ILPTUC in November 1918). The first part of their report described their impressions and reported their conclusions on the Irish reality they witnessed and interpreted. The first section was on 'General Terrorism and Provocative Behaviour'. They were talking about the British forces:

> In every part of Ireland that we visited we were impressed by the atmosphere of terrorism which prevailed. This is due to some extent to uncertainty; people are afraid that their houses might be burned; they fear that they might be arrested or even dragged from their beds and shot.
>
> But terrorism is accentuated by other less direct methods. Lorries of armed men with their rifles 'at the ready' are frequent sights in the towns and even in the country districts. We are aware that the Irish Secretary would have us believe that these 'brave men' might be shot by 'cowardly assassins' in the streets, but we cannot believe that for men to carry rifles 'at the ready' is a means of protection against the possibility of being shot from a window or at a distance. This display of arms assists to spread the feeling of terror. The sight of 'tin hats,' drawn bayonets, and revolvers, and here and there of sandbags, or machine guns, or powerful searchlights, is calculated to terrorise the civilian population.[32]

The rest of the report went on in the same vein. Reporting on reprisals, the Auxiliaries were described as 'undisciplined and virtually uncontrolled'; the Auxiliaries and Royal Irish Constabulary had members who were 'undesirable characters'; the Auxiliaries and 'Black and Tans' had 'got out of hand'. The IRA, on the other hand, was a different story:

> The forces of the Crown in Ireland are opposed by the Republican Volunteers. To speak of the forces of Sinn Féin as an army is

misleading. The Irish Republican Army may consist of 216 battalions, whose strengths vary from 100 to 1000 men, but it is an army only in name. This remark implies no disrespect for the IRA, which, in point of fact, is a far more formidable organisation than any army raised from a population of at most three million could ever be. The IRA is formidable because it is in-tangible; ... in its present form, it is everywhere all the time and nowhere at any given moment. Without the sympathy and support of the vast majority of the population it could not exist. This support is probably more general and effective to-day than it has been at any previous period. Irish Volunteers are fed and harboured by people who, three years ago, were certainly not Sinn Féiners, and some of whom were Unionists. So great has been the provocation by the forces of the Crown that eighty per cent of Irish men and women now regard the shooting of policemen and throwing bombs at lorries with the same philosophic resignation that Mr. Lloyd George displays towards arson, pillage, and the shooting of civilians at sight in the presence of their wives and children.

This must be one of the most respectful assessments of the military opponents of the British state penned by the main British parliamentary opposition party in the twentieth century. Whether it is accurate is less relevant here than what it tells us about the sentiments being expressed by the leadership of the working class movement in Britain on Ireland in late 1920. The Labour Party's general assessment, in this instance, was the same as that of the ILP and the *Daily Herald*, and amounted to unqualified criticism of government policy and sympathy for their Irish opponents. The conclusion of this section of the commission's report summed this up:

Things are being done in the name of Britain which must make her name stink in the nostrils of the whole world. The honour of our people has been gravely compromised. Not only is there a reign of terror in Ireland which should bring a blush of shame to the cheek of every British citizen but a nation is being held in subjection by an empire which has proudly boasted that it is the friend of small nations.

Something had to be done:

Let the people of Britain raise their voices in a united demand for the rescue of the Irish people from the rule of force and for the establishment of peace and freedom and a new brotherhood between the peoples of the British Isles. Only by repudiating the errors of the past and the infamies of the present can the democracy of Great Britain recover its honour. Only by granting to Ireland the freedom which is her due can we fulfil our great responsibilities towards our sister nation.

This seemed to be call to action. The question is whether, during these years, British workers were in the mood for action.

The Home Front

The capability of the British working class to collectively respond positively to the Irish national revolution was dependent on many factors, one of which was the level of its own militancy. Two contemporary assessments of such, and comparing this to Irish militancy, were made in the first half of 1919. The first was at a meeting of the War Cabinet in February 1919 when the release of some interned Irish Republican prisoners was discussed. The suggestion was postponed because, it was concluded, this would be seen as a sign of weakness by trade unionists in England and Scotland who would be encouraged to increase their own agitation.[33] Apparently, the industrial situation in Britain was seen as a greater threat than the Irish revolutionaries; a view also evident in the quote from Lloyd George reported to C. P. Scott, quoted at the start of this chapter.

Another opinion covering the broadly same comparison comes four months later from a contrasting source. This was made by 'a messenger from Moscow', someone who was 'a Soviet member', in an interview in *Workers' Dreadnought* (previously *Woman's Dreadnought*) with its editor, Sylvia Pankhurst. 'Ireland', he thought, 'will be like the Ukraine: it will demand and secure self-determination in the early stages of the [British] Revolution, and it will come to the actual Communist Revolution, as was the case in Ukraine, later than Britain.'[34] This only made sense if, when it was made, there was an assumption that Britain could indeed be in those 'early stages' of its revolution. What fuelled such hopes or, in the War Cabinet case, such fears?

There is certainly a wealth of data which suggests something was indeed going on among the common people. Membership of trade unions affiliated to the TUC rose from 2,851,000 in 1916 to 6,500,000 in 1920;[35] overall membership rose from 2,565,000 in 1910 to 8,347,000 in 1921.[36] The number of working days lost through industrial disputes rose from 2,446,000 in 1916, to: 5,647,000 in 1917; 5,875,000 in 1918; and 34,969,000 in 1919 – before falling to 26,568,000 in 1920, then rising again to 85,872,000 in 1921.[37] Election statistics show a parallel, if less dramatic, growth in support for the Labour Party. In the December 1910 general election, Labour had 7.2 per cent of the total vote. In 1918 it captured 22.2 per cent, and in November 1922 election 29.5 per cent.[38] The working class electorate had increased dramatically during this same period after the franchise extension of 1918, but there is little doubt that support for Labour in the working class also mushroomed. Membership of the Labour Party increased from 2,220,000 in 1916 to 4,360,000 in 1920,[39] and if it could be argued that this rise was due to the growth of unions affiliated to the party, individual membership of the more left-wing Independent Labour Party enjoyed a similar percentage increase, from 21,000 in 1914 to 37,000 in 1920.[40]

For all of this there were international, national and local reasons. Most obvious is the radicalising effect of the Great War and the demands for social and economic change this produced; the Russian revolutions of February and October 1917; the imposition of conscription; the post-war economic boom; the common view that although the Coalition government had triumphed in the 1918 election this was a tarnished mandate informed as it was by war victory; and the emergence and the growth of multi-militancy in specific geographic areas and industries, for example Glasgow and coal mining.

Whatever the reasons, as early as May 1917 Lloyd George reported to his cabinet that a 'highly organised labour movement with seditious tendencies was developing in many industrial centres'.[41] Confirmation seemed to come the following month with the meeting of the Leeds Convention. This had been called by the BSP and the ILP. There, resolutions were passed calling for an end to the war, congratulating Russians on the February revolution and even the establishment of 'councils of workmen and soldiers delegates' for the purpose of 'initiating and co-ordinating working class activity.' It was the usually-moderate Labour MP W. C. Anderson who moved this resolution declaring, 'if a revolution be the conquest of political power by a hitherto disinherited class, if revolution be that we are not going to put up with what we have put up with in the past, then the sooner we have revolution in this country the better.'[42] Approximately 1,200 attended the Convention. They included Ramsay MacDonald, Philip Snowden, Robert Williams, Robert Smillie, Tom Mann, Bertrand Russell, Willie Gallagher and Jimmy Maxton, a who's who of contemporary British socialism. Even though it may be the case, as David Howell has argued, that the proposal from the Convention to establish workers' council was 'smothered in vagueness about its political purpose' and that, 'for many the commitment seemed to end with rhetoric',[43] the heady atmosphere of the time could still encourage Tom Quelch of the BSP to declare, 'the hour of the social revolution is close upon us.'[44]

Such optimism was not reflected in the aftermath of the Leeds Convention. The 'councils' it resolved upon never appeared, yet fresh thinking did continue to permeate the labour movement. The following year the Labour Party adopted *Labour and the New Social Order* as its programme, which has been summed up as Labour committing itself to 'full employment and widespread social reform, the nationalisation of coal, the railways, electricity, land and liquor ... progressive taxation and a capital levy to pay off the national debt, and to the redistribution of wealth.'[45] This was radical, although it was also the case that during the war the intervention of the state into organising and controlling major aspects of British industry had made a common-sense case for such intervention.[46] Nevertheless, as one critical commentator has argued, *New Social Order* may have been 'riddled with limitations and ambiguities', but in it 'the Labour Party appealed to its working class electorate for the first time in history as a socialist party.'[47]

At the same time, some were not convinced. The often-jailed Scottish revolutionary John Maclean argued at the 1918 BSP conference that 'the Labour Party at present was bound up with capitalism', and that such was the temperament of the proletariat that the BSP 'had a chance of developing a force and organisation that would sweep the Labour Party on one side.'[48]

With hindsight, a more sober assessment of the working class movement in 1918 is that 'at the level of political activism, there was little to suggest any mass radicalisation of the working class, but there were centres, and perhaps moments that seemed to offer hope to the left.'[49] Where such 'centres' were located was to become clear the following year. The most spectacular action came in MacLean's Glasgow when the Clyde Workers' Committee organised a mass strike in January 1919.

Engineering and shipyard workers went out in support of a 40-hour week, a demand fuelled by fears of post-war unemployment. Mass demonstrations and clashes with the police followed until eventually a compromise was agreed with the granting of 47-hour weeks, 10 hours less than had previously been worked. Belfast engineers, Yorkshire miners and northeast shipyard workers also went on strike in January 1919, as did miners in other areas in March. In June, cotton workers in Lancashire and adjourning counties were out; the following month it was again the turn of the Yorkshire miners, and in September iron founders and railway workers were involved in national disputes. There was also unrest in sections of the police, army and navy, the latter two witnessing mutinies caused, in the main, by the slow rate of demobilisation after the war.[50] By March 1919, Lloyd George was concerned enough to tell the Cabinet:

> Russia has gone over completely to Bolshevism and we had consoled ourselves with the thought that they were only a half-civilised race; but now even in Germany, whose people were, without exception the best educated in Europe, prospects are very black ... Great Britain would hold out, but only if the people were given a sense of confidence - only if they were made to believe that things were being done for them.[51]

The Prime Minister in this period did have a tendency, almost an enthusiasm, for spotting 'Bolsheviks' and other miscreants around every corner. When the Triple Alliance of miners, railway workers and transport workers threatened strike action in mid-1919, he privately prophesied that if they succeeded 'this would inevitably lead to a Soviet Republic'.[52] When railway workers struck in September 1919, he detected 'an anarchist conspiracy.'[53] When miners were calling for nationalisation of the mines in October 1919, he accused them of 'guild socialism' and 'syndicalism'.[54]

Certainly, 'Direct Action' was being advocated and practised, the most spectacular example of which came in May 1920 when London dockers showed their international solidarity by refusing to load munitions onto the Jolly George bound for Poland and its war against Soviet Russia. On the same theme the Council of Action, hosted by the Labour Party and TUC in August 1920, was established 'to use all the resources of Labour to prevent the British nation being plunged into war, and by all means open to them to restore peace to the world'; specifically, to prevent British intervention against Russia. A general strike was threatened to prevent such a possibility and as many as 350 local councils of actions were formed. 'It is difficult to believe', A. J. P. Taylor has written, 'that there would have been no British aid to the Poles, if the threat of a general strike had not been made – and with such unanimity.'[55] The contemporary observation of Lenin was even more dramatic. For him, the Council of Action was 'a tremendous turning-point in British politics. Its significance to Great Britain is as great as the revolution of February 1917 was to us.'[56]

Aspects of the Council of Action will be discussed subsequently, but Lenin's words are of more value in conveying contemporary impressions than historical judgements. G. D. H. Cole was both an observer and historian, and his assessment of the Council of Action as 'the last national rallying call of Labour before the slump'[57] is more accurate. The following year, the number of industrial disputes fell to 763 in contrast to the 1,607 of 1920. Although, as already noted, the number of days lost through strike action increased, this was due to the national miners' strike of April to June 1921, which, for Michael Foot, proved 'the most painful, tragic and instructive drama in modern Labour history',[58] notable for 'Black Friday' when the leaders of the railway and transport unions declined to fulfil previous pledges to strike in solidarity with the miners.

Although 'Black Friday' marked the effective end of 'a climax of class conscious activity among the workers which has not yet been surpassed',[59] it was by no means the end of social and political unrest. Unemployment leapt from 691,000 at the end of 1920 to 2,171,000 at the end of June 1921, statistics which some have argued underestimates the problem;[60] but, although this may have helped to weaken industrial militancy, it created other manifestations of discontent. In October 1920 there was a violent clash in London between police and unemployment demonstrators, and by early December three town halls, five libraries and numerous other buildings were occupied by the unemployed.[61] Even a year later, in December 1921, the King was concerned enough to write to Lloyd George saying that, because of unemployment, 'the people grow discontent and agitators seize their opportunities, the police interfere, resistance ensues, troops are called out and riot begets revolt and possibly revolution.'[62]

For Walter Kendal, an historian of the left, the immediate post-war period saw a 'crisis' which, for 'British society', was 'the most serious since the time of the Chartists'[63] and, for socialists, 'the greatest revolutionary opportunity in generations'.[64] However, to say that there was an opportunity is one thing, to suggest there was a willingness to take it is something else. As far as the Labour Party was concerned, despite its leadership's support for the Leeds Convention and the Council of Action, it was not difficult to detect moderating influences. It had, after all, been part of the war-time coalition, with Arthur Henderson sitting in Asquith's and then Lloyd George's cabinet until August 1917 when he was succeeded there by George Barnes. More generally, the PLP, said Irish observer Henry Somerville, writing in 1921, 'are a set of respectable, sensible men without much idealism or intellect. They are very British, very patriotic, and many of them have been Sunday school teachers or preachers.'[65]

Just how many were Sunday school teachers was perhaps less relevant than the extent to which those MPs were representative of the class they sought to lead. Eric Hobsbawm argues:

Only a tiny fraction of the pre-1914 radical left consisted of revolutionaries in the Russian or Irish sense ... These few score, or at best few hundred militants played a disproportionately large part in the years 1911–1921, when the British labour movement ... showed signs of rejecting 'the system', including 'politics', the Labour Party and trade union leadership. To say that it was revolutionary would be misleading.[66]

A similar view was expressed at the time by Scotland Yard's Basil Thomson in a confidential report for the Cabinet into 'Revolutionary Feeling During the Year 1919'. He was worried that 'class prejudice ... has a firmer grip upon the working class of this country than ever before', but he also reassured the government that 'the signs are against violent revolution, but in favour of gradual evolution through the ballot box.'[67] Or, as Chris Wrigley has written, 'there does not appear to have been a potentially revolutionary situation in Britain. There was not an overall crisis of the old regime'.[68] And, as another historian has said, 'For all the mass turbulence ... only a minute segment of the British working class, namely that organised in the far left politics and groups had been sufficiently affected by these experiences to reject the British social and constitutional system root and branch.'[69]

Nevertheless, while it can be debated how near British workers did come to 'rejecting the system', or how substantial 'the greatest revolutionary opportunity' was, there was a militancy in this period which indeed had not been seen since the Chartists. Moreover, it is apparent that it was not simply economic struggle that was involved. The Leeds Convention, the Jolly George and the Council of Action confirm the activities and aspirations of the more militant in the labour movement reached beyond bread-and-butter issues. The growth of the Labour Party and its articulation, however vague, of socialist ideas similarly suggest a growth in political consciousness. Militancy may have been on the ebb by 1921 when unemployment was rising and this, as David Howell has suggested, may have undermined the possibilities of an alliance between the Irish cause and the British left,[70] but it would be too mechanical to insist that there had to be an exact conjuncture both in time and pace between the two struggles for one to assist the other. Whatever the intricacies of such propositions, it surely remains the case that as the Irish issue was reaching a climax from 1917 to 1921, those engaged in the struggle there for self-determination would rarely have had a more receptive audience when appealing for assistance and solidarity from the British labour movement.

The Great and the Good and the Irish

The potential of British working class opposition to the government's Irish policy was influenced not just by its own internal political dynamic and what was occurring in Ireland but also by wider public perceptions. General criticism of the government's Irish policy, or aspects of it, could be expected to strengthen the labour movement's self-confidence in expressing and acting on its own opposition. We have already seen there was such criticism within the socialist press and the Labour Party, and there is no doubt there was a more general criticism. Here, for example, is G. K. Chesterton, forever to be associated in popular culture with the Father Brown short stories, but a writer, commentator, philosopher, poet and theologian of a much a much more varied and substantial body of work:

The essential point to realise about our policy in Ireland is that we have crossed a definitive line. It is a frontier and frontier is a fact, not an opinion. It is, among other things the boundary between Christendom and the barbarians ... The Prussians adopted the destructive method in Belgium and the English have now adopted it in Ireland ... It is if the governing class were to walk about naked or drink bumpers of blood. The Irish rebel feels as if he were in a cell with a homicidal maniac.[71]

A contrasting source, if not opinion, is *Irish Exile*:

We find Ireland drenched with blood, her towns and villages devastated by fire; her factories and creameries bombed and razed to the ground and her harvest burned; her national journals supressed; her manhood tortured, shot, hanged, or rounded up by a brutal soldiery into concentration camps; her old men, her women and children shot like pheasants; her churches, convents and monasteries desecrated; her priesthood killed, outraged and thrown into prisons. We find in short, every offence in the catalogue of crime committed against the Irish people.[72]

The *Irish Exile* was the newspaper of the England-based Irish Self-determination League (ISDL). Chesterton's words were published by the British-based Peace With Ireland Council. These opinions represent two sociological ends of a spectrum of opinion in Britain which, certainly from 1920 onwards, was highly critical of the government's Irish policy. That such opposition to British policy in Ireland existed has been well-established by D. G. Boyce, who has observed that 'by the spring of 1921 an influential body of political, intellectual and ecclesiastical opinion was ranged against the conduct of government policy in Ireland.'[73] Boyce's research will be briefly summarised here, as will one original source acknowledged by him, an unpublished account of the Peace With Ireland Council provided by George F. H. Berkeley,[74] one of the Council's principle organisers and one of the few Irish people centrally involved in that organisation. In addition, the work of the ISDL will be outlined, an organisation which although rather neglected by subsequent researchers was, as will be shown, capable of widespread week-by-week activity and, on occasions, of mobilising large public demonstrations.

The Peace With Ireland Council was publicly launched on 29 October 1920 and was designed, writes Berkeley, as 'an English protest against the policy of the government, and not to be confounded in any way with any kind of Irish resistance.'[75] Its architects and leadings spokespersons were, for the most part, well placed within British society. The Chairman was Conservative MP Lord Henry Cavendish-Bentinck and its Secretary was another Conservative MP, Oswald Mosley. Its speakers' list included Tory peers, Liberal members of both houses of parliaments, bishops and leading women members of all three main parties. The Labour Party was well represented with Ramsay MacDonald and Sidney Webb being its most prominent representatives. Bernard Shaw, spoke at its meeting, although he was not formally a member. It was though the Liberal Party which, in the words of Berkeley, was 'well to the fore'[76] and which supplied more of the members of the speakers list than the Conservatives or Labour. Berkeley also testifies that the Council, 'achieved far more success than it was entitled to expect, mainly because of the assistance which it received (and gave to) both the Liberal and Labour party machines.'[77]

The public activities of the Council centred on producing leaflets, pamphlets and organising and sending speakers to public meetings. There were nearly 200 such meetings and as many as 30 pamphlets were produced. As well as G. K. Chesterton, other famous writers included Hilaire Belloc, Robert Lynd and J. L. Hammond. The high point of the Council's activity was the winter of 1920–1921 when there were large meetings in such centres as Oxford, Birmingham, and Cambridge. An estimated four thousand people attended a public meeting in Manchester and an Albert Hall rally whose speakers included Lord Asquith, Cavendish-Bentinck, and the Bishop of Peterborough. 'We had 8,000 people there', writes Berkeley, 'I spent half-an-hour counting them.'[78] Boyce has concluded that that the Council was perhaps 'the most effective and certainly the most committed pressure group to protest against reprisals.'[79]

There were others who protested. For example, on 2 July 1921 the Woman's Freedom League organised a 10,000 strong demonstration in London protesting against the government's Irish policy, addressed among others by the veteran campaigner Charlotte Despot.[80] Berkeley has testified to another initiative from the women's movement, from around late 1920:

> I went out one evening to the Kingsway Hall to a meeting on Ireland under the auspices of the Women's International League. It was

excellently done. The speakers were good, and they had magic-lantern slides representing the sacked town of Balbriggan and other scenes of the sort which brought the true conditions home to the audience. In the end they made a collection. There were about 600 people present, but they seemed far from being rich. Nevertheless to my great surprise they subscribed no less than £67 to the campaign. Of course many of them were Irish! But for all that, here I thought, is hope and sympathy: and I may add that the Women's International League certainly deserved it ... I do not know what political creed these ladies professed. I believe that some of them were considered to hold extreme views. But as regards Ireland, at all events! I know that they were the first body of English people who had the courage to put their names to the truth.[81]

By late 1920, *The Times* and *Spectator* were opposed to reprisals, as were, more predictably, the *Manchester Guardian*, *Daily News* and, of course, *Daily Herald*. Indeed, among newspapers only the *Morning Post* and *National Review* unequivocally condoned reprisals.[82] Such opposition to aspects of the government's conduct in Ireland had its limits. The Peace With Ireland Council did not advocate a specific political solution, and certainly its personnel were not inclined to advocate an Irish Republic. Nevertheless it reflected a widespread opposition to government policy, and it established and reflected an atmosphere which should have encouraged others to take up the Irish issue, and to do so by moving on from protesting against the government to putting forward an alternative policy.

The impetus for the ISDL came from a different direction than that of the Council. In April 1921 its own newspaper, *Irish Exile*, described its origins and activities:

At the express instructions of President de Valera a new organisation was set up to keep exiles in close intercourse with their people in the motherland ... The ISDL was founded at Manchester on March 30th 1919 ... Two simple objects were set before members: (1) To secure the application of the principles of self-determination to Ireland and (2) to secure the release of all Irish political prisoners ... The League is open to all people of Irish birth or descent. All of its meetings are open to the public ... The League's activities consist of branch meetings, public meetings ... and ceilidhe to raise funds ... The League gives practical support to the study and use of the Irish language, history and literature ... issues pamphlet and leaflets ... collects money for the Irish White Cross fund.[83]

The first generation Irish in Britain was, by the outbreak of the Great War and its aftermath, in decline, and indeed had been for 40 years. Census figures say that there were 566,540 Irish in England and Wales (2.49 per cent of the population) in 1871, 375,325 in 1911 (1.04 per cent) and 364,747 (0.96 per cent) in 1921. The figures in Scotland were proportionally higher, but had still fallen from 207,770 (6.18 per cent) in 1871 to 174,715 (3.67 per cent) in 1911 and 159,020 (3.26 per cent) in 1921. Of course, such figures can be deceptive as they do not take account of second generation Irish, many of whom were involved in the Irish community in Britain. Indeed, the vice-president and leading figure of the ISDL, Art O'Brien (Art Ó Briain), was born in London of an English mother and an Irish father who had been a major in the British Army. He came to Irish nationalism through the London Gaelic League, which he joined in 1899.

By July 1921 the president of the ISDL, P. J. Kelly, could claim a membership 'greater than that of any previous Irish organisation in Great Britain',[84] and although this claim has been disputed,[85] certainly there is evidence of a spectacularly successful and active organisation. As well as its own publication, which was established relatively late, the ISDL's activities were reported in the *Catholic Herald*, whose editor Charles Diamond, a former Irish nationalist MP and in this period a Labour Party candidate, was often critical of the League because of its refusal to endorse and call for votes for the Labour Party.[86] The ISDL was also closely observed by Basil Thomson of Scotland Yard, whose weekly reports to the Cabinet on the British left regularly included a section on 'Sinn Féin Activities in Great Britain'. Thomson, Diamond and the ISDL itself concur in their reports and assessment of the League. By 1 November 1919 there were 54 branches, the following November this had risen to 214 and by November 1921 the peak of 294 had been reached.[87] According to the ISDL constitution there was a minimum of 15 members in each branch, and the total membership grew from 7,300 in February 1920,[88] 10,000 by April 1920,[89] 26,000 by November 1920[90] and 38,726 by March 1921.[91] By March 1922, following the ending of the War of Independence, splits in the ISDL over the Treaty and, said the general secretary, 'the great amount of unemployment' with its effect on subscriptions, the League's membership had declined to 20,405.[92] Although Boyce's view is that the ISDL membership was 'never high'[93] it was, for instance, equal to that of the ILP, and the League's growth over such a short period of time was little less than spectacular. The membership figures are all the more impressive as the ISDL did not organise in Scotland where Sinn Féin organised directly. In Glasgow and West Scotland alone there were, according to Basil Thomson in October 1920, 30,000 'volunteers'.[94] What exactly he meant by this is not clear, but it was the case that the IRA was organised in Britain from 1919 and active from late 1920, announcing its arrival with an arson attack on Liverpool docks in November 1920. Over 400 incidents of arson, sabotage, explosion and robberies of guns and armaments were to follow, although many of these were relatively minor; the death toll of one policeman, four IRA members and five civilians was also low.[95] Cumann na mBan, the women's associate of the IRA, also had branches in Britain and there were also branches of the Irish Volunteers before 1914 and after the 1914 split over the war. However, it was the ISDL that was the dominant organisation in the Irish community and which could mobilise large numbers. There was a 15,000 strong demonstration in Manchester in November 1919[96] and a 'packed'[97] rally at the Albert Hall in February 1920 saw 10,000 attending, with another 40,000 'applying for admission', resulting in in a separate overflow meeting.[98] A tour by the Republican-minded Catholic cleric Dr Mannix in November and December 1920, organised by the ISDL, attracted among others 4,000 in Rochdale, 3,000 in Blackburn, 1000 in Wigan[99] and 4,000 in Bolton.[100] When organising support for Irish hunger-strikers in Wormwood Scrubs prison in April 1920 the ISDL, on the same night, brought 10,000 onto the streets of London and 10,000 in Manchester, with other demonstrations in towns such as Bolton and Bradford and on Tyneside.[101] Right up to the signing of the Treaty, the ISDL remained capable of large mobilisations with 10,000 packing the Albert Hall to greet the Irish treaty negotiators in November 1921.[102]

As already suggested, the ISDL was closely monitored by the police. It was also subject to frequent raids and arrests. In the course of 1921 the general secretary, acting general secretary, treasurer, chief clerk, several full-time organisers, and several minor officials were arrested and deported to Ireland without charge or trial, where some were interned.[103]

Despite such difficulties it continued to function, and to address itself to mobilising the Irish community in England and Wales. Its second annual conference, held in Manchester in November 1920, amplified its objectives to securing recognition of the Irish Republic.

That the ISDL was able to mobilise large number of the Irish in Britain, despite the difficulties with the police, surely has some relevance in weighing up the possibilities of labour movement mobilisations on the Irish issue, especially as it was in the Irish working class in Britain that the ISDL had its roots. The *Catholic Herald* complained in February 1920 that, 'the more respectable' of the Irish in Britain 'have not been particularly courageous', and that where 'patriotism' or 'lovers of liberty' existed was, 'in the ranks of the common people.'[104] Basil Thomson reported that those at a 700 strong ISDL meeting in March 1920 in Birmingham 'were chiefly of the poorer classes.'[105]

For its part, the ISDL, as already suggested, was not prepared to enter a formal alliance with any British political party. Its constitution declared 'no Branch or District Committee shall at any time take any action in regard to or any part in English politics'[106] and attempts by Diamond to get this changed with an endorsement for Labour candidates who supported Irish self-determination failed. Nevertheless, the ISDL at times did orientate towards and took part in labour movement activities. For example it participated in a May Day demonstration in London in 1921 which ended in Hyde Park where the ISDL set up two platforms 'right in the heart of the ... labour demonstration', and which attracted 'mostly Irish, but there was a fair sprinkling of British trade unionists'.[107] The following month at an ISDL demonstration in Hyde Park, the principle speaker was a by-election Labour Party candidate.[108] For Basil Thomson, writing in 1919, the trend was ominous: 'under the guise of a Self-Determination League for Ireland there is a tendency all over the country for Irish and Labour Associations to work together.'[109] This was an exaggeration and the controversial historian Peter Hart also over-stated when he located the ISDL and the IRA in Britain as 'an extension of British post war radicalism as much as Irish Republicanism'.[110] There were, no doubt, individuals who were active in both the British labour movement and ISDL, but the ISDL was conceived in Ireland and made a point of its political independence. Moreover, the fact that O'Brien, Kelly and those in the ISDL and IRA in Britain whose participation was later recorded by the Bureau of Military History[111] came to such activity through previous activity in the Irish community, notably the Gaelic League, suggests that this is where their ideological and cultural roots mainly were.

The extent to which cooperation between the ISDL and the labour movement did or did not exist was not just determined by the ISDL's determination to be politically independent. Obviously, the more unenthusiastic or equivocal the labour movement was on Ireland the more unenthusiastic and equivocal the ISDL would be about the labour movement. The judgement given by the ISDL and others in the Irish community on the working class organisations and Ireland will be referred to in the concluding chapter. What is noteworthy at the moment is that both it and the Peace With Ireland Council showed by their activities what could be done on Ireland and how successful this could be. Certainly, by the end of 1920 there did seem to be widespread sentiment for action on Ireland, a sentiment ranging from important figures and opinion formers in the Conservative establishment to the poor Irish. The growth in working class political activity and class consciousness at approximately the same time, together with the escalation of the Irish crisis, would suggest that the labour and socialist movement would be likely to welcome the opportunity to tap into that sentiment, especially given its own criticism of government policy. But how would it do so? That was to become the issue. The *Daily Herald* in October 1920 put it this way:

It is no use for Labour to disassociate itself from the government's responsibility. Labour abhors both the futility and the utter wickedness of the government's policy; but it is not enough to stand aside. Labour stopped the war with Russia over Poland. Labour could equally stop the massacre of the Irish people. If Labour fails to stop the massacre it must share responsibility for it.[112]

And:

Ireland's crime ... is to desire the freedom in whose name British soldiers died ... The duty of the British public is to overthrow by any means whether political or industrial the government that has dishonoured the British race.[113]

This was big talk.

3
The Labour Party

One judgement of the performance of the British working class during and after the Great War was made by Mrs Shirley Williams in 1987. She wrote of the 'extraordinary patience and stoicism of the British people, and particularly of the English.' She noted 'The Clyde workers did, after all, organize and fight', and that 'the Welsh miners on more than one occasion used the strike weapon to protect their fellow workers from victimization'. However:

> But the English working people rarely fought for their rights, or protested against the extreme injustices meted out to them. After the war, when revolution swept like a forest fire through the European continent. The English settled for an extension of the franchise and, in 1924, for a minority Labour government.[1]

When these words were being written, Williams had herself acquired a reputation for political moderation. She had left the Labour Party, on whose behalf she had served as a Cabinet member, saying it was too left wing, formed the Social Democratic Party and then oversaw its merger with the Liberals. So, many would conclude, for her to complain of the temperance of the post-war proletariat, then things indeed must have reached a level of English working class restraint which was beyond timidity.

Yet the securing of votes for virtually all men aged 21 and over, and all women aged 30 and over, was a major reform. Additionally, the British working class had its own political party, the Labour Party, which now at least tiptoed in Westminster corridors, and whose large majority of Members of Parliament came from what was then called 'humble origins'. Also, that party had, by the end of 1918, professionalised itself and defined its purpose. The latter was to found in *Labour and New Social Oder* and the new party constitution, both of which looked forward to significant wealth redistribution and nationalisation of major industries. The professionalisation was also found in the new constitution that moved the party from being an amalgamation of trade unions and socialist organisations to a mass party with local branches. Williams is right to suggest that compared with what had happened elsewhere in Europe's proletariat, most notably the revolutions in Russia and the attempted revolution in Germany, the British working class's ambitions and achievements were modest. Yet compared with where Labour had been a quarter of a century before there had been progress, and with _New Social Order_ in particular Labour had differentiated itself ideologically from Liberalism, where many of the party members served their political apprentice. The issue was, what would Labour do next and how would they wield the influence they had acquired. To take the case of Ireland, which, after all, saw in these years the then British state's very own revolution, is not a bad place to start. This examination of the Labour Party's Irish will focus on its three constituent parts, which the 1918 constitution had re-defined: that is, the Party conference, the National Executive Committee (NEC) and its parliamentary party (PLP).

The Party Conference

Ever since the Labour Party was reconstructed at the end of the Great War, there has been controversy over the power and authority of its annual party conference. Decade after decade, local party activists have sought to use the conference to determine policy and its enactment, and to insist that decisions taken there should govern the wider party and its parliamentary representatives. And decade after decade those parliamentary representatives have said that this is not necessarily so. The wording of the 1918 constitution gives comfort to both arguments. On the one hand it was the 'duty' of the conference to decided 'what specific proposals' should be supported by the party and promoted by the NEC and the PLP. On the other hand the 'principles' agreed by the conference were only to be followed by the parliamentary party 'as far as may be practicable', and even then only if there was a two-thirds conference majority. Nevertheless, and despite this ambivalence, the party conference has mattered and has at least enjoyed a moral authority.

Before 1918, the conference had showed little enthusiasm to exercise such authority as far as Ireland was concerned. The BSP's _Call_ complained in January 1918 that 'the leaders of the British Labour movement are, as a rule, silent on Ireland',[2] but it was a silence shared by many others in the party. The hesitancy before 1916 has already been recorded and it was not until the eighteenth party conference, held in June 1918, when the party or its forerunner, the LRC, debated a policy for Ireland. It is true that the Parliamentary Report presented to the 1917 conference recorded that the PLP 'deplores the failure to give legislative effect to the temporary settlement of the Home Rule controversy'.[3] Accordingly, by endorsing this report the conference did, de facto, adopt an Irish policy in the form of support for traditional Home Rule as set out in the parliamentary legislation of 1912 and 1914. However, the Easter Rising and its aftermath suggested that this legislation needed amending. Indeed, the government admitted as much by establishing the Irish National Convention, which first met in July 1917. The report of Labour's NEC presented to the January 1918 conference was optimistic about the Convention, detecting 'indications of the possibility of a general agreement on a self-governing policy following its deliberations'.[4] Again, in endorsing this report, the conference sanctioned the Irish aspects of it without discussion.

The first specific Irish debate occurred at the June 1918 conference around a resolution supported by the NEC and moved by James O'Grady, MP. O'Grady was an interesting choice. Born of Irish working class parents in Bristol, he had been a union activist and later an official in a furniture workers union. He had been a member of the Marxist Social Democratic Federation, then the ILP, then after the 1906 general election a Labour MP – and the only Catholic one at that time. In his maiden speech he had articulated his support for Home Rule, but insisted on Ireland's loyalty to the wider British state. He was an enthusiastic supporter of the war. In 1918 he received a commission under the Irish Recruiting Council and went to Dublin to help with recruitment. This was not a happy experience, and he complained about the lack of support he received, telling one newspaper, 'I even had to walk through the streets with a servant maid carrying my own portmanteau.'[5] It is fair to suggest both he and his 1918 conference resolution were out of date. The latter said:

That this Conference unhesitatingly recognises the claim of the people of Ireland to Home Rule and to self-determination in all exclusively Irish affairs; it protests against the stubborn resistance to a democratic reorganisation of Irish government maintained by those who, alike in

Ireland and Great Britain are striving to keep minorities dominant; and it demands a wide and generous measure of Home Rule on the lines initiated by the proceedings of the Irish Convention, should be immediately passed into law and put into operation.[6]

The reference to the Convention was amended out of the resolution. The key argument was the sentence limiting self-determination to Irish affairs; not only the key sentence on this occasion, but, in one variation or another, for the next three years. The issue was how independent from Britain British Labour would allow Ireland to be. At the June 1918 conference this was raised, with an amendment moved by the National Union of Shop Assistants, Warehousemen and Clerks, and seconded by the BSP. This deleted 'exclusively Irish affairs'. On behalf of the BSP, Sylvia Pankhurst said that passing the resolution without the amendment 'would be going absolutely contrary to the wishes of the majority of the Irish people.'[7] In reply, one delegate warned of the dangers to Britain if the Irish were allowed to establish an independent army or navy,[8] a concern which was, as will be seen, to become a common one. The amendment was lost and the resolution was carried.

There was no debate at the 1919 conference, but the 1920 one saw a second round in the controversy that had started in June 1918. By now, with Sinn Féin victories in the 1918 general election and subsequent local council elections, Pankhurst's words had proved prophetic. Indeed even before the 1920 conference met at Scarborough, the importance of the Irish issue was attracting comment. Previewing the conference, an editorial in *Labour Leader* maintained, 'the ambiguity about the Labour Party's policy on Ireland should be removed, and it should be made unmistakably clear that the Party stands for the free and unfettered right of the Irish people to determine their own form of government'.[9] Then, when the conference began, the Presidential Address given by Mr Hutchinson of the Amalgamated Engineering Society insisted, 'Ireland must be given the form of government she desires. If it be an independent and separate Republic can Labour deny her that right?'[10]

Answers to that question were forthcoming during the debate on Ireland later in the week. The motion tabled was in the name of the party executive and was moved on its behalf by Sidney Webb. This called for 'withdrawal of the British Army of Occupation', but that was so uncontentious that it attracted little attention and no opposition, an indication of the low esteem in which British forces in Ireland were now held by many in Britain. But there was controversy elsewhere. Even before Webb spoke, a delegate called for reference back and redrafting, maintaining the resolution was 'contradictory'.[11] The objection was that while the resolution demanded, 'that the principle of free and absolute self-determination shall be applied immediately in the case of Ireland', it also said that any Irish constitution drawn up by an Irish assembly should be confined to 'exclusively Irish affairs.'[12] Webb attempted to deal with this ambiguity by arguing that 'whilst they may be quite frank and sincere in offering Ireland complete self-determination for all Irish affairs, that did not mean they wanted Ireland to go spinning along the road like a motor hog, without regard to anyone else on the road.'[13] Seconding the motion, an ILP delegate spoke in favour of no limitation on self-determination, as did a delegate from the Post Office Workers who, in supporting the resolution, asked conference to 'give Ireland an opportunity of saying what form of government it wanted, whether an Irish Republic or not.'[14] By then it was clear that the motion meant different things to different people, with both Webb, who supported qualifications on self-determination, and the ILP, which did not, speaking in favour. Not surprisingly, therefore, a second attempt to refer back the resolution to the Standing Orders Committee was supported by both sides in the debate and endorsed by the conference. When the resolution returned to the conference floor, British military withdrawal remained, as did 'absolute and free self-determination', but 'exclusively Irish affairs' did not. However, the issue was faced squarely when an amendment from the Iron and Steel Trades sought to re-insert this qualification.

Of those who spoke in the debate, Emanuel Shinwell (ILP), Mr T. Cunningham (Ardwick Labour Party), Councillor Bamford (Bermondsey), an unnamed 'Irish Delegate' and Ben Tillett (Dockers) spoke in favour of the resolution and against the amendment. The contrary view was expressed by a delegate from Workers Union and by NEC member J. H. Thomas. When the vote was taken, the amendment was lost by 1,191,000 votes to 945,000. Thus, Labour's party conference had voted that Ireland 'takes its place among the nations of the earth', to quote the words of 1803 revolutionary Robert Emmet. This did not last long.

On 29 December 1920 a special party conference was held to debate two issues: unemployment and Ireland. On Ireland, the conference had before it a report from the Labour Party Commission, which had just returned from Ireland and, as seen, was strongly critical of British government policy, having also supported the withdrawal of British armed forces. More significantly, the main resolution, based on the report, before the conference called for:

> An immediate election, by proportional representation, of an entirely open constitutional assembly, charged to work out, at the earliest possible moment, without limitation or fetters, whatever constitution for Ireland the Irish people desire, subject to only two conditions, that it affords protection to minorities, and that the constitution should prevent Ireland from becoming a military or naval menace to Great Britain.[15]

The resolution had been drafted by the NEC, who decided in advance that no amendment to it would be allowed. *Labour Leader* was to subsequently criticise the conference for being an 'almost entirely platform affair',[16] but with no counter position permitted the resolution was over-whelmingly carried. Although it would be an obvious exaggeration to describe the new policy as 'Home Rule', unqualified self-determination had been dropped. On the other hand, because of the manner in which the debate was conducted it could be argued that neither the party as a whole, nor the conference was given an opportunity to debate that change.

The 1921 conference presented the possibility for further discussion. The ILP submitted a resolution calling for a general strike on the Irish issue, as did three local parties, while a further ten local Labour parties had resolutions well to the left of that adopted at the Special Conference. Yet again, only a NEC resolution was selected for debate. This began by expressing 'detestation and abhorrence at the continued see-saw of crime and reprisals and counter-reprisals', and went on to endorse the Special Conference policy. By then, according to the 1921 resolution, this had been 'adopted at hundreds of public meetings' organised by the party as part of its campaign on Ireland in the intervening period, a factor which would have made the resolution more difficult to amend. In the event, although the 1921 conference did witness Jack Jones, MP, complaining that the NEC motion was 'mild', 'pious' and 'should be stronger', with no alternative permitted it was carried unanimously.[17] Once again, however, it is an open question what the result would have been if a full debate had been allowed.

In summary, Conference policy on the Irish national question in these years was: up to 1918 implicit support for Home Rule, made explicit at the 1918 conference; unqualified self-determination at the June 1920 conference; but qualified from December 1920 onwards. Whether or not the result would have been different had a freer debate been allowed in the last two conferences must remain conjecture. What is clear is that it was the national executive who took the lead in trying to frame policy, and who, explicitly or implicitly, at each conference advised rejection of unrestricted self-determination. Accordingly, the NEC's role was central.

The National Executive

The 1918 constitution had expanded Labour's NEC from 16 to 23 members. Of these, 13 included representatives from affiliated organisations, five local party members, four women and the treasurer. These were elected directly by the party conference where the unions dominated. For the most part, the unions supplied the affiliated organisations positions, although these also included ILP and Fabian Society representatives. For this period that meant, respectively, Fred Jowett and Sidney Webb. The treasurer was Ramsay Macdonald, who had lost his parliamentary seat in the 1918 election. Arthur Henderson had been party secretary since 1912 and was chiefly responsible for the party's 1918 reorganisation.

The NEC made no public comment on, nor did it discuss at its own internal meetings, the 1916 Rising, the executions which followed or the subsequent British security/military measures. The first minuted discussion in this period was on 6 March 1917, just over a month after Count Plunkett had won the Roscommon by-election on a pro-Republican ticket. The NEC recognised things were changing. It urged the government, 'in the interests equally of Great Britain and Ireland' to make to make a new effort 'to reach a settlement of the Irish question'.[18] This resolution did not specify what government action was required, but two months later Lloyd George announced plans for the holding of the Irish Convention. The NEC took no position on this, but it was endorsed by Arthur Henderson.[19] Neither Sinn Féin nor Irish Labour attended the Convention, absences which, for the NEC, probably mattered less than the participation of the parliamentary Nationalists. For, on February

1918 the NEC wrote to the Irish TUC and Labour Party (ITUCLP) defending the practice of the PLP 'accepting the views of the Irish Nationalist Party in preference to those of the Irish Labour Movement', citing the Nationalists' strength in the House of Commons.[20]

After the March 1917 statement criticising the government for inaction, the NEC showed a similar disinclination, not discussing Ireland again until its meeting of April 1918. The context then was the Military Service Act and the application of Irish conscription. Before the Act had been passed, in a joint meeting with the Parliamentary Committee of the TUC and the PLP, the NEC had listed Irish conscription as one of six objections to the legislation.[21] When the bill was passed, the NEC and Parliamentary Committee met again to discuss how to respond. This time the views of Irish Labour were taken into account. Henderson reported on discussions he had with the ITUCLP and its opposition to conscription.[22] J. H. Thomas told the same NEC meeting of similar sentiments expressed to him on a recent trip to Dublin. Accordingly, the NEC and Parliamentary Committee sought and were given an immediate meeting with the Prime Minister at which they presented a *Memorandum on Irish Conscription*. This began with an 'appeal' to the government not to apply conscription to Ireland 'on grounds of principle and expediency alike – not to violate the national conscience, and not to jeopardise the whole future of the country and its Allies in their success in the war, by imposing conscription on a nation without its consent.'[23] At the meeting with Lloyd George, J. H. Thomas appeared to modify the party's position by suggesting the government 'suspend' the implementation of Irish conscription until a Home Rule parliament was established.[24] Lloyd George would have neither the general opposition to Irish conscription nor the particular suggestion of Thomas. In the latter case his argument was that even if there was a Home Rule parliament, it would have no power over conscription because, 'in no scheme of Home Rule that had ever been seriously formulated had it been proposed that military affairs should be the subject of a decision by an Irish parliament.'[25] Labour, as already noted, was starting to struggle with this this very issue and was to do so for the next three years, so a coherent challenge to Lloyd George's premise would have been difficult.

Having been rebuffed by Lloyd George, the Labour leaders proceeded cautiously with their opposition to conscription, agreeing not to make public their *Memorandum*. A majority of the NEC favoured publication, but the Parliamentary Committee did not, arguing Lloyd George should first have the right to reply. The joint meeting of the two leaderships agreed to this by eight votes to six,[26] but the decision was made meaningless when the *Memorandum* was leaked to the press.

This episode suggests that Labour's leaders were not enthusiastic about making a major issue out of Ireland. A similar conclusion can be drawn from the July meeting of the NEC. At this, Henderson reported that he had been approached by John Dillon of the Nationalists with the proposal that the Labour Party should 'co-operate in the holding of Demonstrations throughout the Industrial Centres of Great Britain, during the Autumn urging the application of self-determination to the Irish people'. The NEC stalled, agreeing only to 'pursue conservations with Mr Dillon',[27] and nothing more was heard of the proposal. However, three months later the NEC did express its 'deep misgivings' about the government's Irish policy and warned of 'the dangers that lie ahead unless a determined effort is made to settle the Irish question satisfactorily'.[28] This resolution did not specify how the government should proceed, although the NEC's own resolution had just recently been passed at party conference calling for self-determination in 'all exclusively Irish affairs'. It is somewhat surprising, then, that when the NEC and PLP produced their manifesto for the 1918 general election, it promised:

> The principles which Labour acclaims as Allied war aims it will apply to its own subject peoples. Freedom for Ireland and India it claims, and it will extend to all subject peoples the right to self-determination within the British Commonwealth of nations.[29]

While this formulation left unresolved what would occur if 'subject peoples' did not wish to stay in the Commonwealth, it seemed to go much further than had the party conference on the extent of Irish self-determination that Labour would support. Seven months later second thoughts followed when the NEC discussed and approved another manifesto, this time a by-election in which its candidate was Arthur Henderson. On this occasion the phrase, 'the fullest measure of Home Rule' for Ireland was utilised, to which was added, 'and further, we advocate the establishment of separate local legislatures for England, Scotland and Wales'.[30] This put the Irish policy in the context of the general devolutionary schemes favoured by the party and indeed the Liberal Party in bygone days.

At the beginning of 1920 there was further evidence of the party leadership's hesitancy, even lack of confidence when MacDonald, wrote that, 'the Irish problem may become so hardened that a Labour government may be baffled by it, just as much as this government is'.[31] Signs of a more collective uncertainty were shown at a joint meeting of the NEC and PLP the following month which discussed how to respond on the King's Speech. One proposal was that the PLP should move a specific amendment on Ireland, 'on the lines of self-determination', but this was deemed too radical. Instead the issue was to be 'dealt in general debate and that officers confer with members of the Nationalist Party regarding an amendment'.[32] It did not seem to matter the Nationalists had just been overwhelmed by Sinn Féin in the general election.

The government proceeded to publish its proposals with the Government of Ireland Bill, which included two Irish parliaments subordinate to Westminster. This pushed Labour into clarifying its alternative. A joint meeting of the NEC and PLP on 25 February had before it a report of a recently returned delegation of five MPs to Ireland. The details of this will follow shorty when discussing the PLP, but it included self-determination, with the now familiar qualifications concerning British defence interests and safeguards for Ulster.[33] The NEC and PLP endorsed this. Then, just when it appeared a policy had been agreed, there came both a new challenge and a return to prevarication.

The difficulties arose at a by-election in Stockport, when the Labour candidate Sir Leo Chiozza Money and the NEC were challenged by a group of local Irish on their policy for Ireland. When Money was questioned he found little favour because of an 'unsatisfactory attitude towards the shootings of Connolly and Pearse'.[34] Two of the Irish community subsequently met the NEC who, when asked 'if they were in favour of unqualified self-determination for Ireland' replied, '"No" ... they are only in favour of self-determination for Ireland in Irish affairs'.[35] The NEC then issued a long statement seeking to clarify its attitude. This maintained that it 'is not authorised to lay down policy. The Conference of the Labour Party alone determines policy'. The rest of the statement went on to express a number of formulations, at times contradictory, and at other times ones the party conference had not endorsed. These included: 'the Labour Party is committed to the principle of self-

determination ... the acceptance of this principle implies the right of the
Irish to determine their own future'. But, 'if Ireland were left free to
decide whether she would remain in the Empire or become completely
separated ... the Irish people upon mature consideration would decide
the link should not be completely severed'. Therefore 'an immediate
decision on the issue of Union or Separation might not be a true reflex
of the considered opinion of the majority of the Irish', as it involved, 'a
total repudiation of any form of connection' with Britain. The roots of
this reasoning to defer an Irish vote on leaving the Empire came from
the recommendations of the five MPs who had visited Ireland on behalf
of the PLP.

The Stockport statement then went on to quote the Home Rule
resolution adopted at the 1918 conference, but added that it 'is now nearly
two years old, and both events and opinions have developed since it was
passed.' Even more confusingly the statement then cited a resolution
passed by the Socialist International declaring that 'absolute self-
determination' should be 'applied immediately in the case of Ireland',
by 'the free, equal and secret vote of the people'. The NEC said that
this resolution was 'supported by the Labour Party', but added to the
confusion by saying that the NEC was backing a motion going to the
1920 conference supporting, 'the most complete Self-Determination', but
'in exclusively Irish affairs'.

When Ramsay MacDonald was asked by the Stockport Irish to explain
one of the many contradictions in this statement – that between the
positions of the Labour Party and the Socialist International – he said
the party supported the International resolution 'out of sympathy, and
[it] was not intended as a practical policy'.[36] It was hardly surprising that
the Stockport Irish reacted to all this befuddlement by putting up its own
candidate in the by-election, William O'Brien of the Irish Labour Party
and TUC (ILPTUC), as the ITUCLP had now become, who at the time
was in Wormwood Scrubs jail on hunger strike. He polled 2,346 votes;
Labour lost the by-election by just over 6,000.

The whole episode showed the NEC to be dithering on Ireland.
However, during the discussions it had insisted that party policy was
determined by conference, so, following the Stockport controversy,
the decision of that conference in June 1920 to support unqualified
self-determination that should have given the NEC a new brief. First
indications were that the party leaders were articulating the more radical

policy. Shortly after the conference MacDonald wrote that while he did 'not believe that an Irish Republic is necessary', he also argued that to 'save' Ireland 'from reaction and obscurantism we must trust Ireland with self-determination.'[37] Using a more generous tone, Arthur Henderson, in a letter to *The Times* in October 1920, indicated his willingness to move in the direction of conference policy. He observed that, while in December 1919 'I had reason to believe that Dominion status would have been accepted by a majority of the Irish people ... the latest developments have destroyed the possibility of settlement on these terms.' Henderson called for an Irish constituent assembly, and while he still maintained there had to be 'safeguards for minorities' there was no further qualification on self-determination.[38] But there was a return to inconsistency in November when the NEC issued its own Irish manifesto, accurately described by the *New Statesman* as 'embodying a policy which is practically identical to the new Liberal policy – namely self-determination, subject only to two conditions, the protection of minorities and the strategic security of the UK.'[39] Thus the military/strategic question had reappeared. It was accompanied in the manifesto by a bland, and as it turned out, naive assurance that 'the Labour Party believes that the Irish may now confidently rely on the British people not to make use of that superiority in bargaining power to exact in the terms of the agreement anything derogatory to the effective autonomy of Ireland'.[40]

The policy in the manifesto was, of course, contrary to that of the party conference of June 1920, where indeed it had been specifically voted down, so the assurances given to the Stockport Irish about following conference policy proved hollow remarkably quickly. Fortunately for the NEC, the stage-managed December 1920 conference gave it a new mandate. Also by then, the NEC's position had received support from what was, on the surface, a surprising source. For, as the *New Statesmen* explained, the two qualifications on self-determination had 'already been accepted by the Irish [Labour Party and] Trades Union Congress' earlier in the week in which the NEC manifesto was issued.'[41] This was unexpected because the ILPTUC annual conference in August 1920 had carried a motion supporting 'the right of the people of Ireland ... to choose and decide ... the constitution and form of government, and the social, political and judicial institutions under which they shall live.' There was also a call for the rights of minorities, but only after self-determination was achieved and not as a pre-condition to it. So, how did the Labour Party persuade the ILPTUC to moderating its policy?

The process appears to have started at a joint meeting of the NEC, the PLP and the Parliamentary Committee of the TUC on 18 October 1920, at which a deputation was received from the ILPTUC. This informed the British Labour leaders that 'the Irish Labour Party had been generally satisfied with the terms of the resolution' adopted at the June conference, backing unqualified self-determination, but complained that 'within a fortnight ... Labour members were advocating a policy that fell far short' of the Scarborough conference policy. At the end of the meeting, Arthur Henderson proposed further joint consultation between the leaders of the two movements, 'with the object of arriving at some common policy which could be the subject of propaganda throughout Great Britain', and a possible joint committee.[42] The newspaper of the ITGWU reported the Irish side's reaction to this proposal:

> They could not agree or disagree with it, but they could assure the other side that Irish Labour would not be prepared to accept the Committee unless the movement in England – and all sections of it and its chief spokesmen – meant real business on Ireland and got down to that business.[43]

Two days after the meeting with the ILPTUC, Henderson, in the House of Commons, called for a commission of inquiry into the government's reprisals policy,[44] but was rebuffed by the government. Then, on 10 November, Henderson proposed that the Labour Party launch its own more wide-ranging inquiry to be followed by a national campaign on Ireland, based on the NEC manifesto. He did so at a meeting of the International Joint Sub-Committee of the NEC, PLP and TUC.[45] Only six days later the ILPTUC met in a conference, at the very end of which the new policy on self-determination, with the restrictions on defence and minority rights, was introduced. There was a proposer, a seconder and only one other speaker.[46] The relevant issue of the ITGWU newspaper, *Watchword of Labour*, which was normally critical of British Labour's attempts to limit self-determination,[47] reported this decision in two lines and without comment.[48] For its part, just two days later the NEC endorsed Henderson's initiative and added the secretary of the ILPTUC to its commission of inquiry.[49] He was Tom Johnson, whose own history was more in line with Henderson than with the radical wing of Irish labour as represented by the heritage of Connolly and Larkin. Johnson had been a home ruler and pro-war, and was an Englishman whose early career in Irish trade unionism was as a union official in Belfast. Johnson, says one Irish labour historian, was 'a non-violent socialist at a time of revolution and armed struggle ... he did not fully understand the deep-rooted nationalist feelings of most Irish workers.'[50]

Out of this commission came, as already recorded, the call for British withdrawal, fierce condemnation of reprisals, and even sympathy with the Irish Volunteers/IRA, but also the qualifications of self-determination as outlined in the NEC's manifesto and the ILPTUC conference. Thus, whatever the precise manoeuvres, there is a suggestion of a deal being done, with the ILPTUC modifying its Republicanism in return for the Labour Party having 'got down to business', including launching a national campaign. This willingness of the ILPTUC to politically compromise may also reflect concerns about alienating its Belfast Protestant membership.[51]

Apart from all of this manoeuvring, what is also noteworthy is that when collaborating with the Irish labour movement British Labour Party leaders reversed previous attitudes. As we have seen, for a number of years Henderson, the NEC and the PLP had argued that in formulating their policy for Ireland there was no onus on them to consult their counterparts in Ireland; rather, they would listen to the parliamentary Irish Nationalists because they were the majority party in Ireland. Indeed, as already outlined, the NEC and PLP were still consulting the Nationalists as late as January 1920, even though it could not have been seriously argued then that they were still representative of majority Irish opinion. However, by the end of the year, in working with the ILPTUC British Labour seemed to have reached a similar conclusion – but if the guiding principle had been consultation with majority opinion, Sinn Féin rather than Irish Labour should have replaced the Nationalists as British Labour's collaborators. As this was not even attempted, it can be suggested that a more likely motivation behind the actions of the Party's NEC was to consult with those with whom they had the closest agreement. When the choice was between the Nationalists and the more Republican ILPTUC, the choice was the Nationalists; when it was between the ILPTUC and the even more Republican Sinn Féin, Irish Labour was selected.

Following the decisions of the December 1920 conference and Labour's campaign of public meetings which followed, the NEC reverted to caution. Two approaches from the Peace With Ireland Council to hold a joint campaign or demonstration on Ireland in June 1921 were rebuffed by the executive.[52] This was despite the intensification of the government's pursuit of a military solution in the first half of 1921, despite Labour's demands and campaign for the opposite approach. When the truce came in July 1921, the NEC's passivity over the previous few months was again apparent when it 'agreed to make no public statement on Ireland at the present stage'.[53] In early September, however, when there were signs that the truce might break down, the NEC and Parliamentary Committee issued a joint statement. This spoke of 'a disaster if the deep spontaneous feeling for peace which now pervades the two peoples were allowed to evaporate' and said that the British and Irish negotiators needed to 'escape from verbal controversy to a recognition of the realities of the problem'.[54]

This statement was not the original that had been proposed by the NEC. No copy of that statement survives in the NEC minutes; however, those of the TUC Parliamentary Committee record that it was a 'modification' of an NEC proposal.[55] Nevertheless, in agreeing to the joint statement, the NEC was now adopting what was, in effect, a neutral position in the negotiations between the Irish and British, and declining to put forward its own basis for a settlement. In previous years, there had been limited discussion, prevarication, confusion and a disinclination to abide by what the Irish voted for. There had also been condemnation of the government's version of law and order. Now, it seemed that the dominant wish was that the whole business should be brought to an end.

One further context should be noted. The campaign of public meetings agreed by the NEC followed a similar venture by Asquith's Liberals. Indeed, throughout 1920 the Liberal Party and Labour had clashed over who was most militant on Ireland, with Asquith, for example, saying that Labour had 'no record at all' on Ireland. He went so far as to blame the Labour members of the war-time coalition for sharing responsibility for the crisis, through their decision to threaten Irish conscription in 1918.[56] Given Asquith's own record on Ireland, that was a bit much, but he was playing parliamentary games. How did Labour perform in that arena?

The Parliamentary Party

From Easter 1916 to the close of 1921, there were two distinct Parliamentary Labour Parties. The first, consisting of 42 MPs, was elected in the December 1910 general election; the second, with 63 MPs, in the general election of December 1918. The two parties operated under different political circumstances: the first, when a wartime political truce was observed and when Labour MPs served in a coalition government; the second, when, outside the new coalition, Labour became the official opposition for the first time. This PLP was hampered by the failure of a number of the more prominent Labour figures to get elected in 1918. These included Henderson, MacDonald, Snowden and Lansbury. With only three members of the ILP elected, the left of the party was under-represented. The leader of the party, as chairman of the PLP, was Arthur Henderson from 1914 to August 1917, followed by William Adamson until 1921, who was then succeeded by J. R. Clynes. Both Adamson and Clynes were subsequently assessed by Ralph Miliband as 'extreme moderates and mediocre parliamentarians to boot.'[57] The PLP was also often criticised at the time by the broader party. At the 1920 conference, for example, there was an attempt to refer back the entire Parliamentary Report on the grounds of the poor attendance at the House of Commons of the Labour MPs. There was even criticism of the PLP's attitude to Ireland. In May 1918, *Labour Leader*, when complaining of the PLP's reluctance to oppose Irish conscription, asked:

> How long, might we ask, are we to have the contemptible spectacle of Labour Party conference passing resolutions upon important matters of public policy, and the Labour Party executive issuing manifestos on these questions, and at the same time the official Labour Party in Parliament following a line of action in opposition to the Party policy?[58]

In January 1920, the anti-parliamentarian *Call* was even more scathing, saying, 'The action, or rather inaction' of the PLP on Ireland, 'has been utterly deplorable.' The charge was that:

> Not one brave word of protest has been spoken by any of them against the dragooning of the Irish people and the strangling of Irish liberties.

Totally lacking in initiative, fatally overawed by the legislative atmosphere, and totally ignorant of Irish aspirations they might ... have been dead and buried for all the effect they have had.[59]

This was certainly good invective, and it is the case is that even before Labour entered the war-time government its parliamentary representatives expressed support for the most important aspects of government policy. When the Government of Ireland Act was suspended at the outbreak of war, Arthur Henderson told the Commons that 'the whole of the country, every part of it, not only Ireland, but the other parts will say there was no other course open.'[60] The Easter Rising suggested such optimism was misplaced, but there was no full scale Irish debate in the Commons after the Rising until October 1916. The occasion was a Nationalist motion declaring that the 'system of government at present maintained in Ireland is inconsistent with the principles for which the Allies are fighting in Europe, and has been responsible for the recent unhappy events and for the present state of feeling in the country'.[61] Two Labour MPs spoke: J. H. Thomas who confined his remarks to a railway strike then taking place in Ireland, and James O'Grady. He congratulated the Nationalists in 'getting men to join the Colours', criticised the execution of James Connolly ('a friend of mine'), argued that the government reaction to the Rising had 'not diminished the support of the Sinn Féin movement in Ireland, but increased it', and proposed 'the formation of an Imperial Council' at which representatives of South Africa, Australia, New Zealand, Canada and the UK could 'discuss a question of this kind'. O'Grady concluded by saying, 'the Irish people have been sold by the British government', but that 'though I am speaking like this and speaking in the name of my party ... we will not do anything to embarrass this government in carrying out the War.'[62]

The proposal of an Imperial Council to discuss Ireland was certainly not the policy of the Party Conference, and there is no record of the NEC proposing it. But O'Grady did underline that he was speaking in the name of Labour, so perhaps it was sanctioned in advance by the PLP. Either way, no more was heard about an Imperial Council. Instead, when the government established the Irish Convention, the PLP's support for the government returned, saying it 'holds out ... a reasonable change of settlement.'[63]

As it became clear that the Convention's prospects were slight, PLP speakers in the Commons became more critical. In October 1917, O'Grady maintained that 'there were no white people on earth ... that would put up with the government that Ireland has had for the past hundred years.' Again, however, he placed such criticism second to supporting the war effort, saying, 'if the government ... would only give justice to the Irish people you would get the whole of the Irish people on your side, which would be in the interests not only of the British Empire, but also of the cause of the Allies.'[64] Even by October 1917, this suggestion of a possible Irish rush to the British war effort was becoming somewhat delusional, and was a reflection of just how distant the Home Ruler O'Grady was becoming from the contemporary Irish sentiment. As to what his 'justice' would entail, O'Grady was not clear, and even nine months later Labour's leader, William Adamson, speaking in the House of Commons was both moderate and vague, calling for 'a measure of Home Rule as will be satisfactory to the aspirations of the Irish people.'[65]

At least it can be said that Adamson reflected conference and NEC policy; but what of the complaint by *Labour Leader*, quoted above, regarding the PLP's attitude to Irish conscription? The NEC's and Parliamentary Committee's opposition to this, as contained in their *Memorandum* of April 1918, has been described, but so has the lack of enthusiasm when it came to making it a major political issue. Labour's George Barnes did argue against conscription in the Cabinet,[66] but, when it came to the parliamentary debate on the Military Service Bill, the PLP declined to move any amendment in opposition to the Irish clause or in respect of any of their other objections to the measure. The specific complaint of *Labour Leader* was that when an amendment was moved declaring that conscription should only be approved if agreed by an Irish parliament, only seven Labour MPs voted for, six actually voted against and the rest abstained. Then, on the third reading of the bill, nine Labour MPs voted for, including those in government and only seven against, with the rest abstaining. However, the minutes reveal that the NEC specifically agreed beforehand that the PLP was not mandated to oppose Irish conscription in the Commons.[67] Thus the specific criticism from *Labour Leader* that the PLP was acting unilaterally was on this occasion, unjustified.

With the end of the war and Labour leaving the government, the PLP was free to take a more independent line, and with Sinn Féin's election victory needed to do so. Clynes, in a debate in the Common on Ireland on 3 April 1919, had an opportunity. Instead, he was nostalgic. He began his speech by calling for the enactment of the Home Rule legislation of 1914. He then mourned the passing of the Nationalist, noting:

> The party which stood for constitutional action and for law and order in the affairs of their country and in the affairs of its government, was nearly destroyed at the polls, and the party which treats this country and this House with contempt, and refuses to come near it, has received the support of the great majority of the Irish people.

Despite this, when asked, he said that he was opposed to independence, saying instead that the Irish should be allowed to 'govern themselves in their own country, in their own Parliament, and be responsible to their own people for all those daily domestic and other affairs which materially affect the well-being of that country.' And, as to the demands of Sinn Féin, Clynes assured the Commons that the Irish were 'not now placing their claims so very high as to actually want the national aspiration to be met by conceding to them an extreme form of government which was, perhaps, never previously in the mind of British statesmen who have faced this question.' What he appeared to be saying was: Home Rule, probably; independence, no; and despite the 1918 election, well, the Irish didn't want that anyway.

The following month, the main Labour speaker in debate on Ireland was James Sexton. Sexton was another Labour MP with an Irish history. In his biography, he was to recount that his father was 'a member of a band of Irish gypsies', who had migrated to England, while his mother was second generation Irish whose parents 'had experienced the horrors of the Irish rebellion of 1798 when pitch-cap and gibbet were the certain fate of any priest celebrating mass as they were of any peasant who dared to take up arms against injustice.'[68] Indeed, according to Sexton his father had himself 'taken up arms', in his case stored them for the Irish Republican Brotherhood during their raid on Chester Castle in 1867. Sexton implies he had also dabbled in Brotherhood activities until, in the late 1880s he had 'realized the utter hopelessness of the physical force movement and I joined the constitutional movement that eventually almost superseded it.'[69] He later directed his political activity into the British labour movement, but, by the early twentieth century, he was another of those from an Irish background who had difficulty coming to terms with the new Ireland that was emerging. Thus, in the May 1919 debate he also called for the enactment of the 1914 legislation, claimed that that was what the Irish still wanted and declared that if legislation had meant Ireland leaving the UK he would have voted against in 1914.[70] There matters laid until, for the first time, the PLP took the initiative in February 1920. This was in the form of the PLP Commission of Inquiry (as opposed to the later, more general party commission), already referred to, whose brief was to 'obtain the fullest information regarding the present methods of the British government in Ireland' and to 'ascertain the opinions of representative Irishmen and representative organisations ... on the question of the government of Ireland'.[71] The inquiry team was one of leadership, headed by Adamson, Clynes and Henderson. Its political conclusion was cautious and equivocal, putting forward two alternatives which the commission believed 'would be acceptable to the majority of the Irish people'. One was for 'Dominion Self-Government' with 'protection for minorities' and Westminster control of foreign affairs and defence. If the Irish wanted a more radical break from Britain they could adopt a new constitution, but only after 'number of years', by when the Irish 'would have an opportunity to return to a more normal state of mind, free from the prejudices and animosities engendered by the failure of British governments in the past to satisfy Irish demands'.[72] To interpret harshly, the Irish were not yet in a good enough mood to know what was good for them.

The second suggested alternative was for the election of an Irish constituent assembly which would draw up a new constitution, but again with the understanding that defence and foreign affairs would be reserved for Westminster and that minority rights would be guaranteed. As already noted, the PLP delegates' report went to a joint meeting of the PLP and the NEC on 25 February. The policy that had been agreed there was later outlined in the House of Commons by Clynes. It was 'the maximum of self-government compatible with the unity of the Empire and the safety of the UK in time of war' and 'adequate protection for the Ulster people'.[73] The political conclusion of the PLP's commission was roundly denounced by the ITGWU. Its newspaper headline was 'English Labour Fails on Self-Determination for Ireland'.[74] The *Daily Herald* proclaimed that placing the conditions they did on self-determination was 'illogical and impolitic. Self-determination of its own nature excludes such reservations.'[75]

At least the commission was evidence that the PLP was, on this occasion, prepared to take its own initiative on Ireland, more than nearly a year before the NEC's own inquiry team was dispatched. It is also the case that the PLP commission's policy was broadly in line with 1918 conference policy, possibly even a little more radical. However, when the party policy was changed to unrestricted self-determination by the conference of June 1920, the PLP was not prepared to reflect the new brief. In July 1920, J. H. Thomas, speaking in the House of Commons, continued to limit his demand to one of 'Dominion Home Rule'[76] and, in November, the PLP resolved to support self-determination with the familiar qualifications on 'protection to the minority' and measures to 'prevent Ireland becoming a military or naval menace to Great Britain.'[77] Although this was against conference policy, it was in line with the policy as adopted by the NEC. Accordingly, while the PLP could be criticised for breaking with conference policy, as with the issue of conscription, the party executive had set the precedent.

The other significant initiative taken by the PLP was a censure motion against the government debated on the Commons on 20 October 1920. This,

> Regrets the present state of lawlessness in Ireland and the lack of discipline in the armed forces of the Crown, resulting in the death or injury of innocent citizens and the destruction of property; and is of opinion that an independent investigation should at once be instituted into the causes, nature, and extent of reprisals on the part of those whose duty is the maintenance of law and order.

The motion was moved by Arthur Henderson who began by tracing back what he called 'a British government ... policy of military repression and aggression in an intensified form' back to 1917, when, somewhat ironically, he was actually part of that government. His main criticism however was of the more current policies of 1919–20. For him:

> What does stand out beyond question is that a policy of military terrorism has been inaugurated, which, in our opinion, is not only a betrayal of democratic principles and not only a betrayal of the things

for which we claimed to stand during the five years great world War, but is utterly opposed to the best traditions of the British people. Such a policy, it seems to me, can only be characterised as being akin to the policy of frightfulness which was associated with the doings of the Germans, and the doings of him whom we described as the Hun during the War, and which all sections of British people most emphatically condemned.[78]

This and what followed was Labour's powerful sustained condemnation yet of government's military campaign in Ireland. Henderson did not advocate a political policy, but this was not the case for all of Labour's speakers in the debate. Perhaps with remembering the Scarborough conference policy, Jack Jones said:

> I happen to be an Irishman, and I am not ashamed to express my opinion on the subject of Ireland, which has as much right to her independence as Belgium. She is as much a nation. Ireland's relationship to the welfare of this country is no different to the relationship of Belgium and Germany. What did the Germans say about Belgium? They said that the independence of Belgium would interfere with the independence of Germany, and it was necessary to make Belgium a vassal State. In as far as you are the friends of British Prussians, you are taking up the same attitude to Ireland.[79]

The censure motion was, of course, unsuccessful. Nevertheless the very fact that it was moved, together with Henderson's criticism of British policy and Jones's argument for the validity of independence may suggest the PLP was showing a new militancy. There is, however, an interesting comparison. First, if Henderson's comparison of British repression in Ireland with that of Germany in the Great War appears severe, for one speaker in the same debate it was letting the British off too easily:

> It might have been said that the method employed in Ireland is the same as that employed in Belgium during the War by the Germans. The method is not quite the same. Germany had a method which was outlined before the War by its leading military authorities. They entertained the policy of collective punishment ... That is not our method. It is not openly admitted. Our method is far more reminiscent

of the pogrom of the more barbarous Slav, and it represents a far greater breakdown of law and order and justice than did the German method in Belgium.[80]

Second, Jack Jones was implying support for Irish independence, the following, again in the same debate, was more explicit:

It is held over us that if we gave self-government to Ireland, Ireland would be a thorn in our side and would be a strategical danger to us. I do not believe it for a moment. I think if Ireland would only give a guarantee to enter into the League of Nations we need not bother our heads whether we give Ireland the command of an army or a navy or not.[81]

The first quotation comes from Oswald Mosley, then a conservative MP. The second from Lord H. Cavendish-Bentinck, from the same party, who described himself in the debate as 'a very old Conservative'. These two individuals may have been somewhat maverick Tories and both, as we have seen, were active in the Peace With Ireland Council, but nevertheless their words do rather put those of Labour's speakers into a rather tame perspective.

A further comparison can made in respect of the speeches made at the Third Reading of the Government of Ireland Bill the following month. In this case, the speakers are Asquith for the independent Liberals and Adamson for Labour. Both enunciated the same policies of self-government with the now familiar conditions of safeguards for minorities and Britain's defence interests. However, in respect of the latter, Asquith called for the government to adopt a 'generous and ungrudging spirit.'[82] Adamson was less wishy-washy, insisting, 'We recognise that an independent Ireland would be a grave menace to this country, and it is self-determination on our part to say that the peace and safety of this realm shall be safeguarded.'[83]

Where this eventually took Labour was shown in the run up to and the early stages of the negotiations between the government and Sinn Féin, which got underway in October 1921. Just before they began, but when a truce was in place, J. H. Thomas, hot from a visit to Belfast, in an interview with the *Daily Herald*, offered a series of remarks directed to the Irish. He warned them, 'No greater mistake could be made than to assume that England are on⨍ the run', and to prove it added that 'the assumption that the English people or any political party in England can hold out any hope on the Irish Republic' was 'foreign to the facts.'[84] These words were forcefully condemned in the same issue of the *Daily Herald*, but it was now as though Labour had reverted to its wartime coalition mentality of lining up with government against a foreign foe. As already described, the NEC was by now declining to disassociate itself from Lloyd George. The same tendency can be detected in a Commons debate on Ireland on 21 October. The occasion was a censure motion moved by the Tory right criticising Lloyd George for even negotiating with Sinn Féin, a motion Labour opposed. But during the debate Arthur Henderson laid down three conditions for supporting the government in the event of a proposed settlement. The first was Irish majority support for the outcome, and the second was protection for minorities. The third, he told Lloyd George, was, 'We shall examine the proposal from the standpoint of the security of our country'. The implication was that if the potential Irish 'menace' was not sorted out, Labour would oppose any settlement. Not that Henderson seemed to have much doubt that Lloyd George and his fellow negotiators would not let the country down. He promised, 'While continuing to oppose' Lloyd George's other polices 'with regards to Ireland, [we] are determined to assist the government all we can' in its 'honest attempt to examine the difficulties'. Accordingly, 'we are prepared to trust those who are carrying out the difficult negotiations.'[85] Then, in the same debate, and just to ram home the point as to where Labour was coming from, J. R. Clynes insisted, 'We have as great a regard for the British Empire as the rest of you.'[86]

Further aspects of Labour's political thought on Ireland will be examined later in this book. For the moment, a number of observations can be made. The first concerns the PLP. Its record suggests a lack of enthusiasm about raising Ireland as an issue, wariness about advocating unqualified Irish self-determination and a lack of clarity about what to propose instead. But in all this the PLP was doing no more than reflecting attitudes and uncertainties commonly held within the upper echelons of the Labour Party. Indeed, in that the PLP send its own delegation to Ireland, it had pre-empted the NEC in at least doing something.

The second observation concerns the party generally and to question how far it had strayed from Lib/Lab past. The truth is that there was no distinctive Labour voice on Ireland, either in parliament or outside.

Self-rule, but with safeguards for Ulster and British defence, was shared with the Liberals; the protest meetings held by Labour over Ireland were held after the Liberals had held theirs. Furthermore, when Asquith returned to the Commons in February 1920, he was often more critical of the government over Ireland than his Labour counterparts. Roy Jenkins has written that it was 'mainly Ireland which engaged [Asquith's] attention' in this period,[87] a priority which no one could accuse Henderson, Thomas or Adamson of sharing. The third observation is that in terms of the desired political outcome Labour's leadership not only shared polices with the Liberals, both also shared the crucial one with the Liberals and the government. None were having the Irish Republic.

4

The Trades Union Congress

James Henry Thomas was born in Newport, Monmouthshire in 1847.
Like many of those who became labour leaders, he was born into the
working class – in his case, a single parent family. He went to work at
the age of twelve in the railways. He became an active trade unionist
and Labour Party activist. He progressed in both, eventually becoming
a Labour MP for Derby in 1910 and general secretary of the NUR in
1918. He supported participation in the Great War, which he saw as
'being fought in the sacred cause of liberty',[1] but opposed conscription.
In his biography, written in 1937, in describing the pre-war period
he said, 'Those were the days when Labour was striving to convince
Capital that it had a right to place in the sun',[2] and that could sum up
his political ambition. His commitment was to secure for his labour
movement what he considered was its just reward, not replacing 'Capital'
but given due recognition alongside it. In some ways, by the end of
the war organised labour was well on its way to achieving that. The
political side of the movement had participated in coalition government,
the industrial wing had grown to over six and a half million members,
and it, too, through backing the war had been given national responsibilities and a say in how some industries were run. Accordingly, it is not
difficult to imagine Thomas, MP, when, in 1920, he was president of the
TUC in a member of its leadership body, the Parliamentary Committee,
and of Labour's national executive, deriving some satisfaction for what
he and his movement had achieved. As for Ireland, he had always
been a supporter of Home Rule and believed that the failure to enact
Gladstone's first Home Rule Bill was 'mainly responsible for much of
the trouble that has since taken place.'[3] But again, writing in 1937, he
looked back with some pride on the achievement British trade unionism
had made even in Ireland. He wrote, 'We had succeeded in the industrial
field in bringing Roman Catholic and Protestant together'.[4] That was
a selective memory.

Conference and Leadership

In 1915, the executive body of the TUC, the Parliamentary Committee, was described by the leading Fabian Beatrice Webb as 'conventionally warlike'.[5] At its 1916 Congress, the TUC's President, Harry Gosling, confirmed such an impression when he declared:

> Labour on its part has been the personification of real patriotism. Every conceivable sacrifice has been made, and made ungrudgingly. We of the working people have every pride in the fact that millions of our best in strength, efficiency and manhood have voluntarily given all they have (their lives) for the defence of their country.[6]

Accepting, that such sentiments were generally held within the TUC, its members would hardly have been expected to look kindly on Ireland's Easter Rising, with its opening of another front against Britain. However, Ireland was not discussed at the 1916 Congress, although resolutions which were moved and carried at it included one on electoral reform and one which called for 'political and civil rights for Jewish people'.[7] Nor was the Irish issue raised at the 1917 Congress. Indeed, when a resolution favouring Irish Home Rule was moved at the 1918 Congress its proposer, Ben Tillett of the Docks and Riverside Workers, testified that 'this is the first time the Congress has considered a proposition of this character',[8] and indeed there had been no debate on Ireland since the TUC had first met in 1868. The Parliamentary Committee, from Easter 1916 to the 1918 Congress, was also silent: there are only two minor references to Ireland in its minutes. The first was in August 1916, when representatives of the ITUCLP, on the eve of Congress, asked for visitors' credentials. The committee agreed unanimously that the delegates in question 'would not be received' as 'no invitation had been sent to them'.[9] This was possibly a consequence of the frosty relations that then existed between the British and Irish movements. The background here is that some Irish unions and, in 1912, the ITUCLP had split from the British movement in pursuit of its variation of self-determination. Furthermore, the 1913 Dublin lock-out had witnessed massive rows between the leaderships of the two movements over the alleged failure of the British unions to support the Irish workers involved in that gigantic struggle.[10] Nevertheless, the Parliamentary Committee's refusal to allow the Irish delegates to observe their deliberations at the 1916 Congress does, on the face of it, seem somewhat uncomradely. The second occasion when Ireland featured in the Committee's minutes prior to the 1918 Congress was in August 1918, when the British Army wrote to the TUC asking for its support in promoting recruitment in Ireland. Support for the sentiment behind such efforts in Britain had already been noted in Harry Gosling's remarks quoted above, but on this occasion the Parliamentary Committee demurred. Outright refusal could have been embarrassing, so this time the existence of the ITUCLP came in handy when the Army was re-directed there.[11]

So, the debate on the resolution moved at the Congress held in September 1918 was the first substantial discussion the British trade union movement and its leadership had collectively held on the Irish issue. This began by calling 'upon the British government and Parliament to establish Home Rule in Ireland under the most generous and free conditions of democratic self-government.' This was followed by a plea for Irish self-determination, 'consistent with democratic principles and unity.' What came next was more a political tract than a conference resolution: 'This Congress is of the opinion that the industrial classes of any and every country should be joined in direct industrial interest.' There followed the observation that 'the workers of Ireland are equally with ourselves under capitalist rule', and that therefore 'the exploiter of Labour whether Irish, Scottish, English or Welsh or any other race, is one and the same enemy.' There was the assurance that 'our fellow industrial workers of Ireland have our sincere sympathy in their objectives of self-government', but the statement ended with a sentence directed at the Irish themselves:

> In this war profiteering and Prussianism have been the upper and nether millstones of human crucifixion, and we ask our Irish brothers and sisters to help us in winning the war for peace and peoples, and for the establishment of democracy and the subjection of militarism.[12]

This was a rather exceptional resolution, combining as it did support for Irish Home Rule, an internationalist sentiment which seemed to place the workers of the world in one camp and the capitalists in the other, yet also an insistence on the priority of fighting 'Prussianism' and accordingly a call for the Irish working class to join the British war effort. Of course, many British, and indeed Irish, trade unionists did see the Great War as a fight against oppression, but the thinking behind this resolution was indicated when Ben Tillett moved the motion. He began: 'We were hoping that, instead of Sinn Féin or anything else trying to separate the working classes of Ireland from this country, the workers of Ireland will realise that they are in the same bondage as ourselves, and that the better wages and conditions they enjoy today are due to the work of trade unionists in this country.'[13] Tillett also maintained that 'bread-and-butter politics are the only politics we should be interested in', and went on to warn the Irish that 'the Irishmen working with us are brothers, and we view with great concern the psychology of Irishmen at home and in this country', an apparent attack on the growing separationist sentiment in Ireland and among the Irish in Britain. He added, 'I honestly believe that we shall have to force Home Rule upon Ireland. There are a good many Irish politicians who do not want Home Rule. They would rather have a grievance than Home Rule.'

Perhaps the kindest interpretation that could be given to such opinions, and indeed those in the resolution itself, was that they were a product of the times. A terrible war was being fought, with both passions and prejudices raised, when those supporting the war effort were always liable to have their patriotism give way to a holier-than-thou sentiments. One of the two other speakers in the debate, an Irishman representing Liverpool dockers, addressed himself to such feelings when he assured the Congress, 'If you give Irishmen Home Rule, you will have them flocking-to the colours in their thousands.'[14] The overwhelming message of the resolution and the debate was very much that Ireland should take second place to the war, and that too was understandable. The resolution was carried 'by general assent'. The irony is that, just as with the Labour Party in the same year, when the TUC had finally debated and called for Irish Home Rule, the Irish themselves were moving on from that to endorse complete self-determination and independence. Moreover, both the absence of Ireland from previous TUC's agendas and the rather grudging manner in which the TUC had supported even Home Rule suggested that there were mixed messages being delivered. There was support for Irish reform, but no great enthusiasm for making an issue of such matters. This seemed to be confirmed in early November 1918 when the Parliamentary Committee came out against Irish conscription. They sought a meeting with the Prime Minister to press home this opposition, but Lloyd George reacted by saying he was 'too busy' to receive this deputation. The Parliamentary Committee's response to the rebuff was to agree to leave the matter 'in abeyance'.[15]

No further discussion on Ireland by the Parliamentary Committee is minuted for just over a year. Before then the September 1919 Congress did debate its preferred political solution. That contrasted to the absence of debate at the Labour Party conference the same year. There was also a policy change from the 1918 Congress, for the 1919 resolution said:

> This Congress views with alarm the grave situation in Ireland, where every demand for freedom is met with military rule. The Congress once again reaffirms its belief that the only solution is self-determination, and calls upon the government to substitute self-government for military rule, as the only means whereby the Irish people can work out their own emancipation. The Congress expresses its profound sympathy with our Irish brothers in their hour of repression.[16]

Perhaps somewhat surprisingly, this resolution was in the name of NUR and was moved by its leader, J. H. Thomas. He asked delegates to 'recognise quite frankly that the situation in Ireland today is radically changed from what it was four years ago when Mr. John Redmond made his plea and demand for justice for Ireland.' He concluded by arguing that 'the only justice' for Ireland now 'is to grant the power of self-determination to her people so that they may have perfect freedom to work out their own salvation in their own way.'[17] The resolution was carried unanimously after two further speeches, both from Irish-born delegates, including Robert Smillie of the Miners Federation. The motion was later described as 'pious' by an ILP member, Harry Campbell. He maintained that the TUC should have responded to events in Ireland by organising 'large indignation meetings ... and if necessary direct action should be taken.'[18] A similar call had come the previous month from the Irish Labour Party and Trades Union Congress (the ITUCLP had now become the ILPTUC), when it unanimously passed a resolution that invited 'the workers of England to use all the forces at their command to compel their government to withdraw the Army of Occupation from Ireland immediately.'[19]

Compared with such requests, the TUC resolution may indeed have been 'pious'. Also the resolution was somewhat vague about the form of political solution it favoured, mentioning both 'self-determination' and 'self-government', a euphemism for something more restrictive than unqualified self-determination. Nevertheless, in his speech Thomas had specifically recognised that history had moved on from the era of Redmond's plea for Home Rule, and, compared with the resolution and speeches of the previous Congress, there was a noticeable and radical change of emphasis. In explaining the change, the political context can again be noted. Britain was no longer at war by the time of the 1919 Congress, so the pressures that produced the chauvinist tendencies evident the previous year were no longer present. The ending of war had also, as noted, produced a resurgent radicalism. Indeed, the 1919 Congress witnessed significant manifestations of this with support for direct action for political ends, and the censoring of the Parliamentary Committee for failing to call a special congress to deal with what was seen as a growing political and economic crisis.[20] Then there was the situation in Ireland itself and the sweeping victory of Sinn Féin in the 1918 election. All of this can explain both Thomas's apparent militancy and the complaint that this did not go far enough. Yet it is worth remembering that, given that the Labour Party did not even discuss Ireland in conference in 1919, the TUC could now be judged as being in advance of the party on the issue. However, as far as the Parliamentary Committee was concerned, this was not a leadership it was inclined to exercise. This was evident at its meeting at the end of December 1919 when it received a deputation from the ILPTUC on a drivers' strike in Ireland, associated with the national struggle. When the deputation asked for support for the strike from the British movement it was, 'referred to the Labour Party who were sending a deputation to Ireland.'[21] To be precise, it was the PLP commission of inquiry referred to earlier.

A discussion on Ireland was held by the Parliamentary Committee in April 1920, when 'the question of the arrest and imprisonment without trial of Irish trade unionists' was raised. There was no decision taken on what to do or say about that, but instead there was a general resolution which 'deplored' the 'present state of affairs in Ireland' and gave the opinion that 'there will be no real solution of the Irish problem until the people of Ireland are given the powers to work out their own salvation.'[22] As with the resolution adopted at the 1919 Congress, this was more a general sentiment than a specific policy and, of course, it was not accompanied by the TUC actually doing anything to press home these sentiments. However, when in May 1920 a political/industrial dispute began in Ireland which was to force the Irish issue to the top of the TUC's agenda, such quiescence was no longer sustainable.

The Special Congress and its Aftermath

On 22 May 1920, 400 members of the Dublin branch (North Wall) of the NUR refused to unload what they thought were munitions for the use of British security forces in Ireland. 'War Train Derelict' was a subsequent headline in an Irish newspaper.[23] Although the action was halted when it was discovered the consignment for the British Army was food not weapons, similar action by other railway workers followed. As general secretary of the NUR, J. H. Thomas soon sent a telegram urging his Irish members to return to work in order, he said, 'to give the labour movement an opportunity of acting on their behalf'.[24] Thomas's return to characteristic caution was understandable. The railway workers' actions did have far-reaching implications for the British and Irish trade union movements, as was evident by the time the Parliamentary Committee met on 16 June. By then, NUR members in Dublin had been sacked for 'blacking' British munitions and, as Thomas told the meeting, the NUR was 'being pressed by other trade unions to assist its Irish members.' Consequently, the Parliamentary Committee agreed to call a special congress, 'to discuss the application of direct action to Ireland.'[25] Less than a month later, on 13 July 1920, the TUC met. While this Special Congress was principally concerned with Ireland, unemployment and Russia were also briefly discussed. Coincidentally, the congress was within one month of the Labour Party coming out in favour of unqualified self-determination, a decision which J. H. Thomas had spoken against at the party conference. It was his union which moved the major resolution at the TUC's Special Congress. This was a deliberate choice made by the Parliamentary Committee, who, when deciding on the Special Congress, had specifically asked the NUR to submit a motion so that it could be 'placed on the Agenda with the resolution sent in by the Miners' Federation'.[26] The miners' motion declared:

> That this Congress protests against the British military domination of Ireland, and demands the withdrawal of all British troops from the country, and demands the cessation of the production of munitions of war destined to be used against Ireland and Russia, and in case

the government refuses these demands, we recommend a general down-tools policy, and call upon the Trade Unions here represented to carry out this policy, each according to its own policy, by taking a ballot of its members or otherwise.[27]

Given the cautious attitude the Parliamentary Committee had shown up to now, it is hardly surprising that the NUR was invited to submit an alternative to the miners' militancy. The railwaymen's motion said, 'the present position in Ireland ... does not warrant any section of workers being allowed to fight alone a battle for freedom.' In other words, the NUR was not going to take direct action by itself. It did not suggest an alternative course of action for either British or Irish trade unionists, but called for a truce in Ireland and for the government to open negotiations with the Irish on the basis of 'full dominion powers in all Irish affairs, with adequate protection for the interests of minorities'.[28] As to what action the TUC should take to promote this, 'It is unwise to commit ourselves to anything at this stage.'[29]

The other rail union, the Locomotive Engineers and Firemen (ASLEF), was critical of such circumspection. It also called for a truce, but if this was agreed by the Irish and not the British then 'an immediate ballot [should] be taken of the members of affiliated unions as to a general strike to compel the withdrawal of troops from Ireland.' In moving this resolution, John Bromley, the union's general secretary, complained that the NUR's motion was 'pious ... merely causing the government to believe they were gasbags.'[30] Bromley's resolution was defeated by a large majority on a show of hands and an amendment to the NUR resolution was then taken. This sought to delete the reference to a truce and Dominion Home Rule, and to substitute 'the withdrawal of the Army of Occupation' and 'Recognition by the government and immediate application of the right of the Irish people themselves to determine the form of government they desire.'[31] The amendment was lost by 2,676,000 votes to 1,916,000. The NUR resolution was then put and passed, but by a small majority of just under 200,000. Then the miners' more militant resolution was put and this, too, was carried, by 2,760,000 to 1,636,000.

If there are a number of apparent contradictions in these proceedings and votes, there were those who choose to downplay them. Reporting the next day, the _Daily Herald_ was jubilant. Under the headline 'General Strike to Free Ireland', there was the comment: 'Emphatically the

Congress warned the government that, unless it ceases to coerce the Irish people ... the trade unions in this country will ballot their members on the straight issue of an immediate general strike.'[32] The *New Statesman* was not so sure. 'It has been pointed out', it said, 'that there was confusion in the resolutions, that there was no agreed solution, that some delegates wanted an Irish Republic and some Dominion Home Rule and that on the question of direct action there was enough division of opinion to make it an idle threat.' Nevertheless, the journal continued, 'for the first time in the history of the Labour movement in this country a definite vote has been carried for direct action for a political end – and carried by an enormous majority.'[33] With the benefit of hindsight, a subsequent interpretation was more cynical than jubilant. Nine months later Henry Somerville, an Irish critic of British Labour's attitude to Ireland, saw the Special Congress as 'a shameless exhibition of insincerity.' His view was that 'By passing both resolutions' – the NUR's and the miners' – 'the delegates knew that an absurd situation had arisen ... the position was so complicated that nobody could say with certainty what was decided and what was not.'[34] And indeed, when, at the close of the congress, a delegate asked its chairman, J. H. Thomas, when the date for direct action would be set, he replied, 'Wait and see.'[35]

There was not a long wait. Shortly afterwards, Thomas led a deputation from the Parliamentary Committee to the Prime Minister. At the meeting he reported that the decisions of the Special Congress represented 'a declaration in favour of Dominion Home Rule, with a recognition of the Ulster problem ... provision being made for ... protection for the interests of minorities.' More remarkably, he said that as far as he was concerned, the Ulster counties should have the right to permanently opt out of the jurisdiction of an Irish parliament and stay with the British one, an opinion which did not reflect the TUC resolutions and was contrary to what was then Labour Party policy. When Lloyd George responded by observing that 'it was idle to discuss such a matter unless with somebody they knew was in a position to deliver the goods', Thomas replied, 'We will go to the Irish Trade Union Congress.'[36] The following day representatives of the national executive of the ILPTUC, who were in Britain, reacted angrily to Thomas's words. 'We are not here to make a deal with Mr Lloyd George or the British government', they said. If Lloyd George or Thomas were 'deeply concerned about the state of Ireland' then, they urged, 'relinquish your authority, withdraw your forces, leave the Irish people the responsibility and power, and we shall show then whether we can "deliver the goods".[37] The short shrift given to Thomas by the representatives of the ILPTUC is hardly surprising. They were in no position to negotiate with the government, and even if they had been they would certainly not have favoured the Dominion Home Rule policy of Thomas. As to Thomas's general behaviour, it is worth remembering that ostensibly he went to the Prime Minister to report not just the resolution on Dominion Home Rule but also the one threatening direct action to secure British withdrawal. There is no evidence that he raised this issue. Perhaps the shrewdest comment on the whole affair was that made by Scotland Yard's Basil Thomson, then spying both on the labour movement and the Irish in Britain: 'A deputation from the Parliamentary Committee ... presented the resolutions to the Prime Minister and then endeavoured to bury them with as little publicity as possible.'[38] Thomas told his version of events some months later at the annual congress of the TUC. He recalled the Special Congress and its resolutions, and explained that the failure for anything to come of it was all the fault of the Irish:

> These views were submitted to the Prime Minister of the day who, while not rejecting them, agreed to meet any section of the Irish people in a position to make a settlement. Your Committee believed, and still believes, that the Irish Labour movement fulfilled the requirements of the Prime Minister's stipulation, and accordingly invited the Irish Labour Party Executive to meet us. The body made it perfectly clear that they did not intend to have any negotiation with the British government, and therefore our efforts have so far failed.[39]

Shortly after these remarks were made, Arthur Henderson and the NEC of the Labour Party, as outlined in the previous chapter, did attempt a more conciliatory approach to the Irish labour movement. The Labour Party delegation to Ireland was one consequence. The TUC was invited to send three representatives on this delegation, but in the words of the minutes of the Parliamentary Committee, 'It was decided not to take part therein.'[40]

Leaving aside the issue of the carpenters' dispute, which will be dealt with next, no further substantial discussion was held on Ireland by the Parliamentary Committee, its successor the General Council, or the Congress. What, then, is to be made of the Special Congress, the one occasion when the TUC did appear resolved on a course of action in support of some form of Irish self-government?

First, J. H. Thomas was unquestionably correct when he told Lloyd George that it was Dominion self-government which the TUC was supporting. For those who hoped to see some concerted and united policy and action by the labour movement on Ireland, this was particularly unfortunate in that, as been shown in the previous chapter, the month before the Labour Party conference had rejected such restrictions on self-determination, despite the opposition of Thomas. On the other hand, where Thomas had no mandate from any labour movement body was for his opinion that Ulster should be allowed to opt out of the jurisdiction of an Irish parliament. To be fair, he did tell Lloyd George that when he advocated this solution he was speaking for himself. Even so, to make such a suggestion when he was leading an official delegation was hardly warranted. Thomas could also be criticised for declining to press the resolution on direct action passed by the Special Congress. However, in this he was not alone. The resolution had called for unions to organise ballots in order to carry out this action. There is no record of any of the affiliated unions doing so. This unanimity suggests it would be wrong to see the reason for the unwillingness of the TUC to act on Ireland residing in the figure of J. H. Thomas or the Parliamentary Committee in general.

Henry Somerville placed the debates at the Special Congress in a wider context. It was, he said, 'one union ... trying to score a point over another union ... The miners sought to make the railwaymen choose between the acceptance of a policy of direct action or confession to the fact that they had no policy at all'.[41] This was a reference, not just to Ireland but to the general debates within the labour movement on direct action, and specifically between the two unions mentioned. This was to climax the following year when on 'Black Friday', the NUR refused to carry out a pledge to strike in support of the miners. If Somerville's explanation for the debates at the Special Congress is accepted, that is, that Ireland was simply a peg on which other issues were hung, then the failure of any union to pay heed to the Congress resolution for direct action on the issue makes sense: Ireland merited attention only so far as it was relevant to more general debate; it was a minor skirmish in a general conflict, and, accordingly, not worth prioritising. But then, almost to the day of the Special Congress meeting, a train of events began in Belfast which did not allow the policies and practice on Ireland to be so easily subsumed.

The Belfast Carpenters' Dispute

The 1920 Belfast carpenters' dispute is a unique and under-told episode in British and Irish labour history. The story has three aspects. First, the glimpse it provides into the political and religious sectarianism of the contemporary Belfast working class. Second, how one British trade union strongly contested that sectarianism, even within its own membership. Third, the insight it provides into the attitude of the TUC leadership towards this contest and this sectarianism.

An appropriate place to start is a speech by Edward Carson, leader of the Ulster Unionists, at an annual 12th of July rally in Belfast in 1920. The former member of Lloyd George's War Cabinet said:

> We must proclaim today that, come what may, we in Ulster will tolerate no Sinn Féin – no Sinn Féin organisation, no Sinn Féin methods ... We tell you [the British government] this – that if, having offered you help, you yourselves are unable to protect us ... we tell you that we will take the matter into our own hands ... And these are not mere words. I hate words without action.[42]

These were spoken when the War of Independence was being strongly contested. They were spoken in a city which had witnessed serious sectarian clashes for half a century. They were spoken by a Dubliner who saw Ulster Unionists' resistance to Home Rule, never mind Irish independence, as a means to defeating Home Rule in its entirety. Passions among Belfast Protestants, to whom the remarks were addressed, were already raised, both by the events elsewhere in Ireland and the very occasion on which Carson's speech was made, that is, the annual 12th of July celebrations commemorating the victory of a Protestant King over a Catholic King for the throne of England and beyond at the Battle of the Boyne, Ireland, in 1690.

Several days after Carson's speech, the IRA shot dead Colonel G. F. Smyth in Cork. Smyth was a member of the Royal Irish Constabulary and a native of the Ulster town of Banbridge. On the day of his funeral on 21 July, 'action', to use Carson's word, was initiated at one of the smaller Belfast shipyards by a group called the Belfast Protestant Association. Some of its members produced revolvers, and declared their intention to drive from the shipyard every 'Sinn Féiner' they could find. 'Sinn

Féiner' proved a very elastic terminology. Those attacked were not just supporters of Sinn Féin, but every known Catholic, trade union militants and socialists. The violence soon spread to other workplaces. By the time it ended, over 10,000 Catholic men and 1,000 Catholic women had been driven from their place of work. The vast majority were never to return.[43] Among those so affected were several hundred members of the Amalgamated Society of Carpenters, Cabinetmakers and Joiners. The leadership of the Carpenters' Union, as the Society was known, had only recently come under fire from some of its Belfast members after passing a resolution on Ireland and Russia which included a condemnation of the government for 'refusing to allow the form of government chosen by the Irish people', and added that 'the most effective way in which protest can be made is for the organised workers to refuse to manufacture or transport munitions of war for Ireland or Poland.'[44] Two Belfast branches of the union voiced their disapproval of this motion. One voted 14 to two, out of a membership of 105, to 'strongly protest',[45] the other by 22 to nil, out of a membership of 283, to 'strongly object'.[46] A mass meeting of the Carpenters' Union membership in one of the smaller Belfast shipyards said the executive should 'leave politics aside', otherwise it could, 'cause dissension in our ranks.'[47]

The person who chaired this meeting was William Barclay, a member of the Unionist Party's Ulster Unionist Labour Association. He himself was not too wary of causing such dissensions when the following month he chaired a further meeting which resolved 'That we, the Unionist and Protestant workers ... will not work with disloyal workers ... Also, that in all future applications for employment we respectively suggest that the first consideration be given to loyal ex-servicemen and Protestant Unionists.'[48] Thus, while some members of the Carpenters' Union were being driven from their workplace, other members were openly encouraging such sectarianism. August saw attacks on Catholics and Catholic-owned property reach new depths. The London *Daily News* described it as, 'five weeks of ruthless persecution by boycott, fire, plunder and assault, culminating in a week's wholesale violence, probably unmatched outside the area of the Russian or Polish pogroms.'[49] A 'loyalist' shipyard worker boasted at the start of August that 'they had gained a great victory and they had struck Sinn Féin and the red flag of socialism the worst blow it had received in Belfast for 30 years',[50] while another claimed that 'since the Sinn Féiners were cleared out of the shipyard over five hundred loyalists ... had been taken on.'[51] The loyalists organised themselves in the workplace into Vigilance Committees and it was these which were influential in determining who worked and who was taken on to replace the victimised workers.

Such was the difficult situation into which the Carpenters' Union decided to intervene. On 24 August, members of the union executive went to Belfast and met the management of the largest shipyard, Harland and Wolff. The union made a series of proposals. These included a reinstatement of the expelled workers, the outlawing of religious or political discrimination in employment in the shipyard and protection for the victimised workers on their return to work. In response, the management, while saying they deplored the violence and expulsions, promised only to consider the proposals at a future date. The union judged this as prevarication and called a mass meeting of their members to discuss the situation. The meeting was to be private and held indoors. Nevertheless, the British military authorities judged that it would 'give rise to grave disorder'[52] and banned the meeting. During the next two weeks, further expulsions occurred. Among the victims was D. A. Boal, who was a member of the Carpenters' Union executive, a Protestant and 'moderate labour man'.[53] Such was the situation facing the TUC when it met at the start of September in Portsmouth for its annual congress. An emergency resolution on the events in Belfast was moved on behalf of the Standing Orders Committee, after it had received a deputation from Belfast trade unionists, by J. H. Thomas. 'Men are being prevented from working', he explained, 'because of their religious and political opinions', although he went on to explain this by 'the anxiety to uphold the union jack in Belfast.'[54] The resolution instructed the Parliamentary Committee 'to call together the executives of the various Trade Unions affected by the recent disturbances in Belfast with a view to taking a common line of action for the reinstatement of all the Trade Unionists expelled from their work.'[55] Despite the protests of a delegate from the Ship Construction and Shipwrights' Association, a Mr Swan from Sunderland, who wanted to 'leave the situation to the workers of Belfast',[56] the motion was easily carried. Meanwhile, in Belfast, on 12 September, Harland and Wolff management responded by letter to the Carpenters' Union proposals of 24 August. No specific reply to the suggestions therein was made; instead, a further meeting was proposed between the management, all the unions involved and, more controversially, the Vigilance Committee.

That organisation clarified its attitude when it said that any expelled worker who wished to return to the shipyard would have to sign a declaration of loyalty to the British Empire and further state, 'I do not belong or sympathise with Sinn Féin, and I deplore and abhor all murders and outrages inflicted upon humanity by this dangerous and disloyal movement.'[57]

Thus, two months had passed since the expulsions had begun. During that time the Carpenters' Union had seen hundreds of its members driven from their work. It had also recognised that some of its members were engaged in these attacks. The union's attempt to consult with its Belfast members had been banned by the military authorities. Rather than reply to the union's proposals, management had called for a further meeting in which an openly sectarian organisation would participate. The union leadership now decided to act. At an executive meeting on 18 September, an instruction was issued to all their remaining members in the shipyards and other firms affected by the victimisations to come out on strike. The executive explained:

> We have taken this drastic step to preserve the freedom of our members and the solidarity of our organisation. The victimised men have observed the rules of our society and conformed to the working rules agreed upon between our Belfast members and the employers. It is a gross violation of these rules for employers to allow men to be driven from their employ because they are suspected of not holding certain political or religious opinions ... If the employers elect to discriminate between our members, then we have no option but refuse to allow them the use of *any* of our members. All or none must in ordinary fairness be our rule. We are convinced that the Belfast employers could, if they had so desired, have prevented this disgraceful and vindictive boycott of sections of their workmen. The test of the value of our society is its ability to keep the avenues of employment open to all our members.[58] [Original emphasis]

In taking this action, the executive must have known the problems it faced given the divisions within the union membership in Belfast. It could be accused of a further lack of realism for attacking the management when it was the actions of sections of the workers themselves which had offended. Yet evidence of management complicity in the sectarianism came at the meeting suggested by Harland and Wolff in its letter of 12 September. At this, the Vigilance Committee agreed to drop the demand that any returning workers had to sign an Empire loyalty oath and anti-Sinn Féin declaration. However, while there was also the pledge to work 'with any workers irrespective of their religion', there was the addition of 'putting them on their honour that they are not associated with Sinn Féin or any disloyal organisation.'[59] More significantly, Harland and Wolff management agreed to the somewhat bizarre suggestion that in the future the Vigilance Committee would be given the role of defending any Catholic in the shipyard from assault.[60] Henceforth, management permitted the Committee to meet in work-time, and even set aside rooms from which the Committee could operate. In short, management gave de facto recognition to this sectarian grouping. All this suggests that there was some validity in the Carpenters' Union holding management responsible for what went on in its workplace. One Belfast engineering company, MacLaughlan and Harvey, had agreed to ensure that all religious and political tests on employment were withdrawn, but neither Harland and Wolff nor the other companies affected by the Carpenters Union similarly complied with what were, in effect, these same demands as presented by the union. Accordingly, the test for the union then was how many would obey the strike call. Only a minority of the members did so: 600 out of 2,000.[61] The stakes were raised even higher when the 'strike-breakers' were promptly expelled from the union. This action attracted support from Carpenters' Union branches in Britain. Even before the executive acted a branch in Eltham had passed a resolution favouring such expulsions.[62] After they did occur, only four branches of the union are on record for opposing the action. The contrary view can be summed up in a motion from a branch in Carlisle, passed by 58 to nil: 'That we, in realising the difficult task our E. C. had to face in tackling the Belfast religious unrest among the members of our organisation, heartily congratulate them in the action they have taken and express our full confidence in their judgement.'[63] The December edition of the union's journal records 45 branches passing such a resolution. In justifying its action, the executive maintained it had 'taken up the only possible position to preserve the union of our organisation.' It added, 'we deeply regret that the other unions whose members have been flung out on the streets have not yet thought fit to stand by us in this important struggle.' The statement ended, 'In our judgement the trade union movement, if it will act boldly, can by firmly insisting on the observance of its own principles, end the internecine strife in Ireland.'[64]

So, what of the rest of the trade union movement and, in particular, the TUC leadership whose Congress policy had instructed the Parliamentary Committee to formulate a common policy on behalf of the victimised workers? Initially, the Committee appeared to take its instruction seriously. At its meeting of 21 September, three of its members were appointed with 'plenary powers' to go to Belfast with a view to 'bringing about such a change in the situation as would at least be helpful to trade unionists in Belfast involved in the present conflict.'[65] These were J. Hill of the Boilermakers and Iron and Steel Shipbuilders, A. A. Purcell of the Furniture Trade Association and A. Pugh of the Iron and Steel Confederation. After these appointments, the pace of the initiative slowed. The October meeting of the Committee was told that 'it had not yet been found convenient' to go to Belfast,[66] and it was not until 6 December that the deputation arrived there. The brief given to the deputation by the 1920 Congress was to formulate a line of action to win back the jobs of the victimised workers. However, as the three members of the Parliamentary Committee went about their work, that issue appeared to become a very subsidiary one. As Pugh was later to say, 'We came to the conclusion' that 'there was one problem that had to be overcome in view of the general situation', which was not the re-employment of those forced from their workplace, but 'the dispute which existed between the executive of the woodworkers [Carpenters' Union] and their people in Belfast',[67] by which was meant those members of the union who had been expelled for refusing to obey the strike call. Given both the Congress resolution and the suffering the trade unionists forced from their work had endured, this seems a peculiar priority, but it was one that was sustained in those the delegation met. Although these included the District Committee of the Carpenters Union, which was loyal to the union leadership, and two committees representing the victimised workers, the rest of those the TUC representatives consulted were generally unsympathetic to their cause. These included the managements of the two shipyards, the Unionist Lord Mayor, a group representing the strike-breakers/now expelled members of the Carpenters' Union and the 'Joint Vigilance Committee of the Shipyards'. The TUC representatives met this final group twice.

When the three Parliamentary Committee members submitted the report of their visit to Belfast to the 1921 Congress, it reflected the fact that a majority of those they had met were unsympathetic or hostile to the victimised trade unionists. In a section of their report entitled 'Cause of the Trouble', the delegation gave three reasons. First, that during the war 'there was a large influx of men from the South and West of Ireland' into the shipyards, although just how 'large' this 'influx' actually was, the report did not say. However, it was maintained that 'of those a number were either active Sinn Féiners or were strongly sympathetic to the Sinn Féin movement', but, again, it was not estimated how big this 'number' was. What the delegation did add was that 'it was alleged that many of these have openly avowed their intention of obtaining the domination of the Sinn Féin movement in Belfast', although instances of such avowals or their frequency were not recorded. A further unsubstantiated allegation reported was: 'that a number of Sinn Féin supporters carried arms.'[68] Thus the presence of alleged Sinn Féin sympathisers was the first reason given for the victimisations. The second was 'the murder at Cork, of Colonel Smyth, D.S.O., an Ulsterman who had served in the war';[69] the third and fourth were, 'on 22 August District Inspector Swanzy was killed on the streets of Lisburn ... [and] on the 25th September two policemen on duty in the Falls Road were shot.'[70] In enumerating these as the causes of the pogrom the TUC created the impression that the loyalists had been provoked by the activities of Republicans. No mention was made of Carson's speech or of the presence of organisations such as the Belfast Protestant Association.

The most uncharitable interpretation of the TUC's explanation was that it came close to justifying the victimisations and that in reporting that 'representative bodies of workmen were emphatic in their declaration against working with adherents of Sinn Féin',[71] the TUC had decided it was useless to challenge such attitudes. Certainly its explanation of the pogrom was at variance with other contemporary ones. There is the evidence of James Sexton, who as well as being a Labour MP was also the general secretary of the National Dock Labourers union, and, as already noted, was no friend of Sinn Féin. Speaking in the House of Commons, he said that Carson's speech 'is alone responsible for the dissension and division amongst the members of my own organisation'[72] which had a mixed religious membership in Belfast.

The alternative version of events given by the TUC was also apparent in its assessment of the Vigilance Committee. On this, the 'point of view of business management' was relayed without comment: 'the present position under which firms have in fact conceded the right [to the Vigilance Committee] of deciding on the question of reinstatement of their workmen ... is but the least of two evils'.[73] Even more illuminating is the account of the meetings the delegation held with the Vigilance Committee. 'We found men with strong prejudices but claiming intense loyalty to the British flag and Empire', the TUC reported. The conclusion was that 'the existence of such a body and the methods employed in regard to suspected men' – that is, those driven from their workplaces – 'can hardly be regarded as constitutional machinery of law and order, but in view of the fact that constitutional government has broken down in Ireland generally, its reflex in Belfast need not occasion any surprise.'[74] With such a generosity of tolerance, it is hardly surprising that the TUC delegation could add that its meetings with the Vigilance Committee were 'conducted in a perfectly friendly spirit'.[75] In concluding, the subsequently endorsed delegates' report covered both the issues of the victimised workers and of those expelled from the Carpenters' Union. On the former the advice was unspecific, even facile. 'The most broad-minded of the men on both sides should be brought together for the purpose of discussing the difficulty',[76] was the recommendation. However, on the dispute between the Carpenters and their former members, the TUC was prepared to be a little bolder. Referring to the decision to expel those who disobeyed the strike call, the report claimed to 'express no opinion'. But it did say, 'throughout our stay we were continually met with the view that in the circumstances it was a mistake.' So much a mistake meant that 'means should be found whereby the relationship between the [Carpenters' Union] and their expelled members should be renewed',[77] a thinly disguised call for reinstatement.

Soon after the Parliamentary Committee members returned from Belfast, the Carpenters' Union met a delegation of their ex-members from Belfast. The central requests from the union were that they should withdraw a circular they had sent saying they would only work with 'loyal subjects' and those who 'gave their word of honour that they were not connected with Sinn Féin', and reject a reduction on wages imposed on them by management in September. At a subsequent mass meeting, the former members of the union turned these down by 1000 votes to

86.[78] They remained expelled from the union. The leadership of the TUC made further, unsuccessful, attempts to persuade the union to take the men back, including the convening of a meeting in London of representatives of the executives of all the unions affected by the 'disturbances', a meeting which again ignored the issue of the victimised workers.[79]

There are two other significant references in the minutes of the Parliamentary Committee and its successor the General Council to the Belfast disturbances and the Carpenters. The first was in June 1921 when it was recorded, 'It was decided to comply with a request from Mr Gorman, secretary of the Vigilance Committee, that he should be supplied with the report of the delegation to Belfast as a confidential communication.'[80] Then, a few months later at a meeting discussing arrangements for a special congress on unemployment and the international situation, it was reported that a delegate 'had applied for permission to take a collection in the Hall in aid of the Catholic workers expelled from Belfast.' The General Council's minutes record: 'Resolved: that no collection of any kind be taken in the Hall.'[81]

A comment on the Parliamentary Committee's handling of these events was made at the annual congress of the TUC in September 1921. A delegate from Belfast, ILP councillor James Baird, not a member of the Carpenters' Union, referred to those driven from their workplace:

By the inactivity of the English Trade Union movement during the past year you have been supporting Sir Edward Carson and the Orangemen ... We thought that the great English Trade Unions would come to our assistance. We looked with confidence to the action we hoped they would take, but the Joiners' Union [Carpenters] and the Joiners' Union alone took strong action ... Had the other trade unions took similar action ... had they then if the Belfast trade unionists continued to refuse to obey the union order, prevented goods and raw materials going to Belfast, and coal and steel and other things required for the industries, I fearlessly assert that one fortnight of that action would have settled entirely the troubles in the North of Ireland.[82]

Whatever the value of this last assertion, it can be said that the attitude of the TUC on Ireland in these years excluded the possibility of the type of action Baird recommended. The Parliamentary Committee and General Council minutes are evidence of a leadership seeking to avoid the issue.

The outcome and aftermath of the Special Congress on Ireland show a trade union movement in general which declined the invitation to act. The story of the Carpenters' dispute suggests that when at last the TUC did feel the need to intervene into the troubled situation in Ireland, its leadership did so, at least as far as Belfast was concerned, on the side of the sectarians. Such an outcome may not have been the conscious intention. Perhaps the Parliamentary Committee, well aware no doubt that the majority of trade unionists in Belfast were from the Unionist community, decided that expediency and realism should substitute for the principles contained in the instructions it had been given by the 1920 Congress to evolve 'a line of action for the reinstatement of all trade unionist expelled from their work.' Or perhaps the Parliamentary Committee deputation that went to Belfast was too easily persuaded by the majority of those it met. But whatever the mitigating circumstances, a plea made by Baird at the Congress went unanswered: 'We the victim of intolerance in Belfast … demand the protection that we think we have the right to receive. We demand that strong action be taken and speedy action.'[83]

There is one contextual point which is worth making. From 1918 to 1921, both the Labour Party and the TUC had conditioned their acceptance of Irish self-determination on protection for minorities in Ireland. By this, they meant the Unionist population of northeast Ireland. And yet it could well be argued that the non-combatant minority that suffered most in Ireland in these years was the working class Catholics of Belfast and surrounding areas. What the Carpenters dispute in particular suggests is that when this minority needed defending, the TUC preferred to look the other way.

5
Alternatives

What is already clear is that both the Labour Party and TUC, while critical of the British government policy in Ireland in these years, were reluctant allies of the Republicans. But there were others in the British working class movement who might be expected to show greater sympathy. For example, in 1920, The New Statesman, founded in 1913 'as the organ of the Fabian Society' published 'Easter 1916', by W. B. Yeats, which as well as becoming the most quoted poem in the Irish historiography also recognised the transformation that the Rising had engendered. For example, the editor of *Labour Leader* at the time of the Rising was Fenner Brockway, who had to give up his editorship after being jailed for anti-conscription activities and who throughout his later life was a prominent and active anti-colonialist. For example, the *Communist*, the newspaper of the Communist Party of Great Britain (CPGB), saw T. A. Jackson analysing what was happening in Ireland, and Jackson's book, *Ireland Her Own*, republished in 1971, was to become a reference book for Irish history for many British socialists. All of this suggests that there was some understanding and even support for the Irish insurgents of 1916–21 within the ILP, the CPGB and its predecessor the BSP, and the Fabians.

The Independent Labour Party

The ILP had a good war, or rather a good anti-war, with its pacifism attracting a more sympathetic hearing as the great adventure turned into the great catastrophe. That and the spread of radical ideas are behind its membership growth of approximately 50 per cent between 1914 and 1920. Less helpful, the re-organisation of the Labour Party in 1918 had posed the question of what exactly the role of the ILP now was. For the first time, Labour had organised itself into local branches, thereby duplicating and challenging the ILP's own organisational structure and purpose. The ILP was, generally speaking to the left of Labour, but it now needed a distinctive voice more than ever. That voice was heard at the annual party conference, the discussion within the leadership body, the National Administrative Council (NAC) and the ILP's press. These were its weekly newspaper *Labour Leader*, its quarterly journal *Socialist Review*, and the Glasgow newspaper *Forward*, which it dominated.

The party conference only debated Ireland in the latter half of the period, at the 1919, 1920 and 1921 conferences, and the quarterly meetings of the NAC only discussed Ireland on three occasions in the entire period. Accordingly, the bulk of the evidence on Irish policy is found in the party press, but all three, the conference, the NAC and the press, will now be examined together and chronologically. As early as 21 April 1916, and in the aftermath of the Easter Rising, the NAC discussed 'the advisability of issuing a manifesto on the Irish question.' The minutes also record, 'no definite agreement was arrived at',[2] and the suggestion was not raised again. This did not prevent *Labour Leader* and its editor Fenner Brockway from making the occasional comment on events in Ireland. The execution of Roger Casement was attacked, and with it the accusation that the government was making 'criminals of many of its noblest citizens', and condemning 'some of its sweetest souls to die.'[3] The possibility of extending conscription to Ireland was also denounced, and, in the same article in October 1916 there was the more general complaint of 'serious mishandling' of the Irish situation by the government which had, 'undone all the good which had been done by the Home Rule Bill.'[4] This implicit support for Home Rule was confirmed later in the same month. *Labour Leader* was now under the editorship of Katherine Bruce Glasier, but it hosted a weekly column written by the party chair Philip Snowden, a Labour MP since 1906, a pacifist and temperance advocate. He said Ireland's 'best hope' was to put the Home Rule Bill 'into operation'.[5] By the end of the year the newspaper appeared less attached to that particular legislation, calling instead for 'self-government for Ireland.'[6] Certainly, there was an increasing recognition that the old Home Rule solution was in difficulty. In March 1917 Snowden complained that the arrest and imprisonment of Sinn Féin leaders was 'playing into the hands of the revolutionary sections in Ireland', and was 'making the position of the constitutional Nationalist Party impossible.'[7] His conclusion was stated later in the same month: 'it is doubtful if the time when Nationalist Ireland would have accepted a partial Home Rule scheme has not gone by.'[8] He stated his own position the following month, arguing against partition but calling for 'reasonable protection for minorities'. More dramatically, the general proposal now was for 'the Dominion system of self-government'.[9] What this meant was spelt out in a full-page article the following week by E. D. Morel. Morel had been a leader of the Union of Democratic Control, the leading anti-war organisation and had, in August 1917, been sentenced to six months in prison for anti-war activities. He joined the ILP from the Liberals on his release. He also seemed to breaking from his Liberal past on Ireland, because he now wrote, 'the Home Rule Act ... will not settle the Irish problem.' Instead, 'we must give Ireland the status enjoyed by our self-governing dominions, with the one non-vital exception hereafter mentioned.'[10] In fact, two exceptions followed. The first suggested that in an Irish parliament, 'Ulster should be given a political power comparable to the economic power it wields at present.' A series of suggestions followed, centring on the right of Ulster parliamentary representatives to veto legislation they considered injurious to the interests of the north-eastern province.[11] The other qualification was based on the contention that 'Ireland's geographical proximity to England suggests a modification in the full powers of Dominion self-government.' Accordingly, said Morel, a self-governing Ireland would not have the right to raise its own army or navy, instead the British Army would stay in the country. Here were the two qualifications on self-determination which were later to become of such common coinage within the Labour Party. They were, however, introduced by the ILP in the context of a shift away from its former Home Rule position and towards what was understood as dominion home rule, as enjoyed for instance by Canada, a shift the Labour Party had yet to make. The changed mood was best indicated in mid-May in an article marking the anniversary of the execution of James Connolly. This was written by John Bruce Glasier, Katherine's husband. He, along with MacDonald, Snowden and Keir Hardie was one of the leading lights of the ILP, a member of its NAC almost continuously from 1896 until his death in 1920, and had replaced Hardie as chair in 1900, a position he held for three years. He had a mixed history on Ireland. As a young man he joined the Glasgow branch of the Irish Land League, and in 1881 even wrote a song proclaiming that British 'rebels ... Hand in hand will stand with the Irish, and wear the Green with you.'[12] But when he had toured Ireland for the Fabians in 1898 he came to a rather different conclusion:

The more I get to know the inner meaning of things in Ireland the more difficult, if not hopeless, the problem of its salvation becomes. There seems to be a flaw – a fatal lesion – in Irish character that unfits the people for rational and progressive life. The nationalist movement seems to be largely superstition rather than an intelligent desire for national freedom.[13]

Perhaps, 20 years on, he had got over such prejudice, for he now said of Connolly:

His sudden emergence as the leader of the Dublin Rebellion came as a great surprise to me, as, I think, to most of his old friends on this side. But now we understand better, though far from completely the inner circumstances of that tragic event, and not criticism or blame, but deep sympathy and admiration well up within us as we think of him and so many of the brave young idealists ... who fell with him in the struggle.[14]

This was a different sentiment from that with which *Labour Leader* had initially reacted to the Rising when condemning it as 'a crime', and opposing it on pacifist grounds.[15] The pacifism did remain, with Bruce Glasier adding that Connolly 'lacked ... the higher imaginativeness and idealism of some of his compatriots, especially Sheehy-Skeffington – the purest pacifist of them all'. He had been shot dead by a British soldier during the Rising after being held hostage. Nevertheless, Bruce Glasier now maintained that of all the participants in the Rising none but Connolly 'possessed a more absorbing passion for the emancipation of his class, or a more faithful, utterly sincere and guileless heart.'

As to the way forward in Ireland, Snowden's column in the issues of the paper of 24 and 31 May 1917 welcomed the setting up of the Irish Convention, with the expectation that 'much is hoped from the presence of Labour';[16] a presence which did not even materialise as both Irish Labour and Sinn Féin boycotted the initiative. Sinn Féin's absence, especially after its victory in the East Clare by-election in July, dashed Snowden's optimism. Commenting on that result, his opinion now was that Sinn Féin 'represents an overwhelming majority of Nationalist opinion', and accordingly any decisions made by the Convention would be 'valueless'. He still suggested that any such outcome should be put to a referendum, but more generally he was at a loss what to propose saying, 'It is difficult to see what can be done at the moment to deal with the Irish situation'.[17] The problem for *Labour Leader* was that while it acknowledged the popular support for Sinn Féin, it was opposed to its demands. '*Labour Leader* holds no brief for the extreme Sinn Féin position', said the newspaper in September 1917, 'and certainly holds no faith in the efficacy of armed force',[18] a remark made well before the outbreak of the War of Independence. This comment was inserted as an introduction to an article by 'a former Irish correspondent', who reported that in Ireland 'Home Rule and even Colonial self-government are no longer acceptable to the main body of the people ... nothing short of independence is the demand.' *Labour Leader*'s position as stated in its introductory statement was for 'peace in Ireland and "self-determination", although the peculiar device of wrapping 'self-determination' in quotation marks, together with the statement opposing Sinn Féin's demands, suggests the self-determination *Labour Leader* had in mind was not as espoused by Irish Republicans.

The Morel article remained the formal position of the newspaper, and was referred to as such by *Labour Leader* in mid-February 1918[19] However, the sense of helplessness which Snowden had shown in July 1917 also reappeared. In May 1918 he wrote, 'The government have got the Irish question into an impossible and tragic situation, and there seems no way to escape from the appalling consequences.'[20] However, three weeks later, *Labour Leader* gave over its columns to Nationalist MP Arthur Lynch who did try to chart an escape. He attacked Sinn Féin, and called for 'a large measure of Home Rule' in which 'complete reassurance should be given to Ulster on the religious side.'[21] Two months later, *Labour Leader*'s occasional Irish correspondent, trade unionist Patrick Thompson, attacked both the Nationalists and Sinn Féin and called for 'political self-government',[22] and the following month Snowden complained that 'the government have determined not to deal with the Irish situation by the granting of self-government'.[23] Similarly, in September he observed 'all hope may be abandoned' for a government 'attempt to settle the question of Home Rule.'[24] Finally, in 1918, there was Snowden's own election address, printed in the front page of *Labour Leader* at the start of December in which he simply described himself as a 'Home Ruler'.[25]

Apart from attacks on the government's threats to introduce conscription[26] and a couple of articles reporting what was occurring in

Ireland, the references listed above were the summation of the newspaper's coverage for 1918, which can be described as occasional rather than regular and politically unsure. As for *Socialist Review*, it carried only one reference to Ireland in 1918. This was in the July to September issue, which commented, 'the supreme domestic issue has been Ireland' because of the government's threats to impose conscription. This, apparently, had meant that 'within a day, the work of years of war companionship was undone', and this, together with arrests of 'the leaders of the left' (meaning a number of leading figures in the Irish labour movement) brought the comment, 'We have had many difficulties with Ireland, most of which have been of our own making. But we have never so wantonly and gratuitously slapped Ireland in the face.'[27] That it was the threat of conscription that prompted the greatest criticism from the ILP is not surprising given the party's pacifism, although for the same reason the reference to 'war companionship' seems somewhat out of place. A more important point is that in the 89 articles carried by *Socialist Review* in 1917 and 1918 this was the only reference to Ireland. A similar silence was observed by the ILP's NAC, and again the only discussion in 1918 occurred over the threat of conscription. The NAC statement issued on this concluded with a somewhat grandiose declaration which 'calls upon the Socialist and Labour forces in this country to use every means in their power to prevent the perpetration of this crime.'[28] Again, although never followed up, this was certainly more militant than anything the Labour Party was saying.

The following year, in 1919, the NAC did not discuss Ireland, and nor did any of the 43 articles printed by *Socialist Review* contain any Irish reference. *Labour Leader* that year also repeated the pattern of the previous one with, despite the deteriorating situation, only limited coverage and a lack of political clarity. In mid-April Snowden had an article on Egypt, India and Ireland which supported the general principle of self-determination,[29] but it was not until July that he elaborated what this should involve. 'It is now doubtful whether any proposal short of an Irish Republic would allay the popular discontent in the country', he wrote, but he suggested that this was not the solution he personally favoured when he added: 'But if an honest and genuine attempt was made to give Ireland a full measure of self-government, such as enjoyed by the Dominions, there is just the possibility that the present bitterness might be modified and the revolutionary agitation might be deprived of popular support.'[30] An article by Patrick Thompson the following week also advocated 'Dominion Government', although an Irish navy or army was still ruled out. This repeated one of Morel's two qualifications of two years earlier. As for the other one, Thompson now said 'safeguards' on Ulster would be 'impracticable and undemocratic'.[31]

In mid-September, the *Labour Leader* carried its first editorial of the year on Ireland. This concluded that, because of 'English mismanagement of the Irish problem' the existing Home Rule legislation would be accepted by 'no Party in Ireland.'[32] What the newspaper did not say was what should take its place, and neither did an editorial the following week castigating British 'terror' in Ireland.[33] But, in the same edition of the paper Snowden's column did call for 'a policy which will satisfy the aspirations of the Irish people', and in the last issue of 1919 he concluded, 'until Ireland is a free nation there is and there can be no peace.'[34]

Such was the political direction given by *Labour Leader* in 1919, but what of the party generally? At the ILP conference of the same year, held in April, no debate on Ireland was initially tabled, but the issue was raised when a Glasgow delegate objected to the omission of Ireland from the NAC's report on the war settlement. This brought the announcement that Ireland would be dealt with in a special resolution to be debated the following day. When this appeared, Ireland was only part of a longer motion, which also included Egypt and India. The Irish part called for 'the withdrawal of British troops from Ireland, and the recognition of that form of government which is desired by the Irish people'.[35] The Standing Orders Committee said there should be only one speaker on the Irish section of the resolution, and when it was voted on it was so uncontentious that it was passed unanimously. An editorial in *Labour Leader* in early 1920 included similar wording to the 1919 conference resolution, supporting the 'right of Ireland to determine in her own way what form of government she should adopt.' This time there was clarification, and it was a break with both past fudging and the position of the Morel article. The editorial declared, 'We may say for the ILP that we stand by the right of [Irish] self-determination with all the consequences that the conferring of that right involves.'[36]

The changed position was repeated in a comment by Snowden the following week when he advocated 'the full right of self-determination',[37] and although two weeks later in an article 'An ILPer in Ireland', Charles Roden Buxton said 'I personally believe that complete constitutional independence – in the sense of separation – would be a bad policy for Ireland', he implied that if the Irish wanted this, then they should have it.[38] Indeed, the following month Snowden was showing how zealous a convert he now was when he called upon the Labour Party to 'demand that the settlement of the Irish question should be handed over to the Irish people', with a 'fully empowered' constituent assembly.[39] An editorial two months later summed up what that position of *Labour Leader* now was. There was regret that British policy 'has had the effect of driving the more reasonable Nationalists in Ireland into the ranks of the extreme section'; there was the hope that 'if the government, even at this late hour had the courage to rise to the height of true statesmanship it is not impossible that they could bring a change of feeling towards Great Britain among the great mass of Irish people'; but there was the declaration that the ILP 'stands for the full right of self-determination without reservation and without qualification.' There was, however, one additional comment, which objected to any attempt to 'impose upon the Irish people a Republic'.[40] The notion that Britain would 'impose' a Republic seems far-fetched. An explanation for this comment may be found in the proceedings of the ILP annual conference of the previous month. As with the 1919 conference Ireland was not, at first, debated separately but was rather included in a motion which called for 'complete autonomy' for Ireland, Egypt and India. Then an amendment was moved by John Scurr from Poplar ILP. This called for 'recognition of the Irish Republic'. In his speech, Scurr made it clear it was not advocating recognition of the Irish Republic already unilaterally declared, but rather if 'an Irish constituent assembly should freely decide ... in favour of a Republic, it should be recognised.'[41] Even this proved contentious, because when the amendment was put it was only passed by 268 to 207 votes. If the article objecting to the possible imposition of a Republic on the Irish was a coded side-swipe at this amendment the newspaper nevertheless stuck to the party line for the rest of the year. Others were urged to adopt the same course when an editorial on the eve of the Labour Party conference said that 'it should be made clear that the Party stands for the free and unfettered right of the Irish people to determine their own form of government.'[42]

Despite such declarations, there are indications that there were those in the ILP leadership who remained highly sceptical of a Republican Ireland. Ramsay MacDonald wrote in an editorial in *Socialist Review* in the summer of 1920 that he did not believe an Irish Republic was 'necessary or will bring out the best that is in Irish Nationalism. But I am not afraid of it and if we are to allow Ireland to save itself from reaction and obscurantism we must trust Ireland with self-determination.'[43] Given the rather patronising tone employed here it is hardly surprising that apart from this, which was part of a longer editorial not specific to Ireland, *Socialist Review* only included one article on Ireland out of 45 printed by the journal in 1920. This was in the final edition of the year, it was written by Margaret Newboult and it declared that while 'it would almost be an impertinence in us to declare for an Irish Republic' nevertheless, 'we must clear out of Ireland and leave the decision to her'.[44]

So, by the end of 1920, the ILP conference, its newspaper and its quarterly journal were speaking with one voice advocating unqualified self-determination. In early 1921, this reaffirmed with *Labour Leader* asserting 'there will be no permanent settlement of the Irish question until the Irish people themselves are able through their own Constituent Assembly to decided what the future government of Ireland shall be.'[45] What statements like this left out, indeed what *Labour Leader* and the ILP in general had not touched on for some time was the military question: whether a self-governing Ireland would be permitted its own army or navy. This was taken up in July 1921 when a front-page article declared that 'there should be no limit' on Irish self-determination because 'England has nothing to fear from a free Ireland ... she could not be dangerous to Britain in military or naval matters.'[46] Yet, in the same article where this old bogey was finally laid to rest, the other familiar limitation on self-determination re-emerged. 'Everybody now recognises that some special provision will have to be made for N.E. Ulster',[47] said *Labour Leader*, although 'everybody' had not included the 1921 conference which in March had again called for 'self-determination without qualification ... even if it means granting to the Irish recognition of the independent Republic.'[48] Yet by and large the ILP leadership and press did follow the decisions of their party conference. Indeed in opting for self-determination in January 1920 *Labour Leader* had anticipated the decision of the conference of later that year. Similarly, the NAC had attempted to provide leadership to the party in October 1920 when it suggested that party branches should hold meetings on Ireland.[49] The effect of this advice will be examined subsequently (see Chapter 6), but again this was before the Labour Party ran its campaign of meetings, just as the ILP policy of recognition of the Republic was beyond what Labour was advocating. In summary, until the summer of 1921 the ILP leadership and press had steadily evolved to a position of support for unconditional self-determination, almost to the point, to echo J. Bruce Glasier's youthful promise of standing 'hand-in-hand' with 'the Irish rebels'. Then, they pulled away their hand and went to stand on the other side.

The prompt came with the Republican leadership's rejection of dominion status in August 1921, when the truce was in operation. *Labour Leader*'s front page article began, 'On the face of it the Sinn Féin leader's reply to Mr Lloyd George's offer seems to destroy all the hopes one had built up during the six weeks of truce.' The article then spoke of the Irish/British conflict as 'a war between two rights ... in the British case this is the unquestionable supremacy of the imperial throne, in the Irish case the right of a nation to be free and contract such alliances as it deems fit.' The call was for the decision on dominion status to be put to a plebiscite, through which the Irish would decide 'whether they will take the peaceful plunge into the new sphere offered to them by the British government, or allow themselves to be stampeded back once more into the bloody horrors of resistance and persecution.'[50] This new thinking was firmed up the following week under the front page headline, 'ENGLAND'S OFFER TO IRELAND: WILL SINN FÉIN RELEASE US TO LOOK AFTER OUT OWN BUSINESS?':

Mr De Valera and his Republican adjutants are thrashing out a tremendously important question in the Dublin Mansion House this week. They are now deciding whether they shall allow England to cast off the Irish incubus, and be free to get Home Rule for herself, or whether they shall continue to tax the English resources in men and money, in pains and patience and pugnacity to keep the Irish down. Bound up with this, of course, is the question of Ireland's own immunity from British interference, and her freedom to develop as a self-governing nation. But this is a comparatively minor issue for the people of England, Scotland and Wales who have had the mortification of seeing their own social reform measures shelved in session after session to make way for Irish legislation, and their military arm devoted more and more to the odious task of Irish repression. The Sinn Féin South has a valid grievance in that it is asked to sign a treaty for a dismembered Ireland, with apparently only a very outside chance of ever being able to come to a working agreement with the chopped-off province. But what does Mr De Valera suppose would happen if he did … wrest an independent Republican status from the British government. Ulster would still be there and his writ would not run in Belfast. These are, for good or ill, 'immutable facts.' If the offer is not accepted and the Irish never-enders win, then Mr. Lloyd George may be trusted to plunge this country into another Khaki election for the purpose of obtaining a mandate to 'settle' Ireland with the sword. The forward section of English Labour would be powerless to resist the wave of anti-Irishness which would sweep the country, and incidentally, their own programme would be submerged in the flood.[51]

On the face of it, compared to the previous five years, especially the last 18 months, this article and its predecessor seem so exceptional that it can be asked how seriously they should be taken in assessing the general and overall position of the ILP from 1916 to 1921. The opinions expressed were dismissive, even contemptuous of the right of self-determination, a right which was ILP conference policy. It now criticised the Irish struggle for self-determination for getting in the way of English reform, placed the interests of British socialists, as those interests were perceived, above those of the people of Ireland, and in the process used language which was guilty of the very anti-Irishness of which it accused others. The party had, on occasions, criticised the Labour Party for its failure to attack the government on Ireland, and yet here it was siding with the government. So is it best to see these two articles as an aberration, unrepresentative and indicating little more than the inability of those involved to stay calm under pressure? Possibly, but there is another analysis available, one that sees the two articles, and the second in particular, as exceptional only in the sense that they were an exaggeration of what had gone before: a magnification of existing trends. The most obvious is disinterest. Listed in these pages have been all the major editorials in *Labour Leader* and *Socialist Review* on the desired political settlement of Ireland. In total, stretched over five years, they do not amount to a great deal either in the extent of coverage or its intellectual clarity. Neither did the ILP conference show any great desire to break through this apathy. Accordingly, the overwhelming impression the articles quoted above gives – a wish to be rid of the whole Irish issue – 'a minor issue' – does reflect a history into which it can fit with some consistency. Then there is issue of self-determination. True, the ILP did come round to advocating this in January 1920, six months before the Labour Party, but that was still over a year after the Irish had voted for it in such overwhelming numbers. Finally there is the support for partition, which in the second above article the Irish were told they now had to accept. This too had a history in the ILP. The Morel article of May 1917 detailed at length special measures Ulster should be given in a Home Rule parliament, a position again endorsed by *Labour Leader* in its edition of 14 February 1918. After this, separate provisions for Ulster were no longer proposed, until that is the article of 21 July 1921 and its support for 'special provisions' for Ulster. It is true that neither that article nor Morel's supported partition, but they had both trod the road in that direction. Thus, the article entitled, 'ENGLAND'S OFFER TO IRELAND: WILL SINN FÉIN RELEASE US TO LOOK AFTER OUR OWN BUSINESS?' was less an aberration, but rather a confirmation that the ILP never really had any enthusiasm for seeing the struggle for Irish self-determination as 'our own business'.

Where it may have been more 'our business' than most other places was in Glasgow, with its large Irish population and history of Protestant/ Catholic strife. What then of *Forward*, where most of the Irish coverage in these years was written by William Regan in his 'Catholic Socialist Notes' column? Regan was an ILP councillor, appointed ILP Glasgow organiser in early 1919.[52] Therefore, he wrote from a position of some authority. In contrast to *Labour Leader*, as early as the immediate aftermath of the Easter Rebellion, Regan was saying that Ireland should be 'granted independence',[53] and, as already noted, John Wheatley was writing in the same newspaper that the 'only way out of the situation' was by 'boldly handing over the difficulty to the Irish people themselves and tell them to find a solution.'[54] Two months later, Regan was even more explicit, saying Ireland was a 'separate country' from England, that 'the Irish are entitled to complete separation if they wish it' and that 'the English have no moral right to say what the relations of the two countries should be'. The same article went on to attack John Redmond's Home Rule proposals for having 'reduced his country to the status of Yorkshire and its claim to Home Rule proportionally.'[55] This article, together with the other earlier references quoted could be seen as the earliest call within the British working class movement for a separatist solution, if so desired by the Irish. However, it was soon abandoned. By November 1916, Regan was writing that the Home Rule solution was 'very desirable', and that 'this does not mean a separate Irish state' but only 'the right to manage all purely Irish affairs.'[56] Ten months later, in an editorial written by G. B. Clark which came out against a separate Irish state, *Forward* also adopted the familiar worry about defence, saying, 'It would be a great mistake for Ireland to burden itself with an army or navy'.[57] A more forthright analysis of this issue came two months later with Regan writing that 'capitalist Britain' would never agree to 'severance of the link' because 'so long as Britain may be menaced from without she will not voluntarily hand away a military base as a free and hostile Ireland would be.' A lesson in military strategy followed: 'In alliance with Germany or Japan, Ireland's harbour could be used to throttle Britain; her eastern headland could be used as gun emplacements from which ... Britain would be dominated by long range ordinance.'[58]

While *Forward* attributed such worries to a capitalist Britain, it was almost as if the newspaper was performing the role of a devil's advocate. Certainly, the only possibility offered in the article of such thinking not holding sway was to 'destroy capitalism throughout the world' and 'establish the International' and a 'safe and prosperous European confederacy'. In the meantime, an independent Ireland was not 'practical politics'. This opinion was repeated on other occasions,[59] but if the aim of an independent Ireland was judged impractical it was also condemned on what amounted to moral grounds. 'Republican Ireland', said 'Catholic Socialist Notes' in June 1918, 'would bring that country to the level of Republican America with its squalor, sin and serfdom.'[60] It was not until September 1919 that *Forward* returned to its post-Rising position in calling for 'self-determination ... a settlement such as given to Poland and Czechoslovakia',[61] and in January 1920 the Scottish conference of the ILP called for self-determination and the withdrawal of British troops.[62] This position was repeated a couple of times in *Forward* during 1920[63] with even the defence restriction on independence being dismissed on one occasion.[64] And then, as with *Labour Leader*, a dramatic change came in August 1921 with Lloyd George's terms for settlement. *Forward* saw these as the 'biggest offer ever advanced' by the British to the Irish, whose 'tone is correct' and which 'avoids even the appearance of offence to nationalist aspirations.'[65] This estimation – which was not in 'Catholic Socialist Notes', for the column had disappeared the previous month – was challenged in the subsequent issue of *Forward* in a letter from John Wheatley. While Wheatley himself was not an advocate of Irish Republicanism,[66] he complained that the article 'might be read as expressing sympathy with the government's policy', which he attacked on partition and the threat of coercion.[67] There was a reply to Wheatley in the same issue by the editor, Thomas Johnston. 'The Labour programme', he wrote, 'is to offer the Irish people a free choice as to their own form of government, with guarantees as to British security and protection to minorities – we adhere to that.'

These words are as an appropriate summing up as any of the ILP's position of autumn 1921, a position *Forward* had come to adopt, albeit by a different route than *Labour Leader*. The ILP's own policy, as agreed by conference, of unrestricted self-determination had been dropped by its press. By deciding to 'adhere' to what it called the 'Labour programme', in reality the programme of the Labour Party, the ILP had ceased to offer an alternative to that programme or party. To return to the issue of what the ILP was for, as opposed to the Labour Party, at least as far as Ireland was concerned, in August 1921 that question was difficult to answer.

The Communists

The attitude of the Marxist left in Britain towards Ireland will be examined here through the words and policy of the BSP and the CPGB, into which the BSP dissolved itself when the CPGB was formed in July and August 1920 at the Communist Unity Convention. At this convention, the BSP was by far the major influence, having 96 out of the 152 to 157 delegates who attended.[68] Thus, the BSP and the CPGB were the largest Marxist organisations in this period, and this analysis will consist of examining their Irish policies. The views of other Marxists, especially Sylvia Pankhurst and the *Workers' Dreadnought*, but also the SLP's *Socialist*, will be referred to subsequently. Pankhurst and the WSF (the Workers' Suffrage Federation became the Workers' Socialist Federation in 1918) did not join the CPGB and the SLP split over joining it.

The weekly public voice of the BSP was, from 1 June 1916, the *Call*, which had previously been the organ of the anti-war faction of the BSP who had won a majority at the party's conference in Easter 1916. When the CPGB was formed, the *Call* gave way to the *Communist*. The first time the *Call* appeared as the official BSP newspaper, it maintained that 'the only solution to the Irish Problem is for Home Rule for the whole of

Ireland.'[69] Although three weeks later it noted the growth of Sinn Féin, and thereby the growth of sentiment in Ireland beyond Home Rule,[70] the following month the policy was still to attack the government for not granting Home Rule[71] and to call for 'the immediate withdrawal of martial law and the application of the Home Rule Act as it now stands on the statute book.'[72] This position was no different from the rest of the working class movement and it was over a year before the policy began to change, when an editorial decried the Irish Convention and supported instead Ireland's 'right to autonomy or even separation.'[73] In a statement on war aims submitted to the Allied Socialist Conference, the BSP repeated the principle informing these words when it maintained, 'the peoples of India, Egypt, Ireland and Algeria should be free to decide their own course of action.'[74] This apparent support for unqualified self-determination was well in advance of both the Labour Party and the ILP, but the effect of this differential can only have muted by the infrequency with which it was stated by the *Call*. The last four months of 1917 saw no repetition or further elaboration of the policy, and indeed there was no significant mention of Ireland in the newspaper, apart from a section in the more general 'Notes and Comments' column in November headed 'Ireland – Approaching Deadlock'.[75] January 1918 did see the *Call* attack the omission of the Irish issue in the war aims of the allies[76] and complain that 'the leaders of the British Labour movement, as a rule, are silent on Ireland',[77] but the newspaper of the BSP was itself hardly loquacious on the topic. The first time since January 1917 that its main front page article was on Ireland was in March 1918. This complained of 'the continued delay in meeting the just demand of the Irish people for the right of self-government', with the main thrust of the article, headed 'Law and Order in Ireland', on the government's 'force and violence, which is met by force and violence'.[78] There was a further front page article on Ireland two weeks later which concentrated on explaining that 'the Irish difficulty is threefold in character – political, agrarian and economic',[79] but it was not until July 1918 that any substantial space was given to elaborating an Irish policy. Then, the front page article included:

> The time has gone for patched-up settlements, either on the basis of the defunct Home Rule Act or the abortive recommendations of the Convention. There is but one solution: to concede to the Irish people the full right of self-determination and to leave them to determine

whether they will enter any scheme of federal Home Rule that may ultimately be devised.[80]

To abide by the wishes of the Irish was to remain the policy, but, as with others in the British working class movement, doubts were on occasion expressed as to the wisdom of what the Irish would choose. 'It is open to much argument whether the Irish people would gain anything worth having by an independent Republic', said the newspaper in May 1919, while conceding, 'but if the Irish people want that form of government it should be open to no argument whatever within the ranks of Labour'.[81] Perhaps this scepticism towards Irish Republicanism explains why the coverage on Ireland throughout 1919 remained irregular. Despite saying in January that 'the capture of practically the whole of Ireland by Sinn Féin is much more significant than the capture of England by Lloyd George',[82] there was not one front page lead article on Ireland throughout the year and only ten significant references to the issue during the same period.[83] Four of these were inclusions in the more general 'Notes and Comments' section of the newspaper,[84] and one was the report of a speech on Ireland at a 'Hands Off Russia' meeting.[85] There were repetitions of the advocacy of self-determination line,[86] but there was also the comment, 'Ireland ... will never recover her nationhood until communism triumphs.'[87]

The attitude displayed by this last remark may explain why the *Call* gave such patchy coverage to Ireland. What was perceived as a dilemma for Marxists was fully illustrated in a front page article in January 1920. Entitled 'An Internationalist in Ireland', and written by Fred Willis, the first half was a stirring defence of Irish resistance to 'foreign oppression', and an attack on the PLP for its 'inaction' on Ireland. Then the article continued:

But there is another and far more important side of the question. However much we sympathise with a people rightly struggling to be free we are forced to recognise that nationalism, wherever it exists, is essentially reactionary. The 'great war', said Trotsky in a luminous phrase, 'is a struggle between two great imperialist capitalisms.' So, in exactly the same manner, the struggle of Ireland from English domination is superimposed upon the struggle of classes in Ireland.[88]

The theoretical issues raised here will be examined later (Chapter 7). What can be suggested now is that however much the *Call* might defend the Republican struggle, or attack the British Labour Party for its inaction, when the newspaper itself argued that the struggle was somewhat theoretically unsound, even 'essentially reactionary', then such words would hardly be likely to encourage the newspaper's readership to agitate in its support. Yet two months later the executive of the BSP publicly called upon 'every section of the working class movement ... to press the government immediately to withdraw the troops from Ireland and take a plebiscite of all adults in Ireland on Separation, Federal Home Rule or the status quo.'[89]

Certainly, the *Call* and its successor the *Communist* gave much more coverage to Ireland in 1920 than previously. There was still a worry, expressed again by Fred Willis that, 'nowhere is the struggle for nationalism an essential principle of communism. It really belongs in the past',[90] but, in a subsequent issue, R. M. Fox drew a distinction between 'the nationalism of a dominant nation and that of an oppressed nationality'.[91] More generally, there were explanations of the Republicans' use of violence,[92] condemnations of the violence of the British,[93] and an attack on the 'treachery of J. H. Thomas' because of his failure to support the 'blacking' of British munitions by railway workers.[94] There was also a call for the government of the Soviet Union to send a 'commission of enquiry' into actions of the British security forces,[95] criticism of the TUC and its lack of a 'sense of action' over the hunger strike of Terence McSwiney',[96] and even a call for a general strike 'to compel the government to withdraw the military forces' from Ireland.[97] All such articles could have encouraged the readership of the *Call* and the *Communist* to take action on Ireland, but by their own admission these words appeared to have little effect. Often the newspapers lamented the failure of such action to materialise. 'The suppression of Ireland is one of the world's great crimes; the silence of Englishmen is one of the tragedies', was the comment in June.[98] In August it was that 'the workers of England have tamely allowed Irish freedom to be suppressed'.[99] In October there was the observation that, 'We common Englishmen of the working class bear a great load of shame upon our souls because of the cowardice that allows our masters to perpetuate unchecked their devilry in Ireland.'[100] The most powerful article came in a three-quarter page statement, issued by the executive of the CPGB in November. It was headed, 'Communists and Ireland', and it addressed itself, both to the argument that had surfaced before on the relevance of the Irish national struggle to Marxists, and to the apparent disinterest in Ireland shown by the British working class:

> A nation is being murdered under our eyes ... There are Communists who say it is not our concern. This is a Nationalist struggle ... we are internationalists ... In such a case as Ireland – the case of a small nation held in forcible suppression – the National struggle and the class struggle are inseparable from one another ... The Irish workers are suffering ... and the British workers do nothing ... From the British working class they [the Irish] expected better things. They see every device of imperialist tyranny employed against them with ... the acquiescence of the British working class ... Not only the Irish but the working class all over the world is looking to us. We are being weighed in the Irish balance, and if we are found wanting, not all the enunciations of orthodox formulae, not all the protestations of the purity of our communist faith will save us from contemptuous dismissal as faithful, though sometimes talkative servants of the British Imperial oligarchy.[101]

The tone of this statement suggests that there were those within the party who questioned the importance of the Irish issue. Four months later the executive again stressed in a public statement its 'pledge to render revolutionary support in assisting the oppressed Irish people in their struggle against British imperialism'.[102] However, in the same period the *Communist* again saw discussions on the relevance or otherwise for Marxists of the Irish struggle,[103] and when, in the process of these discussions it was argued that the 'nationalist aspirations of the Irish workers ... are dangerous illusions',[104] it can again be asked whether the publication of such sentiments served as a disincentive when it came to encouraging communists and the working class in general to take up the Irish issue. Certainly, there was as much discussion in the pages of the *Communist* in 1921 on such theoretical issues as there was on explaining the basic self-determination argument. Only twice was this re-stated in the course of the year. First, in January when the Labour Party was attacked for conditioning Irish self-determination on a constitutional guarantee that Ireland would not threaten Britain militarily: 'De Valera has as good a right to ask that the constitution of Britain should prevent Britain being a military menace to Ireland – and with more reason', was the quip.[105] Second, in October when it was explained that *Communist* support for self-determination:

... was not determined by the fact that the Irish people have shown a preference for a Republican form of government. Did they wish for a monarchy, or oligarchy or an anarchy our attitude would be the same. Having conceded the right of the Irish people to independence, we would have no excuse were we to seek to impose conditions.[106]

But even then this article went on to state, 'We would be best pleased to see Ireland a Workers Republic', and again it can be wondered whether the fact that the Irish revolution showed little sign of ending in a workers' Republic dampened the enthusiasm of British Marxists for that revolution. So, to what extent was the party active on Ireland in this period? There is some negative evidence, notably that in the first volume of the 'official' *History of the Communist Party of Great Britain*, James Klugmann's study sub-titled, 'Formation and Early Years 1919–1924', the word 'Ireland' does not appear in the index. Nor is there any reference to any policy or practice the CPGB adopted on the Ireland in the text, despite sections in the book entitled 'International Solidarity' and 'The Communist Party and the Fight Against Imperialism, 1920–23'. On the other hand, in a pamphlet produced by the Communist Party on Ireland in late 1921 William Paul, late of the SLP, wrote, 'We scorn to hide our opposition to British imperialism. We will fight it by any and every means. Therefore, because Ireland is engaged in a life or death struggle with it, we rally to her assistance.'[107] Even before this, in an article in the *Communist* in September 1920, T. A. Jackson maintained, first that, 'it is a curious fact that an astonishingly large number of members of the Communist Party are directly or indirectly pupils of James Connolly', a reference to former members of the SLP, and second:

In short: the Communist Party, the legitimate heir of the Chartists who rallied to the support of John Mitchell, of the International who materially and morally supported the Irish Republican Brotherhood, and of the Democratic Republicans of the '80s who lent their aid to

Davitt and the Land League, is in keeping with its pedigree, in no wise [way] likely to ignore the struggles of the Irish common people.[108]

There is a suggestion of a defensive attitude here, and indeed at the start of this article Jackson writes, 'The formation of the Council of Action ... has aroused criticism from an unexpected quarter. We are accused of being very eager about peace and self-determination at the far end of Europe but very indifferent about either at home, or next door.' What was this 'unexpected quarter' to which Jackson refers? He does not say, but the following words are instructive:

> The International will not judge the British comrades by the articles that they write in the *Call* and the *Workers' Dreadnought*, but by the number of comrades who are thrown into gaol for agitating in the colonial countries. We would point out to the British comrades that it is their duty to help the Irish movement with all their strength, that it is their duty to agitate among the British troops, that it is their duty to use all their resources to block the policy that the British transport and railway unions are at present pursuing of permitting troop transports to be shipped to Ireland. It is very easy at the moment to speak out in Britain against intervention in Russia, since even the bourgeois left is against it. It is harder for the British comrades to take up the cause of Irish independence and of anti-militarist activity. We have a right to demand this difficult work of the British comrades.[109]

The words were spoken at the Second Congress of the Communist International or Comintern. The speaker, on behalf of the leadership of the Comintern was Karl Radek, a leading propagandist of the Comintern who was later to become the editor of the Communist Party of the USSR's *Izvestia*. He was speaking during a debate on the national and colonial question, and as is obvious, speaking directly to British communists. The date of the speech was 25 July 1920; the debate itself, which saw further calls for British communists to be active on Ireland,[110] ended five days later, just five weeks before the Jackson article appeared. Given the precise nature of the criticism of Radek – that Ireland not Russia should be the priority for British communists; that criticism of this sort from the Comintern would indeed be 'criticism from an unexpected quarter'; and the timing, there is strong circumstantial evidence to suggest that

Jackson's article was indeed in reply to the Comintern's attacks on the failure of the British communists to do more on Ireland. Even if this was not the case, the Comintern's criticism is obviously relevant in assessing the BSP/CPGB's activity in Ireland. An assessment of British communists on their level of activity by their fellow Marxists outside Britain is a credible contemporary judgement. And while Jackson's article went on to insist that communists were active on Ireland, he did admit that for the CPGB the Russian issue was more important, thereby confirming validity of the Comintern's assessment of the party's priorities.

This is not the only evidence concerning priorities. The first annual conference of the BSP was in 1912, but there was no specific resolution on Ireland until the 1920 conference. The Easter Rising and its aftermath were referred to in the address of the chairman, Sam Farrow, in 1917,[111] and at the 1918 conference a resolution calling for self-determination for Ireland, Egypt and India was passed unanimously.[112] The nature of the discussion at the 1920 conference confirms some of the impressions already referred to of the difficulties British Marxists faced in coming to terms with Ireland. A resolution was moved on behalf of the executive in favour of 'complete national autonomy' for Ireland, but it continued:

> The Conference welcomes the many evidences that the Irish workers, rising above the artificial divisions made for them by priests and politicians, are realising the need for a common working class programme, and look forward to the time when the Irish workers will take their rightful place in the international class struggle.[113]

Within this paragraph, the executive managed the co-existence of a simplistic optimism as to the potential for working class unity in Ireland and a downgrading of what was occurring there, which was, by implication, not yet advanced enough to be judged part of the 'international class struggle'. Yet this second assessment did not go far enough for some at the conference. An addendum was proposed from the Southend branch which instructed the executive 'to issue a manifesto to the Irish workers' in which, said the speaker moving the amendment, 'We had to point out to the Irish workers the difference between a narrow conception of nationality, and the broad conception associated with the idea of nationalism.'[114] Even though, on behalf of the executive, A. A. Watts opposed the amendment on the grounds that 'it might be presumptuous to tell the Irish people what to do', it was nevertheless passed. As with other conference resolutions elsewhere there is no evidence that this resolution was acted on by the executive.

The 1920 conference was the last one held by the BSP. Its successor, the Communist Party, did not have a specific discussion on Ireland at the first Unity Convention of 31 July – 1 August 1920. This is not all that surprising as the main business of the convention was establishing the party. Nevertheless other matters were discussed, including 'the massacre of Jewish Communists and Trade Unionists, carried out by the governments of Poland, Romania and Hungary'[115] and calls for the prohibition of alcohol consumption.[116] Neither did the Second Unity Convention, held six months later have a specific discussion on Ireland, although it did endorse the resolutions adopted at the Second Congress of the Comintern, which, as has been seen, included references to Ireland.

All of this suggests that Radek's assessment of the attitude of the British Marxists to Ireland was well-founded. He had stated that the Third International would judge their British comrades by how many of them were jailed over Ireland. There were isolated examples of some who were. For example William Hedley of Sheffield SLP was imprisoned for causing disaffection among British Army in Ireland[117] and Harold Burgess, the business manager of the *Dreadnought* was imprisoned for six months for a similar offence,[118] but British prisons were hardly full to brim with British left Irish protesters. Or referring back to Klugmann's omission of any mention of party activity on Ireland, if that is not totally accurate, given the Paul pamphlet and the statements on Ireland issued by executive of the BSP/CPGB, his neglect is understandable given the intermittent coverage in the party press and at party conferences. For, while the BSP/CPGB did have in its policy of unconditional self-determination a clear alternative to those in the rest of the working class movement who opposed or tampered with this principle, it was only occasionally enthusiastic in its promotion.

Fabians

What has become one of the classic comments on British labour movement history was made by A. M. McBriar in *Fabian Socialism and English Politics, 1884–1918*. This has already been referred to, but it is worth quoting again. His study, written in 1962, concluded, 'The Labour

Party, founded rather by the ILP than the Fabians, had come by 1918 under the Fabian rather than ILP influence.'[119] This extent of the Fabian influence on the Labour Party has not gone entirely uncontested,[120] but it is a useful judgement to test when it comes to enquiring into what it said about Ireland and to trying to assess its influence on the broader labour movement from 1916 to 1921. There are other considerations, including how seriously they took the Irish issue and how the policy they evolved compares to others on the left. A useful starting point is the Fabian Tract, *Local Government in Ireland* published in 1900. This included:

> What the Fabian Society has to say on the Irish Question is exactly what it has to say on the English Question; and that is, that the workers of a nation have no enemies except the idlers of it; that the poor are always oppressed no matter what government they live under; and that nothing will rescue the Irish and English worker except giving them control through their votes and elected representatives.[121]

No good socialist would be likely to disagree with this, but it does, somewhat simplistically, deny the 'Irish Question' a life of its own. Similarly, *Fabianism and the Empire*, edited by Bernard Shaw and also published the same year, promoted a policy of 'Home Rule All Round', without specifically doing so for Ireland.[122] The impression that the Fabians had little to say on Ireland is further reinforced by recording that of the 192 Fabian Tracts issued by the society from 1884 to 1920, only *Local Government in Ireland*, which was unsympathetic to Home Rule, and its immediate predecessor, *State Railways for Ireland*, were concerned with Ireland. 'Englishmen', said the former 'care ... little about the wrongs of Ireland',[123] and there is evidence which suggests that this was as much a projection of Fabian indifference as it was of mass observation. For example, after returning from a visit to Ireland in 1892 Sidney and Beatrice Webb compared the Irish to 'Hottentots', and added, 'Home Rule is an absolute necessity in order to depopulate the country of this detestable race'.[124] Or, there is the case of one of the 'detestable race', Bernard Shaw, who declared publicly when giving a lecture on Ireland in November 1919 that it was the first time in his 35 years of public speaking that he had lectured on the topic. He explained he found it 'a dull subject'.[125] When other Fabians expressed their opinions they could border on the absurd. In late 1916, *Fabian News* printed a report of a lecture by another of the society's prominent members, R. C. K. (Sir Robert) Ensor which dealt with '*Precautions Against Future Submarine Blockades*'. In the course of the lecture, Ireland was dealt with at some length. It was, said Ensor, 'Britain's most important source of food supply', while 'the Irish depended on Britain for practically all their coal and most of their manufactured articles'. Moreover, as 'the military occupation of Ireland ... would be the final ... stage in any blockade of Britain', a special measure had to be taken. This was 'a tunnel between Great Britain and Ireland' which was 'very vital', and without which 'our military defence of Ireland must always ... be unduly costly and precarious.'[126] This opinion has a curiosity value, but it also has a rarity value. The only other time the issue of Ireland had featured in the monthly *Fabian News* was June 1917, when a report of a Fabian lecture by A. Zimmern on 'Socialism and Nationality' was carried, in which Sinn Féin was condemned for 'carrying the idea of national individualism to the extreme.'

To be fair, *Fabian News* was primarily a newsheet of Fabian activities and would hardly have been expected to cover the politics of the Irish situation in any depth. More generally, however idiosyncratic or even foolish the remarks of Ensor, the Webbs or Shaw quoted above may be, when it comes to evaluating the political thought of the Fabians on Ireland there is a great deal more to be taken into account. To take the example of Shaw, the reality is that apart from being reluctant to deliver a public lecture on Ireland he showed very few signs of being bored with the topic. His play *John Bull's Other Island*, published in 1904, was critical both of British attitudes towards Ireland and Irish nationalism; as noted earlier he was one of the first public figures in Britain to protest at the executions of the leaders of the Easter Rising;[127] and he was a leading protagonist in the defence campaign for Roger Casement, even writing a defence for him.[128] Shaw was also the author of two pamphlets on Ireland. In the first, *How to Settle the Irish Question* (1917), he declared he would be 'demonstrating to the entire satisfaction of Ulster that Sinn Féiners are idiots', and then 'demonstrate to the satisfaction of Sinn Féin that the Ulster Impossibilists are idiots.'[129] If the use of such language suggests it was Shaw the wit and not Shaw as a political theorist who was writing, his advocacy in the pamphlet of federal British parliaments surfaced again in his second pamphlet, *Irish Nationalism and Labour Internationalism*, published by the Labour Party in 1920, which also argued, 'it is impossible to treat Ireland as a separate country from Great Britain for military purposes.'[130] Yet on other occasions, Shaw saw Irish self-determination as a 'natural right'.[131] One study describes his attitude towards Ireland as 'complex' and argues that while 'Shaw did dissociate himself from chauvinistic nationalism', he nevertheless 'had a great deal of sympathy with the struggle for self-determination in Ireland'.[132]

Other leading Fabians were also active on the Irish issue. When the Peace With Ireland Council was formed, Fabians Susan Lawrence and Margaret Bonfield were on its governing body, and G. D. H. Cole was another active member. Fabians also played a leading role in formulating the Labour Party's Irish policy. Four Fabians were on the 1920 Labour Party delegation to Ireland of November 1920;[133] as noted earlier, it was Webb who introduced the party executive motion on Ireland at 1920 annual conference; and two of the party's other leading spokespersons on Ireland throughout the period, Clynes and Arthur Henderson, were also Fabians. Indeed, one writer has argued that Clynes 'symbolized the position of the Fabians over the Irish question',[134] while Clynes himself, acknowledging the influence of Bernard Shaw's 1917 pamphlet, quotes it with approval in his memoirs.[135]

Those listed here were, of course, individuals. The Fabians were not an organised party in the ILP or BSP sense, so the fact that there were Fabians active in Ireland does not by itself prove a great deal. However, if it was established that the Fabians produced an intellectual climate that encouraged interest in and activity on Ireland, that would suggest the presence of so many Fabian protagonists on the Irish issue was more than a coincidence. Two ways the society had of influencing this intellectual climate were through the pages of the *New Statesman*, and the different series of Fabian lectures and educational classes. The lectures and classes fall into a number of different categories. There were the King's Hall lectures usually given in late autumn or early winter each year in London, other miscellaneous lectures in London delivered every couple of months and those provided at the Fabian summer school each year. The topic of all these lectures, although only infrequently their content, was listed in *Fabian News*.[136] The King's Hall lectures consisted of five each year under a general heading. In 1916, the heading was 'Life-Labour-Democracy-Art-Conscience'. In 1917, it was 'The Britain Alliance and World Politics'. In 1918, 'The War and the Peace' was the theme, and the following year it was 'A New Phase of Socialism'. In 1920, the lectures were devoted to 'A Constitution for the Socialist Commonwealth of Great Britain' and in

1921 to 'The Limits of Social Democracy'. Of the 25 lectures, only one –
that already referred to, given by Shaw in November 1919 – had 'Ireland'
in its title, being 'Bolshevism, Socialism and Ireland'. However, it would
have been surprising, judging by their titles if a couple of others did not
touch on Ireland. Specifically, there were those in 1917 which dealt with
'The Britannic Alliance and Constitutional Federalism' and 'The Passing
of Nationality', and that in 1921 on 'National Government and Local
Government'. There were 38 other lectures given in London listed in
the *Fabian News* from the edition of June 1916 to that of August 1921.
Two of these had Irish references – the one which suggested a tunnel
between Britain and Ireland, and the one delivered in 1917 on 'Socialism
and Nationalism' by A. E. Zimmern, which included an attack on Sinn
Féin.[137] Finally, of the 27 lectures or classes given in the Summer school,
as listed in *Fabian News*, none seem likely to have dealt with Ireland at
any length, although one held in 1917 with the title 'The Reconstruction
of the Empire' may have had Irish references. The list is not impressive
as far as Irish issues are concerned, although it should be stressed that
the topics covered in all these lectures were very wide-ranging and there
were few topics that were covered with any regularity.

The *New Statesman* coverage is of a different order. The first suggestion
on policy came in late May 1916, soon after the 'miserable and abortive
Sinn Féin rebellion', when the journal declared that the establishment
of a Home Rule parliament, with the exclusion of Ulster 'if she wishes',
would be 'an exhibition of confidence and moral strength that would be
of inestimable value to the cause of the allies.'[138] The position on Ulster
was modified the following week when it was said that it was important to
'keep wide open the door to eventual reunion'.[139] This article also called
for the ending of martial law and the release of all 'innocent prisoners'.
The rest of 1916 saw the *New Statesman* express its opposition to the
execution of Casement[140] and to Irish conscription.[141] The general political
line was repeated in March 1917: 'Ireland can have Home Rule when
she likes, but Ulster must be excluded', with a call for such a solution
to be imposed, 'with or without Irish consent'.[142] The same advice to
the government to impose a solution was offered the following month,
but seven months later, with the rise of Sinn Féin, the attitude changed.
In discussing the general post-war settlement, 'How will Ireland, voting
Sinn Féin be left out of such a peace ?' was one question; another was,
'If the Czechoslovaks shall have independence, why not the Irish?' The

answer to both was, 'it becomes a question purely of Irish choice, not a question of what is best for Ireland or what is best for Empire as a whole'.[143] This article was by-lined, 'by a correspondent'. The policy discussed was, it was added 'said, of course, merely for the purposes of illustration', but nevertheless quite a bold shift in policy, towards self-determination was being suggested. It seemed to be confirmed at the start of 1918 with an editorial comment, 'We prefer, as regards Ireland, to do what Lord Morley says he did throughout his career – take Irish opinion as our guiding light'.[144] Just what this meant in practice was not, for the moment, clarified. However, partition was now ruled out, in April 1918,[145] and while an article in May called for 'an Irish Parliament in accordance with the Home Rule already on the Statute Book', there was the addendum, 'and invite the Irish (including the Ulstermen) to set to work to model a Constitution'.[146] Whether this meant that any resulting constitution should be accepted by the British was not said, but on the conscription issue there was no ambiguity. An article in April went so far as saying that if it was either conscription or the 'fall of the Cabinet', the latter 'will be the lesser of two evils'.[147] This was followed up the next month with a call for the Labour Party, to say it would withdraw from the government if conscription was introduced.[148] This was bold talk, and the *New Statesman* now began to edge nearer and nearer to self-determination. In January 1919, it proposed a convention of Irish MPs in which, of course, Sinn Féin would have had a large majority, with 'the understanding that the British government accepts the principle of the right of every people to choose its own form of government.'[149] In July, a long article, 'The Key to the Solution of the Irish Problem', included the most detailed solution so far. The proposal was for 'dominion self-government', with or without a federal Ulster parliament, and a self-government which would 'control all the functions of government except the Army, the Navy and the Diplomatic Service'. Immediate British military withdrawal when the Irish parliament was convened was also proposed.[150] Six months later, the policy was revised. Referring to dominion home rule it was observed, 'it is not clear that everyone who uses the phrase means the same thing, and a more unequivocal declaration is needed.' Therefore, 'the principle of complete freedom' should be 'conceded'. The only qualification now was that 'no final decision in favour of separation shall be taken until a certain period of years have elapsed.'[151] This proviso was repeated three months later, but the headline indicated a more unequivocal attitude than ever:

'Ireland Must Have a Republic if She Wants it.'[152] The evolution was completed in September 1920. 'We have to put an end to the Irish War, without conditions and at all costs',[153] and what this meant was spelt out the following week: 'Ireland must have full self-determination – which means if she wants such encumbrances as an independent army and navy, she must be permitted to have them.'[154] Despite this declaration the *New Statesman* gave a favourable response to the Labour Party's policy as it evolved in late 1920.[155] This, of course, re-imposed the two familiar conditions on self-determination, although the *New Statesmen* failed to detail this and indeed put a generous gloss on the new policy. It correctly noted that 'the Labour Party does not want an Irish Republic', but added with less accuracy, 'it recognises that affairs have got past the point at which such a solution can be ruled out.'[156] In July 1921 the policy changed once more with support for 'the fact or partition', a tendency which the journal had displayed throughout and which will be fully discussed subsequently.

Leaving that aside for the moment, what would be a general assessment of the development of the journal's policy? In recapping, a comparison with the other major publication of the non-Marxist left, *Labour Leader*, as detailed above, is useful. The *New Statesman* called for the convening of a Home Rule parliament as early as May 1916, *Labour Leader* waited until October of that year. However the latter developed its policy with support for self-determination, with the two familiar restrictions on minority rights and military matters, in May 1917. The *New Statesman* began to give general if vague support for self-determination in October 1917, but this was not detailed until July 1919 when there was a specific call for self-determination with restrictions on military matters. The conversion to unqualified self-determination came in the last week of January 1920 for both journals, except the *New Statesman* advocated delaying a decision on complete separation. This restriction lasted until April 1920. Both journals gave general support to the policy adopted at the special Labour Party conference of December 1920 and in July 1921 both were moving towards accepting some form of partition or, in the case of *Labour Leader*, 'special powers' for Ulster, with the conversion to partition following shortly. There was then not a great deal to choose between the Irish policies of the two publications as they evolved, although both were well ahead of the Labour Party leadership and party conference in moving in the direction of self-determination.

As to the Fabians' influence on that leadership, A specific example is the *New Statesman*'s support in January 1920 for self-determination but with a delay on a vote by the Irish on the separation issue for several years. This call was made at almost exactly the same time as the PLP Commission of Inquiry was reporting and suggesting the same. On that inquiry teams were, as already noted, the Fabians Henderson and Clynes. Two months later, in its statement for the Stockport by-election, the Labour NEC advocated a similar delay. On the other hand the *New Statesman* called for British military withdrawal from Ireland as early as July 1919,[157] well before the Labour Party contemplated such a possibility, and it was much more forthright in opposition to conscription, advocating the withdrawal of the Labour Party from the government if it was implemented. As previously explained, the NEC while opposing conscription excused the PLP from pressing this opposition in parliament.

In assessing the role of the *New Statesman* the quantity of its coverage should also be noted. There was much more than that detailed so far. In 1916, for example, there were regular reports on the Irish situation. If, on occasions, assessments were erroneous, with the assurance in June 1916 that 'the Irish question is virtually settled',[158] corrections soon followed: the situation was 'less and less satisfactory' in July 1916;[159] and 'worse than it has been for a generation' in October 1916.[160] In February 1917 the journal began a four part series entitled, 'The Historical Basis of Irish Nationalism', which ended on 3 March with the observation: 'The Irishman regards himself as the heir of Irish history: the Englishman is inclined to behave as if there was no such thing as Irish history. Irish history however exists as a witness in the Irishman's favour.'

A further long article in April 1918 indicted British government 'blunders' from 1914 onwards,[161] although Sinn Féin had also been analysed and strongly criticised in September 1917.[162] These are only examples, the general attitude was indicated in a comment in July 1919 which argued 'the Irish question becomes what it was in July 1914, the most urgent of all problems with which British statesmanship has to deal'.[163] The *New Statesman* certainly took it seriously. As a further example, there is the coverage during the latter half of 1920. An article after the TUC Special Conference on Ireland commented 'it would be difficult ... to overestimate [its] importance', and the same article went so far as supporting 'direct action' to force the government 'to bring such a struggle to an end.'[164] The following week, it was reported that 'the

Irish situation is very obviously and rapidly going from bad to worse'.[165] September saw three articles: one reported popular support in Britain for the release of Terence McSwiney, the Lord Mayor of Cork then on hunger strike;[166] a second commented, 'The British forces in Ireland are engaged not in "putting down crime", but in something which can only be described as civil war';[167] the third began, 'The likeness between Ireland under the English in 1920 and Belgium under the Germans in 1914 is becoming more obvious every day'.[168] There were three more articles the following month, one, already cited, in support of self-determination,[169] and two others attacking British reprisals.[170] By the end of the year, four further significant articles appeared, two in one issue dealing with the relationship between Labour Party policy and Irish Labour's reactions to it,[171] one commenting on Bloody Sunday[172] and a further one on Labour's Irish policy.[173]

The range and depth of such coverage was unmatched by the journals of the ILP and BSP/CPGB. The difference could be attributed to historical accidents, the interests of individual editors or members. Indeed, it is probably no coincidence that the editor of the *New Statesman*, Clifford Sharp, and Shaw held the same views on Ireland.[174] But it is also true that both were also key figures in the Fabians and that the *New Statesman* itself has been described by a biographer of Shaw as 'a truly Fabian enterprise'.[175] Moreover, the attention paid to Ireland by the *New Statesman* ties in with the interest and activity of leading Fabians, whether on the Labour NEC or the Peace With Ireland Council. The other side of the story is: only two Fabians tracts on Ireland out of 192, a very limited number of Fabian lectures on Ireland and a wide range of opinions expressed by different members of the society. This latter point, as well as the contrast in attention between the Fabian tracts and the *New Statesman*, suggests Fabians and Fabianism were too diffuse in opinions and attitudes to allow any definitive conclusions to be drawn, apart from one that underlines this very diffuseness. On a more positive note, the *New Statesman* does deserve to be singled out from the rest of the left press reviewed here for providing the most detailed weekly coverage on Ireland and being the most consistent critique of government policy. In that respect, to return to the question asked earlier as to how seriously the Fabians took Ireland, the perhaps surprising answer is, as far as the left was concerned, more seriously than most.

6

Voices from Below

Lord Asquith was pulling no punches when he spoke at a public meeting on Ireland in Leicester in October 1920. First, he denounced the government and its 'hideous brutal policy of reprisals', and then the 'outrages ... by the officers of the law in the uniform of soldiers and policemen'. But he also had a target beyond those ordering this policy or committing these acts:

> I am amazed and ashamed of the lethargy and indifference with which English people regarded these things. There was not a man or woman who was entrusted with the franchise who ought not to go home with a bad conscience and a sense of shame that they were directly or indirectly responsible for a government which permitted such things.[1]

For Asquith, whose own government, by his reaction to the Easter Rising had, in many people's eyes set a precedent for what he was now complaining of, this might suggest a hint of double standards. Nevertheless, by the same token, for him to complain of the docility of the people of England in accepting all of this is worth paying some attention to.

Guilty Workers

However much opposition politicians such as Asquith criticised the government, however many attended the meetings of organisations such as the Peace With Ireland Council or the Irish Self Determination League, the reality was that within Britain it was only the working class who had the power to stop the government in its tracks. There were those who thought it could and should. *Workers' Dreadnought*, writing of 'the martyrdom of Ireland' in October 1920, commented:

And British Labour refuses to act. To offset criticism they ask: is public sympathy behind us, can organised labour stand the consequences of a general strike? Well, even Liberal public opinion is in sympathy with Irish freedom ... The issue could be localised – the dockers, the seamen, the transport workers and the railwaymen could prevent the perpetration of this great capitalist crime ... A scheme of local action, properly worked out, to prevent all munitions and all military officers and men being transported from England to Ireland can and should be put into operation immediately.[2]

The proposition presented here is important, centring as it does on whether the ranks of the working class movement would have responded to calls for action over Ireland from their leadership. The form of the action proposed on this occasion is well spelt out, and perhaps it is significant that even *Workers' Dreadnought* did not have the optimism to propose an all-out general strike, but the particulars are not what are most relevant. The general proposition is what matters most, and it has been made many times and in many different circumstances. The question is whether the leaders of the working class do lead, or whether they reflect, or whether they hold back their membership. Often, the more left wing the historian or commentator, the more inclined they are to see leaders as a restraining influence. That was not always the case in respect to British working class and Ireland during the latter's national revolution. Then, even the British communists could blame the workers. Examples of this were quoted in the preceding chapter. There are others. Referring to Ireland, the 'silence of Englishmen' was condemned by the *Call* on 3 June 1920; the timidity of 'the workers of England' was attacked by the *Communist* on 5 August 1920; the same source detected 'cowardice' and 'shame' from 'we common Englishman of the working class' on 28 October 1920; and complained on 25 November 1920 that while 'the Irish workers are suffering ... the British workers do nothing'. A further example comes from the *Call* in May 1920:

The BSP has protested time and again that the government's actions [in Ireland] have not the endorsement of the British workers. But unless they bestir themselves their inactivity will weaken their power to fight the enemy of both ... we urge all Trade Unionists to increase their imagination, shake off their lethargy and cease to view with indifferent eyes the slow murder of a nation.[3]

An even stronger indictment was referred to by Lenin when recording the unwillingness of the British communists, as stated at the Second Congress of the Comintern, to devote their energies to Ireland. 'Comrade Quelch [of the British delegation] spoke of this in commission', reported Lenin. 'He said that the rank-and-file British worker would consider it treasonable to help the enslaved nations in their uprisings against British rule'.[4] A similar, contemporary opinion was given to the British Cabinet by Basil Thomson, Director of Intelligence at Scotland Yard, when describing working class sentiment in respect to Ireland and Egypt in January 1920: 'It remains the fact that the British working man never takes much interest in matters outside his own country, and this insular tendency can scarcely be overcome by agitation in the present generation.'[5]

If Scotland Yard on the one hand and British communists on the other were saying the same thing, it was hardly surprising that those in the leadership of the Labour movement, when asked to explain their unwillingness to act decisively on Ireland, also blamed the workers. J. H. Thomas argued at the 1920 Labour Party Conference that, 'the Labour movement will not agree to the establishment of an Irish Republic'[6] and J. R. Clynes told the House of Commons in March 1921, in the course of a debate on Ireland, 'I can truthfully say that we are conscious of suffering a serious political disability for taking up what, in many parts of the country, is an unpopular cause.'[7] Indeed, even when launching the party's campaign in Ireland in January 1921, Clynes said publicly, 'It may lose us votes'.[8] Those in the Labour Party to the left of Clynes and Thomas were saying much the same thing. In September 1920, Snowden spoke of 'the quiescence of the British people in the face of what is happening in Ireland',[9] and three months later Labour Leader complained, 'the public of Great Britain has been singularly apathetic about the disgraceful doings of the government in Ireland.'[10] Or there is Beatrice Webb's diary entry of 11 October 1918, when Irish conscription was threatened, which records, 'There remains the uncomfortable fact that many of the Labour Party candidates, even pacifists candidates believe that the cry of "conscript Ireland" will be popular with the electorate.' As for the assessment of the New Statesman, with which the Webbs were closely associated, three examples will suffice. In August 1916, referring to Roger Casement's execution, 'which the *New Statesman* opposed', the journal went on to admit 'the "man in the street" undoubtedly felt he deserved everything he got'.[11] By early 1920 the journal was saying that 'everyone is tired of the [Irish] question ... there was probably never a time since it first became a "question" when so little interest was taken in it in England as at present.' Consequently, 'Except where there happens to be a large native Irish vote ... Irish issues cannot be made an issue in any English constituency.'[12] Then, 18 months later on one of those specific issues, 'it will take a long time to reconcile the English constituencies, even those with Labour majorities, to the idea of an Irish Republic.'[13]

Such were examples of the contemporary judgements of the left. They appear to coincide both with Basil Thomson's view, expressed in December 1920, that although 'Mr Arthur Henderson has returned from Ireland with a demand for an armistice', nevertheless, 'Labour, however shows little interest in the question',[14] and that subsequently expressed by the historian D. G. Boyce:

People could not have cared less about Ireland. After 1918, Irish questions were at the very back of their minds, for they had more pressing domestic and foreign problems to occupy their interest ... And through 1919 and the first half of 1920 this atmosphere of boredom with Irish affairs persisted.[15]

Finally there is the personal account of George Berkeley of the Peace With Ireland Council:

To me the most terrible feature of the whole thing was that at first the majority of the English people undoubtedly approved of the programme [of reprisals]. Most of them deliberately turned a deaf ear to what was going on. They did not mean to know. If one told them the truth, they simply said that one was 'condoning the Sinn Féin murders'. One lady, a married woman with children said to me when I tried to convey to her the real state of affairs: 'Oh the Irish are fractious'. A friend of mine at my club frankly defended reprisals. He said: 'If they kill some of the Irish, it will prevent the others; from murdering our soldiers. It will make the people in general turn against Sinn Féin.'[16]

The unanimity of opinion seems impressive. Yet Boyce dates apathy to Ireland to mid-1920; the quote from Thompson on Labour disinterest continues, 'although there seems to be among all classes a growing feeling that the present conditions have become intolerable'; and eight months after the *New Statesman* complained how tired everyone was of Ireland it was observing, 'there is no doubt that the country is overwhelmingly against the Irish policy of the government.'[17] As for Berkely, he did say 'at first' when he was recording his above impression, and in the same unpublished book he has a chapter titled, 'GREATLY INCREASED ENTHUSIASM IN THE SPRING OF 1921'. By the time of the Truce, he records:

> There was no doubt that the political atmosphere was entirely different from that in which we had begun our work nine months before. In every branch of our small organisation we felt it ... People believed what we said. Primarily of course this was due to the extraordinary steadfastness of Sinn Féin and indeed of the whole Irish people. Primarily it was due entirely to them. But we felt as if we had been of some assistance by our work in England, by creating an atmosphere of peace ... We had now about thirty branches of our Council established all over England. .. It was really remarkable that so many local people should have been willing to imperil their popularity by raising and forming local organisations.[18]

So, there is just a finger of doubt that perhaps Ireland was not always as apathetically regarded by the British common people as some suggest. It is therefore fruitful to move on and examine the material evidence.

The ILP Membership

To examine the attitudes among the rank and file members of the labour movement, the most useful organisation to concentrate on is the ILP. The Labour Party did not have constituency organisations or individual membership until after the new 1918 constitution, and although the Marxist organisations did, it was very small and obviously politically unrepresentative of the class as a whole. Thus, the bulk of the active rank and file of the political wing of the working class movement was, for this period, located in the ILP.

The most obvious expression of the opinions of the membership of the ILP was the party conference, the decisions of which have already been recorded. To recapitulate, while the 1919 conference resolution was in line with that emanating from the party press, those of the 1920 and 1921 conferences tended to be more positive in advocating unrestricted self-determination. Therefore, when some ILP members detected a wavering from this policy by the party leaders it is hardly surprising they wrote to the *Labour Leader* protesting at such back-sliding. A persistent critic was Harry Campbell, who was appointed as an ILP organiser in December 1917 and subsequently given the label 'the champion ILP recruiter' by *Forward*.[19] Campbell attacked *Forward* for supporting the Irish Convention in early 1918,[20] and, in a September 1919 letter to *Labour Leader*, he wondered, 'how much longer are the organised workers of Great Britain going to remain indifferent and stand by and watch their rulers crush their brethren in Ireland?'[21]

Seven months later, and barely a month after the ILP conference voted for Irish self-determination a row broke out in the pages of *Labour Leader* in which Campbell and others indicted not so much the workers, but the leaders, including the ILP leadership. This was prompted by the dispute in April 1920 between the Labour Party NEC and the Irish community in Stockport. As we have seen, this was when the local Irish refused to support Labour because the party declined to endorse unconditional self-determination. Writing in his column in *Labour Leader*, the ILP chair Philip Snowden sided with the Labour leadership. He called the Stockport Irish 'English Sinn Féiners', and continued:

Why do they approve the policy of seventy-three Irish Sinn Féin Members of Parliament who absent themselves from the House of Commons? ... If the British Labour Party were as blameable as the Sinn Féiners allege for not forcing the government to adopt the Sinn Féin programme, surely Sinn Féin is even more culpable ... The Labour Party Executive declined to declare in favour of an Irish Republic. But it is not the business of the British Labour Party to declare the Irish people must establish a Republic. It is for the Irish people to decide.[22]

This raised heckles. Two weeks later, *Labour Leader* printed a letter from a D. Fox in Stockport, who reported, 'The deputation asked the Executive of the Labour Party if they were in favour of unqualified Irish self-determination for Ireland and the Executive reply was an emphatic "No".' The main criticism however came from Campbell, who, no doubt ironically echoing Snowden's terminology, described himself as an 'Australian Sinn Féiner':

> The people of Ireland have already chosen their own form of government ... At the general election held in Ireland, in December 1918 the electors of Ireland voted in favour of an Irish Republic ... What more does Mr Snowden and the Labour Party want more than that? ... The Sinn Féin Party was elected on a pledge to ignore the English Parliament. The English Labour movement will have to do more than pass pious resolutions before they can gain the confidence of the Irish people.[23]

The following week, *Labour Leader* reported its 'letter bag this week contains many letters' on the Snowden/Campbell controversy, but that, 'our space permits only a summary.' Four letters were quoted, all backing Campbell. Labour was accused of 'shilly-shallying' and 'giving lip-service to self-determination', and of being guilty of 'shuffle and qualify' on self-determination.[24] As for Campbell, in December 1920 he announced his resignation from the ILP because:

> The ILP has never made any serious attempt to organise a vigorous campaign of indignation and protest [on Ireland] ... the decision to recognise and support the Irish Republic has been ignored and violated by ILP representatives ... by its indifference, apathy and inactions in this matter the ILP like other British organisations, must take its share of the blame and shame of the Irish atrocities.[25]

Campbell received support from F. Seymour Cocks, whose letter two weeks later commented, 'the ILP is not doing all it should to expose and denounce the unspeakable proceeds of Lloyd George and his hired thugs and murderers',[26] and the following month the Lancashire divisional council of the ILP passed a resolution calling upon the leadership to give 'a more vigorous lead for Ireland'.[27] Then, when *Labour Leader* published the article of 18 August 1921, quoted in the previous chapter describing the Irish situation as 'a war between two rights', the following week a letter from Jas F. Williams asked the rhetorical question, 'is the unquestionable supremacy of the Imperial throne *right* then?''[28] [Original emphasis]

How widespread such criticism was is difficult to estimate, but it is interesting that during the Snowden/Campbell debate no letters were printed or quoted supporting Snowden, despite there being 'many letters' received on the topic. And, of course, as far as support for unconditional self-determination was concerned, conference resolutions were on the side of the critics.

There is another test available on rank and file sentiments, or at least on what was happening at branch level in the ILP. This can be seen by examining two weekly features of *Labour Leader*, the branch reports and the classified columns advertising ILP branch meetings and discussions. The former were often a report of the latter, and of course there must have been branches that never sent in reports or advertised their meetings. This is especially true of Scotland and Glasgow, in particular where the local ILP had *Forward* to use for advertising meetings and reporting activities, and which will be referred to shortly. However, there was a good deal of detailed activity from the branches reported in *Labour Leader*, describing what was discussed at meetings, what resolutions were passed, and what public meetings were held and on what subject. From 1917 to 1921, there were between 1000 and 2,000 such reports each year, and between 300 and 700 classified advertisements for branch meetings and public activities. Tabulated here are these advertisements and reports, with a count of how many were on Ireland or even contained references to Ireland. Thus, not only do the figures for meetings on Ireland include those given over to the topic, but also those that passed resolutions on Ireland or coupled discussion on British policy on Ireland with, to the take the commonest, possible British intervention in Russia.

The results are in Table 6.1. They conclusively point to a widespread apathy and disinterest in Irish matters at branch level of the ILP. Over the five and three-quarter years, whether judging by branch reports or classified advertisements, just over 1 per cent of these had Irish references. In no year did this figure even reach 5 per cent.

One footnote can be added. As previously noted, towards the end of October 1920 the NAC of the ILP suggested that branches should hold meetings on Ireland. The effect of this advice was discernible, but not great. In the nine weeks before this advice was given, there were three branch reports and one classified advertisement with an Irish reference;

in the ten weeks afterwards, there were five and two. If nothing else, this suggests that the rank and file was not always eager to do as their leaders asked.

Table 6.1 ILP branch activity in Ireland as advertised and reported in *Labour Leader*, 1916–21 (Belfast ILP excluded)

Year	Branch Report	Irish Reference	Classified Advert	Irish Reference
1916 (from April)	975	4 (0.41%)	386	2 (0.52%)
1917	1724	0 (0%)	696	2 (0.29%)
1918	1515	10 (0.66%)	602	7 (1.16%)
1919	1224	6 (0.49%)	426	6 (1.41%)
1920	1250	39 (3.12%)	378	13 (3.44%)
1921	1009	20 (1.98%)	249	12 (4.82%)
Total	7697	79 (1.03%)	2737	38 (1.38%)

To complete the picture, there is the evidence of activities by the ILP in Scotland, as available in the pages of *Forward*. Both the advertising of meetings and the branch reports in this newspaper's 'Around the Country' column were less systematic than in *Labour Leader*, varying widely week-by-week. It is not therefore possible to establish what was going in the branches as accurately through *Forward* as through *Labour Leader*. Nevertheless, there is some evidence. Their first period is from the start of July 1916 to the end of June 1917, and covers ILP meetings listed in the classified advertising columns. In all, 250 such meetings were advertised; of these, 131 gave details of what the meetings were about. Only one of these, advertised in 3 March 1917, had an Irish association, being a lecture on 'Irish Revolutionary and Folk Songs.' The advertising of ILP local meetings in *Forward* becomes increasingly unsystematic after this date, so the next reference point is the 'Around the Country' for the years 1918 to 1920. Again it should be stressed the amount of reports varied, but for 1918 there were 492 branch reports with three Irish references (0.6 per cent); for 1919 there were 324 and two (0.6 per cent); for 1920 there were 200 and 19 (9.5 per cent).

A word of explanation can be given about the number of meetings in 1920. Eight of these were in Glasgow on 12 December, when Glasgow ILP called for a day of action on Ireland from their branches[29] – a rare example of regional leadership on the issue. However, if that figure is excluded, the percentage figure for the year drops to five. Overall, again excluding Glasgow's day of action, there is little significant difference in these figures and those in *Labour Leader*. Unfortunately, the *Forward* reports become so inconsistent in 1921 that they are statistically meaningless.

The general picture is of an ILP membership disinterested in Ireland and unwilling to take up the issue, even when their national leadership suggested otherwise. The wariness of the Irish issue by the ILP leadership has already been detailed; the evidence produced now suggests the rank and file were of the same mind.

One further issue in this general area needs to be probed. Could it be that both the ILP national and local leaderships did not adequately measure the interest in Ireland among their political constituency? A clue to answering this is found by assessing how those meetings which were held on Ireland were received. Again, the *Labour Leader* branch reports provide some evidence.

The first details given of an ILP meeting on Ireland was one held in Leyton, London, in September 1916. 'A large and interested' audience was reported.[30] There were no branch reports with Irish references in 1917, but details were provided for an ILP meeting in Leicester in May 1918 on Ireland and conscription, at which the speaker, an NUR organiser, attracted an audience of 2,000.[31] However, a meeting on Ireland held by the Gateshead branch five months later did not seem to fare so well, for although an 'interesting lecture' was reported, no figures were given for how many attended; but, as the report concluded with a plea for 'unattached socialists – come in and help our victory',[32] the implication is that the meeting was not particularly popular. A similar inference can be drawn from a report of a further Gateshead ILP Irish meeting in May 1919, which, although saying the event was 'splendid', added, 'we are still rolling the old chariot along. Who will help?'[33] Similarly, five months later, reporting an Irish lecture in Lewisham, London, the plea was, 'will members and sympathisers please support ... our lectures'.[34] So, what evidence there is suggests that the few meetings that there were in 1919 on Ireland were not notably successful. Reports of the many more ILP Irish meetings in 1920 told a different story. For although a 'small gathering' was reported for one at Derby in July,[35] two in Edinburgh in succeeding weeks in February and March were 'crowded',[36] there was a 'monster' demonstration and march by Birmingham ILP in July[37] and

3,000 marched and 1,000 attended a meeting in Manchester the following week.[38] Two reports of meetings in September (one in Barnsley with a 'large attendance',[39] the other 'a very large meeting' in Jarrow)[40] tell the same story. So does a 'crowded' meeting in Coventry in September and, in the same week 'one of the biggest meetings we have ever had' was reported from Norwich.[41] There were no details given of a meeting held by Consett ILP in December, but it was reported that 60 copies were sold of a pamphlet, 'The Crucifixion of Ireland', written by Harry Campbell, who just two weeks previously had announced his resignation from the party over its alleged inaction on Ireland.[42]

The popularity of ILP meetings on Ireland continued in 1921. In February, Briton Ferry in Wales reported a 'great meeting' – 'the building was crowded',[43] and the following week there was 'a packed house' in Birkenhead and a 'large attendance' in Newcastle-on-Tyne.[44] In March, Dartford's meeting also saw 'a large attendance',[45] while Stockton's meeting was 'crowded and enthusiastic'.[46] Dartford had a further meeting in April which was 'crowded',[47] a 'good crowd' was at Gloucester in May,[48] there was a 'better attendance of members than usual' in West Salford in July[49] and a 'mass meeting' in Middlesbrough in September.[50]

While there could be an element of exaggeration in such reports, the fact that previous ones did allude to a lack of success argues that, in general, they can be trusted. The sum of this evidence suggests that in 1920 and 1921 there was a growing interest in, even enthusiasm for, the issue of Ireland among the community in which the ILP operated. That this proposition cannot be tested more comprehensively than the meetings listed here is, obviously, due to the reluctance of more local branches of the ILP to organise such meetings. Nevertheless, there is now reason to wonder whether, at the very least, it is time to qualify the argument of both left and right that the working class was apathetic about the issue of Ireland. The evidence so far suggests it would be worthwhile to inquire further into the possibility that such a qualification is particularly relevant to the period 1920–21.

Councils of Action

A columnist in *Labour Leader* in December 1920 reported:

> Today I have asked several prominent Labour speakers what their experiences has been when dealing with Irish questions this weekend.

All of them say that their audiences have been remarkably ready to accept the policy of self-determination, and have shown great restraint when references have been made to the recent outrages.[51]

As well as the anecdotal evidence of popular sympathy for Irish self-determination, the most interesting aspect of this sentence is the use of the word 'remarkably': apparently the expression of such sympathy was not to be expected. Such an assessment could say more about the person making it than anything else, because certainly by December 1920 there was a good deal of evidence suggesting support for Irish self-determination in labour audiences. After all, the Labour Party conference of six months earlier had voted for such a policy, indeed in stronger terms than the leadership desired. By December 1920, there was another experience which strongly pointed in the same direction: that of the local councils of action.

Only the briefest of introductions to the Council of Action is necessary here. It was initiated at a joint meeting of representatives of the Labour Party, the PLP and the Parliamentary Committee of the TUC on 9 August 1920. This, fearing 'that war is being engineered between the Allied Powers and Soviet Russia on the issue of Poland', warned 'that the whole industrial power of the workers will be used to defeat this war'. The meeting summoned a national conference so that 'a Council of Action be immediately constituted to take such steps as may be necessary' to stop the threat of war.[52] The conference met on 13 August at which the formation and aims of the conference were approved, as was the establishment of local councils of action. Viewing these developments from afar, Lenin saw the establishment of the Council of Action as 'a tremendous turning-point in British politics. Its significance to Great Britain is as great as the revolution of February 1917 was to us'.[53] Although hindsight allows cold water to be poured on such enthusiasm, there is no doubt that at the time many saw the threat of the Council of Action as influencing the government in stepping back from intervention against the Soviet Union. As Basil Thomson put it, 'a majority of the working men believe that the formation of the Council of Action prevented the government from going to war with Russia.'[54] Subsequent research has cast severe doubt on this conclusion,[55] but what matters here is the perception at the time. Indeed, even as the national conference was meeting on 13 August the chairman of the Council was claiming it had 'rallied' public opinion so that 'up to the present time the government had been kept back from the slippery slope that would lead to another European conflagration'.[56] Whatever the truth of this remark, by the time the local councils of action were established the threat of war against the Soviet Union had subsided. That raised the question of what these councils and the national council would do now. What many at the local level wanted to do was take up the Irish issue. An early example was Hendon council of action, which in September called upon the national council to 'extend the terms of reference to the unofficial war with Ireland'.[57] A blunt refusal from one of the three joint-secretaries followed. He cited 'the fact that a special Trades Union Congress was held in July last, when the policy of direct action to secure an Irish settlement was discussed and very heavily defeated',[58] an interpretation of the Congress decision which, as we have seen, was rather selective.

The Hendon resolution was the start of a deluge – so much so that after Birmingham council of action had circulated a model resolution calling for a further national conference, 'to consider the strengthening of the national council and the extension of their scope to stop the war with Ireland', a joint secretary of the national council noted that 'the majority of our councils' endorse the Birmingham position.[59]

This opinion was never tested because there was no recall conference, but judging by the letters and resolutions sent to the national council proposing a recall conference on Ireland or a simple demand for British withdrawal and a 'down tools' policy to enforce such a withdrawal, these sentiments were widespread. In all, there were calls from 78 local organisations, as recorded in the Labour Party archives, demanding action on Ireland.[60] In total, there were 350 local councils of actions,[61] so obviously this list did not constitute a majority. Neither were all those who wrote to the national council local councils of actions; some were Labour Parties or trades councils, although it was usually through these that councils of actions were established, so the personnel involved was probably not dissimilar.[62] This in itself is important because it clarifies who exactly was involved in these local councils. This was alluded to by an assistant secretary of the national council who complained when Methil District council of action called for 'the forceable takeover by councils of action of all factories' if British troops weren't withdrawn from Ireland and Irish self-determination wasn't granted'.[63] He replied, 'it is one thing to get the resolution ... adopted at a meeting of your local council of action, but

I should like to know what are the views of the individual members of your branch'.[64]

Yet it does seem that many local councils were representative of the local labour movement and did not, in the words of the *New Statesman*, 'usually differ much from the existing Trades Councils and Local Labour Parties'.[65] They were certainly not 'fronts' for any one political current and Marxist parties, those most likely to seek to intervene in the councils, often had difficulty gaining affiliation to them.[66]

Adding to the unlikelihood of the local councils being some unrepresentative red plot, it is also improbable that the Irish resolutions were the product of a conspiracy. As already noted, it is true that Birmingham council of action did circulate a model resolution on Ireland, but it is also the case that the majority of those sent in to the national council went much further than the Birmingham demand for a recall conference, and there were few instances of identical wording in them. So although an assistant secretary of the national council could write, 'I do not know who is circulating this resolution to Labour Parties and Trades Councils, but I venture to suggest that it is being too readily accepted by these bodies',[67] there is no evidence to suggest there was any manipulation of local councils. Accordingly, the conclusion that remains is the probability that the resolutions were a spontaneous expression of significant rank and file feeling; albeit of a rank and file drawn from the politically active.

Climax and Anti-climax

In some of the evidence presented so far there are surface contradictions. For instance, the inaction of the local branches of the ILP contrasts with the enthusiasm for action of the councils of action. Given that the same political influences, indeed if not the personnel, were likely to be involved in both that contrast is heightened. There are, however a number of explanations for apparent differences, the most important of which, as already suggested, is chronological. While it is true that the ILP branches throughout the period were generally inactive on Ireland, they were less inactive in 1920 than in 1919. It was 1920 when branch reports began to testify to the popularity of meetings on Ireland, especially the latter half of 1920. And this was also the period of the local councils of action, and when the Labour Party had its most radical policy on Ireland in the entire period with the endorsement of unqualified self-determination at the June 1920 conference. The contemporary judgement of the ITGWU newspaper *Watchword of Labour* is instructive. Writing in August 1920, its conclusion was based on observing the Labour Party Conference and the TUC Special Congress and from 'our personal observation up and down England within the last eight months'. As far as Ireland and the British working class movement was concerned: 'We believe we see a rising of the tide, slow and weak, but fairly steady and fairly general. It is yet far from revolutionary, far from actual, far from satisfactory. But we believe it is there.'[68]

If it is correct to make chronological distinctions, public opposition to the government's Irish policy can possibly be explained by events in Ireland at this time: the outbreak of anti-Catholic sectarianism in Belfast in the summer of 1920; the death on hunger strike of Terence MacSwiney in October 1920; 'Bloody Sunday'; in November 1920; the sacking of Cork by British forces in December 1920; the beginning of official government-authorised reprisals in January 1921. All of this surely put pressure on the labour movement leadership to respond to and constructively channel growing working class sentiment against the government's Irish policy. The Labour Party's official campaign on Ireland, launched after the special December 1920 conference on Ireland, and running from 17 January to 25 February 1921, provided the opportunity. The party itself was later to describe this campaign as 'one of the most remarkable series of meetings ever held by any political Party on any great public question in the history of the country'. During the campaign, 'over 130 large meetings were held, with audiences of thousands in each case, and, in addition, the local parties in the smaller towns and scattered districts organised a series of small meetings, and the total of meetings during the month numbered well over 500.'[69] Similarly, Mary Agnes Hamilton, a biographer of Arthur Henderson, the main organiser of the campaign, was later to write of a 'large scale series of most impressive demonstrations' for which 'the response, everywhere, was tremendous'.[70]

Hamilton's book is somewhat idolatry, and neither can the Labour Party be judged as the most objective reporter of its own campaign, so what do other accounts say? Basil Thomson was not over-impressed. He attended one of the opening meetings in Glasgow, attended by 2,000 people in a hall with seating for 4,000. He reported to the Cabinet of how 'blows were exchanged between opposing factions', essentially those who were 'supporters of the government tactics' and 'advanced Sinn Féiners who would accept nothing but an Irish Republic'.[71] The same evening another meeting took place in Manchester, attended, said Thomson, by 4,000, 'composed of persons of Irish birth from all over Lancashire.'[72] The following week Thomson reported that, 'the Labour Party's "Peace with Ireland" campaign has so far not aroused great interest', but he did record 4,000 attending a meeting in Preston. Also, 'a somewhat dull meeting' at Wakefield attracted 2,000, although 'very few' purchased the Labour Party's commission report; and at Tonypandy there was 'an audience of about 800'.[73] On the final meeting in the Albert Hall, Thomson quotes without comment Arthur Greenwood as saying that campaign was 'the most successful in the history of the Labour movement'. In the same report he notes 'a large number of meetings have been held in London', and that 'meetings have also been held in the South Wales coalfield' although, 'except where there is a strong Irish element they have been attended only by revolutionary miners.'[74]

Overall, Thomson did not appear too worried by the campaign. He seemed more concerned about the activities of the Irish Self-Determination League, who a month after the Labour campaign ended held 'many meetings' in London which were 'enthusiastic and well-attended'.[75] Yet other accounts paint a more impressive picture of Labour's meetings: specifically those reported in the *Daily Herald*. The opening ones, those in Manchester and Glasgow as well as one in Cardiff were 'three big meetings', with the Glasgow one in particular described as 'crowded'.[76] Three days later the same adjective was used for the Wakefield meeting, while one in Aberdeen was 'large and enthusiastic'.[77] Then there were 'great' meetings in Preston[78] and Carlisle[79] and a 'crowded' one at Marylebone.[80] The start of February saw a 'crowded' meeting at Sunderland and a 'very enthusiastic' one in Dundee,[81] while the following day Dunfermline's and Mexborough's were again 'crowded', while Peterborough had a 'mass meeting'.[82] Next came 'three notable meetings' in different parts of London[83] and 'crowded' ones at Rotherhithe[84], St Helens and Aldgate, London[85] and another 'crowded' one at London, this time at Bow.[86] Finally, 'the Labour Party's nationwide campaign for peace with Ireland – regarded as the greatest platform campaign in the history of the party – culminated gloriously in the Albert Hall'.[87]

These reports were of only a minority of the meetings held. Others which did appear in the *Daily Herald* gave no estimates of attendance.[88] That at least suggests there was not a conscious policy by the newspaper to inflate the success of the meetings. The general impression of a popularly supported campaign can also be contrasted by Thomson's disparaging remarks and his apparent disinterest in reporting the campaign at all. For this however there may a number of explanations. First is that his reports were meant to be on 'Revolutionary Movements in Great Britain' or, the Irish agitation part, 'Sinn Féin in Great Britain', and although he often extended these briefs he did tend to avoid going into great detail on the activities of the Labour Party, which was, after all, the official Opposition after 1918. Also, Thomson's own biography testifies that during this period he felt 'labour leaders' were bringing 'pressure to bear upon the Prime Minister' to have him removed from his post.[89] Accordingly, he may have felt it unwise to send spies all over the country to report on this Labour Party campaign. Anyway, it is the *Daily Herald*'s reports and those contained in the Labour Party's own annual report which offer the most detailed evidence of the party's Irish campaign. Although it would be too much to expect these accounts to be totally objective, the optimistic tone of them does match up with the other evidence of the growing interest in Ireland, specifically the councils of actions and the popularity of ILP's Irish meetings in the same period. This also tallies with the subsequent judgement of G. D. H. Cole, another contemporary and interested eyewitness, who writes of the 'strong public backing' for the Labour Party's Irish policy that emerged during the campaign.[90]

Other indicators of the public mood point in the same direction. Perhaps the most interesting is a series of by-elections which took place in the spring of 1921, and in which the Labour Party had considerable success. Local and national newspapers reported that Ireland and unemployment were the main issues in three out of the four by-elections,[91] and *The Times* attributed what the *New Statesman* called, a 'remarkable series of Labour victories' to unemployment and Ireland.[92] Tom Johnson of the ILPTUC even wrote to the Labour Party, congratulating it on these victories and saying they justified the party's Irish campaign.[93] As for the party's rank and file, the *Agenda* for the 1921 party conference shows that more resolutions were submitted on Ireland than on any other topic. There were 14 in all, most of which were to the left of the party's policy. This figure compares with the ten submitted on the most popular topic (housing) in 1920 and the five on the most popular one (conscription) in 1919.[94]

There were those who were prepared to take the initiative and go further than attend meetings or pass resolutions. In late January 1921, 400 miners at Giffnock colliery near Glasgow staged a 24-hour strike 'as a protest against the [British] terrorism in Ireland and to demand the withdrawal of all British forces used against the Irish people.'[95] This was reported in the inside pages and in a few words in both the *Daily Herald* and *Forward*, suggesting neither were enthusiastic about the walk-out: it may well be that the strikers were by and large from the local Irish Catholic community and the socialist press was worried about what they feared would be the divisive implications of the action.

Similarly but more ambitiously, the Liverpool branch of the ISDL in April 1920 attempted to organise an unofficial dock strike in their port against the imprisonment of Irish political prisoners in Wormwood Scrubs. One of organisers, Michael O'Leary was later to claim:

> The dock labourers and the crews of the cross-Channel boats – B. & I., Cork, Limerick, Dundalk and Newry – came out to a man; and several of the Transatlantic ships, if not actually tied up, had their personnel very much reduced. In the case of the coal heavers ... the number employed was 5,024 and out of that number 5,016 came out on strike, completely crippling the movement of all ships in the Port of Liverpool. Our pickets (Volunteers) were at work at each dock, and the docks only looked a shadow of what they usually were.[96]

The *Daily Herald* was delighted, reporting in its issue of 30 April that '7,000 dockers are reported to be out, as well a number of coal heavers.' This and O'Leary's claim were exaggerations. The *Liverpool Echo* reported that the National Dock Labourers, headed by James Sexton who opposed the strike said that only 500 struck, while the newspaper reported that that 'a striking feature of the stoppage is the amused aloofness of the majority of dockers. On the other hand it did admit that dockers who usually worked the shipping lines from England to Ireland 'did not turn up today.'[97] The leading historian of the Liverpool Irish, John Belcham, estimates that 2,000 dockers and 300 coal heavers struck. He also notes that Special Branch reports said the strike led to a 'deteriorating relationship between the Irish and the [local] labour movement', and that on May Day, which came two days after the strike began, and after which the strike was called off, the Liverpool Trades Council refused to allow the ISDL strike organisers onto the official platform.[98]

More generally, however, there is little indication that the war in Ireland produced a significant anti-Irish backlash in Britain. What incidents there were seem few and far between. In August 1916, farm labourers in Lincolnshire and Yorkshire refused to work with Irish migrant labourers who, as usual, had come over for the harvest.[99] In January 1920, an Irish Self-Determination League club in Earlestown, Lancashire, was attacked by 'a gang of local "tough boys".'[100] In April 1920, in London, a series of ISDL demonstrations outside Wormwood Scrubs, taking up the same cause as the attempted Liverpool strike, were severely attacked by what appears to be a mixture of the police and a local mob.[101] What is also interesting about this, however, is that in the course of these the local trades council and a local NUR branch marched in support of the demonstrators.[102]

Ugly as some of the anti-Irish activities were, it does not at all compare to the sort of sustained anti-Irish violence that was displayed by English mobs in the nineteenth century.[103] In short, there is no substantial body of evidence to suggest a widespread presence of anti-Irishness within the British working class in this period. Indeed, the evidence presented so far indicates there was public sympathy with Ireland at least from mid-1920s.

An opportunity to put that sympathy into action came, coincidently, at the very climax of the Labour Party's public campaign, with a new controversy which casts further light on the whole relationship between leadership and rank and file. This was sparked by the killing of three railway workers by the police in Mallow, Cork in early February 1921 after they had been taken into police custody. Two of the slain men were members of the British-based rail union ASLEF (the Associated Society of Locomotive Engineers and Firemen), whose executive was soon demanding an inquiry into the shootings. More dramatically, the executive threatened a national strike if such an inquiry was not forthcoming. It was, said the union's general secretary, John Bromley, 'no idle threat'.[104] Certainly, ASLEF's actions were taken seriously by others in the labour movement. The *Daily Herald* hoped it would be the start of more general action: 'If ASLEF can protect its members by a strike threat, British Labour can save Ireland by the same weapon. Only the threat must not be a bluff. One society has shown the way. It is for Labour as a whole to follow.'[105] In the pages of *Labour Leader*, G. D. H. Cole was even then putting the events in an historical perspective:

> The strike threat of the A.S.L.E.F. whether or not it leads to actual strike action, is for the Labour movement one of the events that really matter. Despite the national campaign which the Labour Party has been conducting ... the apathy of the working class movement in this country in relation to Ireland is a disgrace. This is, no doubt partly to be accounted for by more pressing concerns – with unemployment, with the employers' campaign for a reduction of wages, and so on; but this while it may be an extenuation, is certainly not an excuse ... During the past two years the Labour movement has been very largely frittering away its strength on minor troubles ... the action of Mr Bromley's union is a fresh awakening ... The British workers have been in the past inclined to say that, while they sympathise with the 'wrongs' of Ireland there is nothing they can do to bring effective help ... The locomotive engineers have shown them what they can do – if they will.[106]

A number if the issues raised here by Cole are of obvious relevance to this study, but for the moment the key phrase is the last one: 'if they will'. As far as the ASLEF rank and file was concerned, the first initial signs were for support for the leadership. 'Branches of the union are rallying to the stand taken by the Executive Committee', reported the *Daily Herald*.[107] It cited branches at Kings Cross (which had voted for strike action with only one against), Leamington, Southall and West Ham. However, Rugby, while supporting the demands for an inquiry, was also 'deprecating strike action'. A more substantial opposition came from the familiar figure of J. H. Thomas and the leadership of the NUR who also had members attacked in the Mallow shootings. Its executive met on 11 February. The result was what *The Times* called 'a distinct setback to any development of the strike movement on the railways'. The report explained that, as far as the NUR was concerned, 'the issue is now transferred to the Parliamentary arena', because, as Thomas said, 'the executive have instructed me to raise the whole issue in Parliament.'[108]

Bromley's response was to stand firm, saying the NUR decision 'makes no difference to our action which has definitely been decided on',[109] but the pressure mounted. On 15 February, the executive of the Labour Party met and called for an inquiry, but significantly made no mention of strike action. The next day, the Parliamentary Committee of the TUC took an identical line. In effect, the ASLF threat had been disowned by the leaderships of both wings of the labour movement. The union executive met, with Bromley absent, on 17 February and withdrew the strike call. *The Times* summarised that 'sane and constitutional action by Mr Thomas, M.P., and his union, and the Labour organisations generally has contributed to bring about this result.'[110] The veteran trade union leader and Labour MP Will Thorne, who, to recall, had called for Casement to be put on trial after the Easter Rising, criticised the ASLEF's original action as 'a mistake in tactics'; James Sexton said that 'the question was a political one, for the Labour Party in the Houses of Commons' and J. R. Clynes' view was that 'Bad as the situation is in Ireland, public opinion is not prepared for a settlement of Irish troubles by means of a strike.'[111]

As to the significance of this episode, one indication of how important it was is the swiftness with which the labour leadership moved to isolate ASLEF. This alone suggests that the strike threat was not only real but was possible to implement, and, indeed, it seems unlikely that the ASLEF leadership would have gone so close to the brink as it did if it was not confident of its membership's support. Of course this was for one union, over one specific issue, and it would be ridiculous to draw a general conclusion on the lines that given the right lead the entire trade union movement would have downed tools over Ireland. Yet two other considerations should be remembered. First, as has been shown, despite the mythology it is unlikely that the entire labour movement would have downed tools over British intervention against Russia. Indeed, a national demonstration called by the Council of Action against such British intervention in August attracted only 6,000:[112] the figures for Irish demonstrations and meetings in Britain around the same time do not compare unfavourably with that. And yet despite the unlikelihood of a national strike call over British intervention being successful, the Labour leadership was still prepared to threaten it. The contrast with its attitude to Ireland is obvious.

Second, if ever the labour leadership was going to move further than protest meetings on Ireland, the time of the ASLEF action provided such an opportunity. It was at the height of the Labour Party's Irish campaign, and when the other indications that have already been mentioned – the Peace With Ireland Council campaign, the ISDL meetings, the ILP meetings, the calls from the local councils of action – suggest that public displeasure at the government's Irish policy was at a peak. Clynes may indeed have been right when he said public opinion would not have been sympathetic to strike action over Ireland, and to reiterate, a general strike over Ireland was unlikely to have been supported throughout the movement, but there were other options, including the limited action proposed by ASLEF which the evidence suggests could have won support at the base of the labour movement had such a lead been given at that particular time. Instead there was the Labour Party's campaign of public meetings and it can be suggested this, at least in part, was a counter-initiative to more militant action being demanded by many in the wider labour movement. As for those Labour Party meetings, the judgement of the Irish Labour Party displayed is significant. 'The meetings were large and sympathetic', reported three leading members of the ILPTUC who participated in them, which again attested to an interested and concerned labour constituency. However, they also showed 'a lamentable ignorance of the conditions of affairs in Ireland; but even more lamentable was the sense of helplessness which seemed to pervade every meeting.'[113]

To generalise from this remark, the labour leadership was, throughout the period, not averse to encouraging such a sense of helplessness, and usually its rank and file reacted to it with compliance or complacency. Such conclusions need to be registered; but so does one that points to between mid-1920 and mid-1921, and suggests that at that time many in the rank and file of the labour movement were politically in advance of their leaders on Ireland. Perhaps then, to return to that old controversy stated earlier whether labour's leaders led, reflected or restrained their members, as far as Ireland was concerned, from 1916 to 1921, the most considered judgement might be all three.

7
Socialism and Nationalism

In March 1920, Katherine Bruce Glacier, still editor of the ILP's *Labour Leader* visited Ireland, then a year in to the War of Independence. She reported:

> Already in many a Labour procession, the industrial towns and cities of Ireland have seen the cruelly informed memories of the Green and Orange flags ... yield to the magic of the Red ... And recently tens of thousands of young Irishmen, by their policy of passive resistance, steadily pursued throughout the war, bore triumphant testimony of our most cherished I.L.P. faith in the invincibility of Right so long as it refuses to stoop to the weapons of lawless might.
>
> Even now nothing can hinder the cause of Irish freedom, save an armed rising, which would give to our British Junkers the opportunity they long for of drowning Sinn Féin in the blood of the noblest leaders and disciples.[1]

There was, at this time and throughout the struggle for Irish independence, plenty of evidence to support the contention that what was happening in Ireland was not simply a case of the British armed forces versus Irish guerrilla forces. Irish resistance took a variety of forms, from elections, to boycotts, to strikes which were indeed examples of passive resistance. But here, Katherine was over-egging the pudding. For instance, just two days before these words appeared magistrate Alan Bell was shot dead by the IRA for investigating, on behalf of the British, Sinn Féin and Dáil Éireann funding. And, as for the terror threats of the 'British Junkers', six days before Bell's killing, Tomás Mac Curtain, the lord mayor of Cork and a local IRA commander had been shot dead by the police.

Yet the above words have relevance beyond factual accuracy. They suggest that this British socialist was prone to seeing the Irish revolution as she wanted to see it; that in maintaining the green and orange were giving way to the red she was giving her British socialist readership a reason to support the Irish; and that in advising the Irish to be peaceful in their protest she was recommending how they should conduct their struggle. Such themes were to dominant British socialist political analysis of Ireland from 1916 to 1921. They sought to answer the wider question as to what the Irish national revolt had to do with socialism.

Traditions

Eric Hobsbawm has written that, between 1880 and 1914, 'nationalism took a dramatic leap forward, and its ideological and political context was transformed'.[2] For him, because nationalism 'gained ground so rapidly' in these years and was 'a function of both social and political changes'[3] then, 'virtually every Marxist theorist of importance ... took part in the impassioned debates on this subject.'[4]

The reasons are obvious. The unifications of Germany and Italy were followed by the establishment of new national states in Bulgaria, Norway and Albania and the rise of national movements among many European peoples, including such diverse ones as Finns, Slovaks, Estonians, and Macedonians. There were national tensions in the Russian and the Austro-Hungarian empires, and the spread of other empires, including the British, saw a growth in national pride and/or jingoism in the imperial heartlands. The same period also saw massive labour migration, often followed by a xenophobia in the country to which the migrants came.[5] The ideological inheritors of the Communist Manifesto, which had insisted in 1848 that 'the working men have no country' and that 'national differences and antagonisms are daily more and more vanishing', were not immune from the pressures inherent in the growth of national sentiments. The French socialist Jean Jaures argued well before the outbreak of the Great War that French socialists would be justified in resisting an attack from Germany; on the German side the leading socialist theorist Bebel saw the need to defend the 'German fatherland' from attack by Russia, 'the champion of terror and barbarism';[6] there were Dutch socialists who justified Dutch imperialism;[7] and Italian ones who supported their state annexing Libya.[8]

The European historian James Joll has maintained that British socialists were absent from the theoretical discussions which accompanied these propositions[9] with, 'England standing outside the social democratic world.'[10] Nevertheless, it is appropriate to briefly summarise the theoretical arguments as they emerged. Three distinct positions can be noted. First is that of the Austro-Marxists who argued for federalism or 'cultural autonomy within the framework of a multi-national, multi-ethnic state.'[11] A second position was elaborated by Rosa Luxemburg, the Polish socialist, who argued that it was utopian to advocate independence for Poland, and equally for Ireland and Czechoslovakia; that it subscribed to the 'bourgeois nationalist' perception that the 'nation' was a uniform totality, rather than one divided by class.[12] The third position developed by, among others, Lenin, was agreed both at the London Congress of the Second International in 1896 and the Second Congress of the Third International in 1920. This endorsed the absolute right of self-determination, and insisted that socialists should, in Lenin's words, 'demand the liberation of the oppressed nations, not only in general nebulous phrases, not in empty declamations, not by "postponing" the question until socialism is established, but in a clearly and precisely formulated political programme'.[13] Further:

> The proletariat cannot but fight against the forcible retention of the oppressed nations within the boundaries of a given state, and this is exactly what the right of self-determination means. The proletariat must demand the right of political secession for the colonies and for nations that 'its own' nation oppresses. Unless it does this, proletarian internationalism will remain a meaningless phrase; mutual confidence and class solidarity between the workers of the oppressing and oppressed nations will be impossible.[14]

Here, the importance of socialists in an 'oppressor' nation, which, in Leninist terms, included Britain, supporting self-determination in an 'oppressed nation', including Ireland, is strongly argued. By contrast, and showing some similarity with the views of the Austro-Marxists and the Dutch socialists, there is Ramsay MacDonald writing in the Labour Party pamphlet *Labour and the Empire* in 1907:

> When the expression 'British' is used in civil matters it implies something more than a mere description of racial or national origin. 'British' justice, 'British' honour, 'British' administration carry to our minds certain qualities of justice, honour and administration, and our

Imperial policy has always been commended by our people at home … on these moral and qualitative grounds. The Empire must exist not merely for safety, or order, or peace, but for richness of life.[15]

Thus, for MacDonald, 'the Labour Party therefore no more thinks of discussing whether the Stuarts should be restored to the throne than it does of debating whether we should break the Empire to pieces.' Nevertheless, 'it approaches Imperial problems with the politics of the industrious classes as guide on the one hand, and the internationalism of its nature as guide on the other.' Accordingly:

Its imperialism is … not of the aggressive or the dragging order; it does not believe in the subjection of other nationalities … To its subject races it desires to occupy the position of friend; to its self-governing Imperial states it seeks to be an equal.'[16]

MacDonald sought to reform the Empire and administer it more humanely. He advocated self-governing states, into which were placed Canada, Australia, New Zealand and South Africa, who he saw voluntarily bounded together with Britain by an 'executive authority' of an 'Imperial Conference', made up of the political leaders of the various states. This would also oversee the development, education and government of the 'subject races' in the Empire and, significantly, 'it would express the political problems of Imperial defence, and co-ordinate the opposing desires of self-governing states to have independent forces of their own'.[17]

The necessity of considering British defence interests in relation to Irish self-government, which this book has already documented, is available here in a more general version. The more general arrangements, cited above, would not involve 'the dependencies'. The African colonies and India were not to be granted a self-governing status. MacDonald is vague about what should happen instead. 'In some cases', he writes, 'it ought to be the rule of chiefs; in others a restoration of a kind of semi-democracy in which the people are partly enfranchised or elect part of the governing authority',[18] but in all instances British imperial authority would remain.

There is not then, in MacDonald's essay, any question of elevating the principle of self-determination to that of a moral or political necessity.

Such considerations did emerge elsewhere in the course of the Great War. The Allies professed to be fighting for the rights of small nations, and in doing so cited the invasions and occupation of Belgium and Serbia. The Central Powers replied by citing British treatment of Ireland, Russian treatment of Finland and 'the subjection of North Africa by Great Britain, France and Italy.'[19] The question came more to the fore with the Russian revolution, whose leaders declared their adherence to the right of self-determination. The whole issue was brought to the very centre of the stage by the enunciation in early 1918 of President Wilson's Fourteen Points, which looked forward to a post-war settlement based on the principle of self-determination, although even then there were limits.[20]

It would be natural for the labour movement in Britain to relate to these developments, and in particular to the question of self-determination for Britain's own colonies. Indeed, in December 1917 the NEC of the Labour Party and the Parliamentary Committee of the TUC drew up its own *Memorandum on War Aims* which included 'international trusteeship of African colonies'.[21] Just before then, in August 1917, the ILP said that any peace settlement should include 'the liberation of people held by conquest against their will under the domination of an alien power and the submission to them of the opportunity to decide their own future government.'[22] However, it was in Labour's general policy document, *Labour and the New Social Order*, published in 1918, that the attitude towards the Empire was best clarified:

With regard to the great Commonwealth of all races, all colours, all religions and all degrees of civilisation, that we call the British Empire, the Labour Party stands for its maintenance and its progressive development on the lines of Local Autonomy and 'Home Rule All Round'; the fullest respect for the rights of each people, whatever its colour, to all the Democratic Self-Government to which it is capable, and to the proceeds of its own toil upon the resources of its territorial home; and the closest possible co-operation among all the various members of what has become essentially not an Empire in the old sense, but a Britannic Alliance ... What we look for, besides a constant progress in Democratic Self-Government ... is a continuous partici-pation of the Ministers of the Dominions, of India, and especially of other Dependencies ... in the most confidential deliberations of the Cabinet, so far as Foreign Policy and Imperial Affairs are concerned.[23]

Although, as already noted this pamphlet was written by a committee headed by Sidney Webb, and it has similarities with *Fabianism and the Empire*, edited by Shaw, its more striking similarity is with MacDonald's *Labour and the Empire*, quoted above, another official Labour Party document. Also obvious is the common ground it shares with the contemporary policy put forward by the Labour Party on Ireland. The 'home rule' solution, the concern about defence, and the belief that it was in the best interests of those under the authority of Britain to stay with Britain surface here as they did over Ireland. So, too, does the obvious question: what if the colonies want more; what if they want to have nothing to do with the Empire or Britannic Alliance?

At least there was, from MacDonald in 1907 to *Labour and the New Social Order*, an ideological framework available to British social democracy, to guide it through the troubled and much-changed world that emerged after 1918, although whether that framework was adequate to deal with that world was another issue. Ireland was to provide one test, and it was also an opportunity for others who did not share MacDonald's and the Labour Party's philosophical assumptions.

Ireland Matters

Before and during the drawing up of the peace treaties that detailed the settlement of the allied victory in the Great War, British participants were well aware of the embarrassment Ireland could cause them in the general discussion on self-determination. A memorandum of the British Foreign Office of November 1918 and the personal testament of Harold Nicholson, a British diplomatic representative at the treaty negotiations, testify to such unease. If, as Nicolson pointed out, 'We had accepted a system [of self-determination] for others, which, when it came to practice we should refuse to apply to ourselves.'[24] Even President Wilson, when approached by an American-Irish delegation in Paris for the peace negotiations, said it was 'a great metaphysical tragedy' that Ireland's 'outstanding case of a small nationality' could not be raised at the Versailles discussions.[25]

Some British socialists made the same point more forcefully. As early as June 1917, the BSP's *Call* said that the eventual peace settlement should include 'the principle of all nationalities having the right to dispose of themselves', and that this should include 'Ireland, Egypt, India,

Persia, Morocco etc'.[26] In January 1918, the same newspaper similarly commented that Lloyd George's 'insistence on self-government on truly democratic lines for the Austro-Hungarian nationalities ... as an essential condition for peace raises the question of the subject nations with the British Empire' and cited Ireland, Egypt and India.[27] Seven months later it returned to the issue, saying of Wilson's Fourteen Points, 'is nothing to be said to England about Ireland, India and Egypt?'[28] There were similar references in *Labour Leader*,[29] although these were from correspondents rather than as editorial comment, and, as already noted, the newspaper's own statement on war aims didn't specify an Irish settlement. There was also external criticism of Britain's apparent allegiance to self-determination on the one hand and its treatment of Ireland on the other. When Labour MP James O'Grady visited revolutionary Russia in 1917 shortly before the Bolshevik revolution, members of the Moscow and Petrograd soviets 'insistently' asked, reported O'Grady, 'You say you are fighting a war of liberation, but what about Ireland?'[30]

The Bolsheviks had read their Marx and Engels – indeed, Lenin's writings on colonialism and the national question have frequent references to Marx and Engels on Ireland. Their writings on Ireland are well-documented and have been discussed often.[31] Accordingly, there is no need for a detailed discourse here, but it is worthwhile quoting a paragraph from Marx which is representative of his and Engels' attitude, especially as this seeks to explain why British workers should agitate on Ireland. Writing in 1870 in a private letter and on the First International he said:

> Hence it is the task of the International everywhere to put the conflict between England and Ireland in the foreground, and everywhere to side openly with Ireland. And it is the special task of the Central Council in London to awaken a consciousness in the English workers that for them the national emancipation of Ireland is no question of abstract justice or humanitarian sentiment but *the first condition* of their own social emancipation.[32] [Original emphasis]

Marx is here advocating the promotion of Irish 'national emancipation' as a way in which socialism among English workers can be advanced. This is a consistent theme of his writings on Ireland. Although he did outline his own political and economic programme for Ireland, centring on independence, 'an agrarian revolution' and protective tariffs,[33] his main concern was to relate Irish agitation within the British working class to the development of its consciousness. He and Engels had at one time thought that revolution in England would be necessary for Ireland to be free of England, but then, said Marx, 'deeper study has convinced me of the opposite. The English working class will *never accomplish anything* until it has got rid of Ireland.'[34] [Original emphasis]. Most notably, 'In Marx's and Engels' view, anti-Irish sentiment was an important constituent of the 'false consciousness that helped to prevent the British working class ... from striking the decisive blow against capitalism',[35] because by identifying with English nationalism against the Irish the English working class tied themselves to their own ruling class.

In the century and a half that followed socialists were, of course, to make similar points about the presence of other forms of chauvinism and racism in the British working class, but for both Marx and Engels anti-Irish prejudice was a good enough reason to organise English support for the Irish cause. There were other, practical benefits tied up with the notion that a defeat for the English ruling class in Ireland would weaken it materially, but it was all summed up by a phrase from Marx that was to be long remembered: 'any nation that oppresses another forges its own chains'.[36] Thus, as to why British workers should take up Ireland, their answer was, out of their own self-interest.

What Marx did not do was attempt to link Irish nationalism with the achievement of socialism in Ireland itself. The most significant contribution in this area was made by James Connolly. That, too, has been well-documented,[37] and again it is sufficient to give the briefest of flavours. Just before the Easter Rising, Connolly wrote:

We are out for Ireland for the Irish. But who are the Irish? Not the rack-renting slum-owning landlord; not the sweating, profit-grinding capitalist; not the sleek and oily lawyer; not the prostitute pressmen – the hired liars of the enemy ... Not these but the Irish working class, the only secure foundation upon which a free nation can be reared. The cause of labour is the cause of Ireland, the cause of Ireland is the cause of labour. They cannot be dissevered. Ireland seeks freedom. Labour seeks an Ireland ... the sole mistress of her own destiny, superior owner of all material things within and upon her soil.[38]

For Connolly, this was why working class organisations in Ireland should participate in the national struggle, indeed, for him, the successful outcome of that struggle was dependent on working class leadership, which would take the national revolution to its logical end and secure ownership of much more than existing state institutions. As one of the most famous of all Connolly quotes put it, spoken to his comrades on the eve of the Rising, 'In the event of victory, hold on to your rifle as those with whom we are fighting may stop before our goal is reached. We are out for economic as well as political liberty.'[39]

From the post-Rising Irish labour movement, other arguments were to emerge to justify socialist participation in the Irish struggle for independence. One of the most notable occasions was when the ILPTUC, in association with the Socialist Party of Ireland, attended the International Labour and Socialist Conference, held in Berne, Switzerland, in February 1919, out of which eventually evolved a reconstructed Second International. For this conference, the Irish delegation produced a written report, part of which argued why the International should support the Irish national cause. These included, 'the profession by all national sections of the International of the right of self-determination'; and the example the securing of Irish independence would provide 'for the solution of the national question elsewhere'. Also:

> The independence of the Irish people and the settlement of the issue between a subject people and an imperialist Power are essential for the union of the Irish workers in a class-conscious movement for the conquest by the workers of political power, liberty, land and all the resources, and the ownership and control of Ireland, and everything within Ireland.[40]

The implication is that the national question had to be settled to allow the class question to occupy centre stage. More basically, at Berne, Ramsay MacDonald, true to his record, and on behalf of the British Labour delegation, argued against the very concept of Irish independence, proposing Home Rule instead, not just for Ireland, but for Egypt and India as well. This, the Irish delegates felt, was 'very unsatis-factory'.[41] They reported that 'the feeling of the delegates as represented ... in the Conference and by private conversations was definitely and in many cases enthusiastically favourable to Ireland's demands in full'.[42]

Consequently, as already noted in relating the Stockport Irish and the Labour Party controversy, the International did endorse that 'free and absolute self-determination shall be applied immediately in the case of Ireland.' This was an important endorsement; in short, the Second International backed the Irish.[43]

However, the social democratic world of the European socialism, as represented by the Second International, no longer had the left wing monopoly it enjoyed prior to 1914. The Russian Revolution and the victory of the Bolsheviks were to offer an alternative, in the form of the Third International (Comintern). Indeed, although the Bolsheviks did not attend the Berne conference other experiences persuaded the Irish delegates there that 'we have still grown stronger in our conviction that the Soviet government in Russia is Ireland's best friend'.[44] As already noted, that seemed borne out when the Second Congress of the Third International, held in Moscow in July 1920, insisted that British socialists take up that issue. At this congress there was also a report on 'Revolutionary Ireland and Communism' presented by two Irish delegates, including James Connolly's son, Roddy. This argued that Ireland was 'of primary importance to international communism'. The reasons given included Ireland's 'strategic importance with regards to England, the seat of British imperialism', which of course was one of the major reasons why the British Labour Party did not support independence; and 'the influence of Ireland's political development on the broad masses of its nationals scattered throughout the British Empire'.[45] The document also looked forward to the co-operation between Irish communists and the CPGB leading to a federated workers Republic of Britain and Ireland, although that was so aspirational it was almost meaningless.[46]

Overall, the Second Congress of the Third International accepted the general principles involved in the Irish argument when it agreed to the *Preliminary Draft Thesis on the National and Colonial Question*. This was drafted and introduced at the Congress by Lenin and included:

In all their propaganda and agitation – both within parliament and outside it – the Communist Parties must consistently expose the constant violation of the equality of nations, by uniting first the proletarians and then the whole mass of the working population in the struggle against the bourgeoisie; and second, that all Communist parties should render direct aid to the revolutionary movements among the dependent and under-privileged nations for example, Ireland, the American Blacks, etc) and in the colonies.[47]

Echoing Marx, and even before the 'Irish Question was reformed in 1916, Lenin had written in 1915, 'If Socialists of Britain do not recognise and uphold Ireland's right to secession ... it is solely because they are in fact imperialists, not socialists. It is ridiculous to cherish illusions that people who do *not* fight got the 'right of self-determination' of the oppressed nations, while they themselves belong to the oppressor nations, are capable of the practicing socialist policies.'[48] [original emphasis] Thus, for the Third International, support by the British working class movement for Ireland's self-determination was not just a duty but a litmus test of its own socialism.

From both the social-democratic world of the Second International and the communist world of the Third International, the advice to their British adherents was: support the Irish. But that just might have been easier said than done.

Missionaries

Among those who spoke at the Second Congress of the Third International on Ireland was Karl Radek, who had once held the Luxembourg position on nationalism and socialism and still showed traces of this. He proclaimed, 'it is the duty of British Communists to go to the colonies to fight at the head of the rising masses of the people.'[49] What he seemed to be suggesting was a form of socialist missionary work, with the communists from the advanced capitalist countries going to the colonies to show the natives how to save themselves. Certainly, there were occasions when members of the British left were willing to fulfil this role in respect to Ireland. For example, P. L. Gray, writing in the *Communist*, although critical of that newspaper's policy, listed the tasks of British communists in respect of Ireland. These included: 'to agitate seriously among workers with a view to getting them clearly to realise that they themselves ... are capable of taking over their country, when the opportunity arises, and winning it as a Workers' (Soviet) Republic' [original emphasis].[50] *Workers' Dreadnought* itself sought to so 'agitate' in early 1920:

Irish Communists should clearly differentiate themselves from the bourgeois social patriots of Ireland. Already they should be pointing out that their goal is not Dáil Éireann, which is merely an Irish replica of the bourgeois Parliament at Westminster; but that Irish workers must strive to establish Soviets. Already steps should be taken to establish the Irish Soviets.[51]

A variation of this methodology of telling the Irish what to do was that adopted by the *Socialist*, the newspaper of the Glasgow-based Socialist Labour Party whose reluctance to discuss Ireland in the aftermath of the 1916 Rising has been noted. This was a reluctance that was sustained, with the topic not being covered at all in any of the monthly issues of the newspaper in 1918. This pattern was broken soon after the *Socialist* went weekly at the start of 1919, but in a somewhat exceptional manner. It took the form of a weekly 'Irish Socialist' column, usually written by Selma Sigerson in Belfast. Sigerson, in fact, was the pen name for one Kitty Coyle. The column ran for six months and was used to direct the Irish working class, and to attack anyone in Ireland who was judged not to be following the correct socialist revolutionary path. The first blast was aimed at Dáil Éireann, 'planned ... upon the economic base of a governing class', which the Irish workers were advised to overthrow.[52] Others to feel Sigerson's wrath included the ILPTUC and the more left-wing Socialist Party of Ireland, both of whom were 'like a cuckoo sitting in the nest of a national impulse beyond their comprehension'.[53] When Sigerson and a few others established the Revolutionary Socialist Party of Ireland in Belfast in May 1919 every other organisation was deemed irrelevant: 'Official Sinn Féin, official Labour, official Ulster, official England, are all fat and impotent Canutes against the rising tide of the revolutionary rank and file.'[54]

Tom Johnson of the ILPTUC described this column as 'insane',[55] and certainly its appearance in a British socialist newspaper which had totally neglected Ireland but which now sought to tell the Irish how to conduct their struggle showed little sense or sensitivity. There were those who objected to such lecturing. The *Communist* said in October 1921 that, although it would be 'best pleased to see Ireland a Workers Republic ... we disclaim any desire or intention to dictate to the Irish workers what they shall do or when they shall do it.'[56] Similarly, the *Daly Herald* on 27 June 1921 proclaimed, 'It is not for us to advise the Sinn Féin leadership what to do'; adding, 'We would that the British Labour movement was as coherent and united as Sinn Féin.' The only problem with the first part of this statement was that just five days before, on 22 June, an editorial in the same newspaper discussing 'methods of terrorism' said, 'We would earnestly appeal to our Irish comrades at once to put an end to these insane tactics.' This plea on this occasion not so much motivated by the newspaper editor's pacifism but because 'such violence cannot have but one effect, that is to drive the British worker on this [Irish] question into the arms of reactionaries'. To be fair, the editorial went on to say, '*There would be no Irish terrorism if there was no British tyranny*' [original emphasis], which was not the first or last time this suggestion was made.

To return to the more general point, there is a history of British socialists presenting themselves as consultants to Irish revolution. Fifty years before one such example had prompted Fredrick Engels to ask: 'After the domination of the English aristocracy over Ireland, after the domination of the English middle class over Ireland ... must we now look forward to the advent of the domination of the English working class over Ireland?'[17] The context of this remark is relevant, and highlights another variation of socialist missionary attitudes. It was when the secretary of the British Council of the First International proposed that the Irish section be brought under the jurisdiction of the British one. The proposal was rejected overwhelmingly by the International's general council, but replays of this organisational controversy were to be staged on a number of occasions over the next half-century. At the Paris Congress of the Second International in 1900, delegates from the Irish Socialist Republican Party were given separate delegate status despite objections from the Socialist Democratic Federation and other British socialists who argued that the Irish contingent should be part of the British one. When the ITUCLP, after years of debate, finally decided in 1912 that it was to be fully independent of the British Labour Party the decision was only accepted by Ramsay MacDonald, on behalf of that organisation, with great reluctance.[18] A couple of years later there was a similar discussion on the same lines between Connolly and William Walker of the Belfast ILP. Connolly argued a 'free federation of free peoples' was the internationalist position, while Walker's advocacy of the ILP organising in Ireland was, insisted Connolly 'the merging of the subject peoples in the political systems of their conquerors.'[19] A similar wrangle developed in the ILP when, in early 1917, its Scottish Divisional Council sent William

Regan to Dublin to set up a Dublin branch of the ILP. Regan reported in a letter to *Labour Leader* that 'while the ILP was admired by Dublin comrades, they were convinced that the violent anti-English temper of the people would seriously impede a party having its headquarters in England', and 'to be effective', a new 'self-contained' Irish organisation was needed. Beneath this letter there was a comment from the editor, Kathrine Bruce Glasier:

> We think the decisions reached ... a little unfortunate, and we feel constrained to ask: what of the International appeal of Socialism? Do not our Dublin friends think the solid stand of the I.L.P. for Internationalism and the liberty of peoples justifies the advanced thinkers of the city putting the broad human claims of the I.L.P. against the narrow nationalism before which they are now yielding?[60]

This did not go down well with some. The following issue saw Regan and the editor joining polemical battle once more and after that came a letter from the leading Irish socialist William O'Brien. He gave the example of the separate identity of Connolly's Irish Socialist Republican Party, reminded *Labour Leader* of the decisions of the 1900 Congress of the Second International on separate representation for the Irish, and asked, 'If Germany continues its domination over Belgium, what would socialists of that country think of a suggestion that their movement should ... become a branch of the German Social Democratic Party?' He also wondered why 'should it be necessary to offer any justification, much less apology, for Irish socialists deciding to have a distinct movement of their own, rather than attach themselves to an organisation having its headquarters in a foreign country'?[61] At which point the editor of *Labour Leader* withdrew, commenting underneath O'Brien's letter that 'we cannot resist' his 'pleading' and 'hereby send our unreserved good wishes to our Irish comrades in the work of International Socialism.'

Nevertheless, while there is no evidence of a Dublin ILP branch being established there already was a Belfast branch and this continued despite the implied acceptance in the comment on O'Brien's letter that the Irish should have their own organisation. If there was a consistent policy it seemed to be to let sleeping dogs lie. When, in February 1918, the Secretary of the Belfast Federation of the ILP wrote to the NAC asking if the party would continue to operate there after Home Rule, the reply was 'they should go on as now until the matter [Home Rule] was actually decided and then the N.A.C. should arrange for consultation.'[62] After that, both the Belfast branch and the leadership of the ILP carried on as before. The ILP Conference Reports from 1920 to at least 1923 record the existence of 'Division One' of the ILP, consisting of 'Scotland and Ireland.' So even after the Anglo-Irish Treaty, the ILP, in theory at least, retained a claim to the whole of Ireland.

There is also the case of the Leeds Convention of July 1917, in which all wings of the British working class movement participated but from which was supposedly established an embryonic soviet in the form of a Workers' and Soldiers' Council. At the Convention, following an intervention from the same William O'Brien who three months before had written to *Labour Leader* defending a separate socialist organisation in Ireland, 'full assurances' were given 'that the right of Ireland to govern her own destinies should be granted in full.'[63] Except, that is, as far as a separate workers' organisation was concerned, for the Convention then announced its Workers' and Soldiers' Council 'for Great Britain and Ireland', with the establishment of 13 regional centres.[64] Twelve of these centres were listed, the thirteenth was not, but as the only area not mentioned was Ireland it can be assumed that it was the thirteenth. There was a subsequent announcement of regional conferences with 'further details later' being promised for the Irish one[65] which, not surprisingly, never appeared, although that was systematic of the general lack of follow-up of the Convention.

There is one further case of British/Irish missionary work which turned the whole notion on its head. This again features the *Socialist*, and this time the writings therein of Sean McLoughlin, a participant in the Easter Rising. McLoughlin was toured around Scotland and parts of England by the SLP in 1920 and was, for a short time, a member of the organisation. To say he was a far left militant is, perhaps, an understatement.[66] His message was a reversal of the socialist British saving the nationalist Irish: 'If once a workers' Republic was established in Ireland, the effect in Britain would be tremendous. It would practically mean that the same thing must occur in Britain. The Irish workers might have to assist in bringing that about.'[67]

McLoughlin was expelled from the SLP on suspicion of being a police spy, which is unlikely and, for good or ill, the Irish Red Army never did land on Britain's shores. How their socialists would have responded if it had, goodness only knows: they had problems enough coming to terms with the rebellious Irish.

Doubts

With the international working class movement urging British socialists to take up the Irish issue, it was left to them to explain the relevance of Ireland to their political constituency. While Marx, Engels, Connolly, Lenin and others had offered a body of thought to aid them, many British socialist propagandists had still had their doubts. Here is the *Call* in May 1918:

> We less than anybody suffer from the delusion that the mere substitution of an alien ruling class by one of their own will secure for the Irish masses the complete social and economic freedom that can arise only from the conscious control of their own labour. But we stand for the freedom of all peoples to full self-determination, and Ireland's assertion to her claim to that freedom has the whole hearted support of International Socialists wherever they are found.[68]

This could be sub-titled 'self-determination without illusions': a willingness to support this principle, but not to expect too much from its implementation in way of economic or social change. Or, as *Workers' Dreadnought* put it, 'political freedom for Ireland is all very well, but the workers must not be exposed to a system of despotic industrial control by an Irish Republic.'[69] Others were not even sure that 'political freedom' was worth the effort. *Forward's* early view of Home Rule, as expressed by William Regan in 'Catholic Socialist Notes', was that 'it gives Ireland to a few Irish, and perhaps a few English and a sprinkling of Jews. But for the miserable Irish proletariat ... there will be nothing but cruel disappointment.'[70] At least Ramsay MacDonald did not employ bigotry when he questioned Irish nationalism, but he also was not persuaded of its worth. An editorial in *Socialist Review* arguing against independence in late 1921 said that while 'nationality is a most precious sentiment ... every good thing, however, can be ridden to death', and 'if Ireland secures full freedom while retaining connection with us ... further demands, however dear to Irishmen are not worth the blood of a single Irishman.'[71]

This again shows that when answering why socialists, Irish or British, should support Irish independence MacDonald challenged the very premise. That was not so much the case with the Marxists, many of whom accepted that self-determination was a principle to be supported, but they still had to elaborate why this was important for socialists. One variant has been noted in the Irish delegation report to the Berne Conference, which suggested that the national question needed to be settled to allow the class question to become prioritised. Some in the British left also took up this theme. The *Call*, in August 1918, said that while 'the real solution to the problems that afflict the Irish people cannot be found until the Irish labourer ... is freed from the levy of capitalism', it added, 'the Irish workman cannot enter the larger unity of labour until the question of self-government of Ireland is settled once and for all.'[72] Similarly, the leading British communist Fred Willis said, 'It will be no United Ireland that will be born on the day that the green flag floats over an Irish Parliament. On the contrary the suppressed struggle between workers and capitalists will assert itself with full fury, absorbing to itself the dynamic forces hitherto engaged in other directions.'[73] On the same theme, T. A. Jackson wrote, 'the attainment of an independent Ireland would automatically free the Irish people from the mental and political necessity to subordinate their class interests to the requirements of national unity.'[74] *Workers' Dreadnought* concurred, saying, 'the sooner Ireland gains independence, the sooner Irish workers will be fighting with us for Communism',[75] and the same view appeared in letters in the educational and cultural socialist journal *Plebs*, on one of the very few occasions it carried anything about Ireland. Here, Sean Glickman maintained, 'Not until the last English soldier is cleared out of Ireland will there be a perceptible sign of the movement in Ireland taking on a definite proletarian character.'[76]

The essence of these arguments was that Irish self-determination was a pre-condition for the attainment of socialism. Others went one step further and suggested that self-determination would automatically lead to socialism. In the same Fred Willis article quoted above, he also said 'Ireland freed and independent would like enough become the Irish Socialist Republic'. *Workers' Dreadnought* also developed the theme foreseeing 'the class war, which must undoubtedly arise in an acute form as soon as the Nationalist struggle has been allayed by its success.'[77] Another letter writer to *Plebs*, Andrew Clarke, cited the Russian example when complaining about the 'more abstract school of

Marxist' who 'dismisses the whole [Irish] business as a "petty-bourgeois" affair' and cited the Russian February revolution: 'Did it not, though in itself capitalist, liberate forces that culminated in the complete overthrow of itself and capitalism six months later ... Revolutions are neither started with the word "go" nor stopped to a chalk mark.'[78]

A further extension of this argument, which had already moved from self-determination being a pre-condition for socialism to being a step that would lead to socialism, was that, echoing Connolly, the two struggles were one in the same. A statement from the executive committee of the CPGB in November 1920 maintained that 'In such a case as Ireland – the case of a small nation being held in forcible suppression by a great Imperialist state – the National struggle and the class struggle are inseparable from each other.' This was because:

> Even those who are not Communists or Socialists of any kind have some vision that their job is not merely the ousting of the English government, but the overthrow of the English system – which is the capitalist system. And the workers themselves see in the establishment of the Irish Republic the first step – the necessary first step – to the establishment of the Irish Workers Republic.[79]

At least this was an attempt to develop some sort of theoretical understanding of the link between nationalism and socialism. An alternative, deployed on occasions by the same organisation, was to lapse into vulgar Marxist phraseology and proclaim, as the *Call* did in March 1918, 'Ireland will never recover her nationhood until Communism triumphs'.[80] This suggested that rather than self-determination being a precondition for socialism, the contrary was the case. Others could not make up their minds. In 1916 *Forward* maintained that 'English rule must be cut down before Irish workers will turn their eyes to ravages caused by slum-landlords and wealth-owners of their own blood. National independence must precede Socialism in Ireland.'[81] The same author, William Regan, had 18 months later decided, 'our reason convinces us that the struggle for absolute independence in Ireland is doomed to fail. The destruction of capitalism must precede the achievement of separation.'[82]

Others even saw the struggle for Irish independence as some sort of Irish capitalist plot. P. L. Gray, quoted above on telling the Irish what to do, and writing in the *Communist* attacked the newspaper's own analysis, arguing:

It would be a crime, whatever their mistakes, to refuse the Irish workers our support, merely out of lofty theoretical considerations. Bu the facts remain that these nationalist aspirations ... have become a deadweight ... they are being made use of by the Irish bourgeoisie, and in so far as they prevent the Irish workers from clearly seeing their own revolutionary rule ... they are preparing the way for the rule of an Irish class of exploiters in place of British exploiters.[83]

Condemnations of Irish nationalism were not always wrapped in the language of Bolshevism; indeed, those to the right of the Marxists were more prone to be dismissive. 'An I.L.P.er in Ireland', while attributing the growth of Irish national sentiment to mistaken government policies, still concluded in late 1917 that, while 'Nationalism oppressed and ill-treated becomes Nationalism exaggerated', this became 'a monstrosity' exhibiting 'blind and undiscriminating hatred'.[84] Two-and-a-half years later, another 'I.L.P.er in Ireland', this time identified as Charles Roden Buxton, complained that the national struggle in Ireland was 'maiming men's bodies and warping their minds', and 'distracting the thought and energies of Irishmen from the questions of social transformation'.[85] William Regan in *Forward* said much the same when he wrote that 'nationalism in Ireland has long delayed the concentration of the workers on social matters.'[86] Robert Williams, the General Secretary of the British union, the National Transport Workers Federation, in a 1918 May Day message to Dublin Trades Council, sought directly to warn Irish workers of the direction they were heading. 'Do not allow yourselves to be deluded by claims of nationalism', he said, 'and at the same time be deprived of the heritage of your class, the fruits of your labour.'[87] While Bernard Shaw in his pamphlet for the Labour Party, *Irish Nationalism and Labour Internationalism*, promoted an internationalist reason to oppose Irish Republicanism. Explaining that, 'the Labour Party is not, and cannot be a separatist party', he concluded, 'far from wishing to detach the Irish people from the English, it aims at establishing the closest possible links between both and all the workers of the modern world.'[88]

These political sentiments appeared more often in the social democratic world than in that of the Marxists, perhaps because of the more positive attitude Marxism had to national struggles. But even those on the very left wing of the Marxists showed at times that they wished the Irish could be different. Although Sylvia Pankhurst was one of the most sympathetic of all British socialists to the 1916 Rising, three years later, after sitting through a session of Dáil Éireann, she described how, 'we were wearied indeed by speeches and longed for the Soviets which assemble, not for speech-making, but for constructive work.'[89] At other times, Pankhurst's newspaper was ready to reassure its readers that the national struggle was being overtaken by the class war. Even the rather limited manifestation of class consciousness of a demonstration in Dublin on May Day in 1919 produced this interpretation:

For the people of Ireland it spells a great step forward. It spells the awakening of the people to the fact that political freedom is not the be-all of freedom; that to be truly free economic freedom must be linked with political freedom. With the awakening of a revolutionary spirit (caused by the insurrection of 1916) has come an intensive growth of revolutionary thought ... Since the overthrow of the Czar the Irish people have watched ... the acts of the liberated Russians, and the system they have set up in place of the old tyranny. And they have found it good.[90]

The writer here was Nora Connolly, the daughter of James, and it is in itself interesting that she and *Workers' Dreadnought* should choose to identify with each other. On another occasion she said that the 'doctrines' of her father were, 'all over the country regarded as embodying the true spirit of freedom',[91] and even when she was not writing, *Workers' Dreadnought* could express similar optimism. There was the message in January 1920 that 'Irish workers ... are readier to engage in the class struggle than in that for national independence',[92] and one in November 1920 that, 'with their industries being destroyed by English capitalists, and with their lives always in danger from the military ... Irish men and women are compelled to become Communists in word and deed.'[93] Similarly, *Forward* reported in 1918 of the 'wholesale tendency on the part of the new generation of Irishmen to ally themselves with the Labour and Socialist movement';[94] although three years later it said the contrary when saying that 'only socialism can bring the Irish working class the victory that matters', decided that 'the Irish have not yet shown much disposition towards the social ordering of society.'[95] Equally circumspect was a *Labour Leader* Irish correspondent, Patrick Thompson who reported in May 1919 that while 'socialism, pure and simple, is gaining ground rapidly', added, 'but its adherents are still relatively few.'[96]

All of this shows more confusion and contradictions than consistency. Certainly, the majority of the views expressed would hardly be likely to encourage British workers to take to the streets over Ireland. But there was always the old argument that an enemy's enemy is a friend. And there is no doubt who the British capitalist state's main political enemy was in Ireland.

The Natives: Sinn Féin

By September 1917, it was fairly obvious to keen observers of Ireland, as the *New Statesman* was, that Sinn Féin needed explaining to its readership. With Eamon de Valera winning the by-election in East Clare on its behalf on 10 July, it was clear that things were happening and that Sinn Féin was at the centre of these. So who were they? The *New Statesman* was somewhat dismissive: 'This is clearly a folk movement aided by a few scholars and "intellectuals" and without half a dozen adherents from the privileged classes.' Moreover, 'although the abstentionist Sinn Féin policy is mainly derived from the Nationalist conception of Westminster as a *foreign* Parliament, there is implied in it an opposition to Parliamentarianism ... similar to what was current among European syndicalism in days before the war.'[97] [Original emphasis]. This was all wrong. There were member 'privileged classes' in its ranks; it was rather more than a 'folk movement'; it was anti-British parliament, not anti-parliament in principle; and it had little in common with syndicalism. Indeed, Arthur Griffith, the founder of Sinn Féin, had more than once crossed swords with James Larkin, the man most associated with syndicalism in pre-war Ireland and Britain, describing him in 1908, for example, as 'the representative of 'English trade unionism in Ireland'.[98] That, too, was unfair, and it is also the case that Sinn Féin in 1917 was a different animal than it was ten years earlier, but certainly it had not adopted 'Larkinism'.

That did not prevent some on the British left from placing it firmly in the proletarian camp. When, in the municipal election in January 1920, Sinn Féin won control of 172 out of 206 councils, in a minority of cases in coalition with the ILPTUC, it was described by the *Call* as 'a triumph for the workers',[99] which suggested Sinn Féin was now synonymous with the working class. Similarly, the executive of the CPGB in its statement of November 1920 said the 'Republican movement is essentially a working class movement', and although there were 'middle class men in its ranks … the strength and vigour and inspiration of the movement lies in the workers and workers organisation.'[100] *Workers' Dreadnought* went further. 'Sinn Féin has been learning much from the tactics of the Bolsheviks', it told its readers in August 1920,[101] and two months later there was the assurance that, 'in spite of prominent Nationalists being the leading spirit of Sinn Féin, the movement is fundamentally economic and working class.'[102] Even the *New Statesman*, revising its earlier somewhat contemptuous attitude in February 1919 expressed optimism:

> Labour here … is destined to play henceforward an increasingly important part in politics. Connolly and Liberty Hall men it was, rather than Pearse and his intellectuals, who precipitated the Insurrection of 1916; and the influence of the Labour element in the ranks of Sinn Féin has not diminished during the time which has passed since.[103]

However, the more consistently expressed opinion from the social democratic wing of the working class movement was more hostile. In July 1918 Patrick Thompson wrote in *Labour Leader* that Sinn Féin was 'bourgeois' and 'very dangerously militarist and insular', which 'unites bourgeois and proletarian by its insistence on the single issue of independence.'[104] Such sentiments did not, apparently, prevent the same newspaper three months earlier from printing the views of a member of surely an even more 'bourgeois' party. That was the Irish Nationalist MP Arthur Lynch, who wrote in *Labour Leader* that Sinn Féin, 'really comes in the category of b [bloody] fools … the Dublin Sinn Féiners are intellectuals, poets, long-haired critics.'[105] The opinion of Margaret Newboult, as expressed through *Socialist Review* in late 1920, was more akin to that of Patrick Thompson. 'So far were these people from an international attitude', she said of Sinn Féin, 'that their view was not that all nations should combine to defeat capitalism, but that all classes should combine to achieve nationalism.'[106] The following issue of the same journal saw a different, although similarly patronising complaint from Ramsay MacDonald. He spoke of Sinn Féin's 'militarism' which 'belongs to a primitive reflex motion, action which in reality is not directed to an end, but which is taken as a relief'. He added, 'the attractions of the Third International belong to this kind of impulse.'[107]

This comparison would have come as news to some of the adherents of the Third International. For example *Workers' Dreadnought*, whose readiness to interpret the Irish revolution as a proletarian one has already been noted, did not always see things that way. 'The Irish middle classes ... are the mainstay of Sinn Féin', it said in May 1920.[108] The logic of this position was to view the organisation as a class enemy, which was presumably what lay behind the actions of a group reported by Basil Thomson as the 'Glasgow Communist Group'. In April 1920, they refused Sinn Féin the use of its rooms because, 'they consider the Sinn Féin movement an organisation of Irish political capitalists who do not intend to free the Irish people from economic bondage.'[109] The complaint of the fluctuating *New Statesman*, on the other hand, was that Sinn Féin was 'the war party in Ireland',[110] and although it was 'one of the best organised and most determined national movements that the world has ever seen', it was still a disappointment because 'it has thrown up no leader of outstanding intellectual distinction or moral authority.'[111] It was all so unsatisfactory, as R. G. Murray, speaking at the BSP conference in 1918, complained: 'The Sinn Féin movement is not all we would desire it to be'.[112]

Others went further. The most sustained attacked on Sinn Féin came from William Regan's 'Catholic Socialist Notes' in *Forward*. As early as November 1916, Regan said Sinn Féin 'deserves no sympathy from Irish socialists' and accused it of 'entrenching and consecrating ... a dirty selfish Irish capitalism on the Irish people.'[113] The following month came the complaint that the organisation 'failed to recognise the class war',[114] and indeed, four weeks later, Regan said Sinn Féin's 'main object was to bolster up and strengthen capitalism in the country.'[115] Soon afterwards it had become 'a national conspiracy to obtain cheap labour slaves for Irish capitalists.'[116] The attacks became less frequent as Sinn Féin's popularity grew, but they never ceased entirely and as late as July 1920 Sinn Féin was an 'octopus of gombeen men and politicians.'[117] In passing, it is worthwhile to record that Harry Campbell who left the ILP over Ireland maintained that Regan's 'insults' stemmed from a pandering to Glasgow's Protestants.[118]

What the remarks of Regan and much of the rest quoted above have in common is a superficiality that, among other things, failed to recognise that Sinn Féin did not fit into neat categories; and that it was both evolving and at times contradictory. The nearest British socialism came to appreciating this was in the CPCB's pamphlet *The Irish Crisis* published in the latter half of 1921 when the truce was in operation. The author was William Paul:

> The heavy mailed fist of the British ... drove the workers who had been influenced by Connolly into a working agreement with the more militant elements in the Sinn Féin movement ... The fusion of the revolutionary workers with the Sinn Féin movement made it a more vigorous organisation ... the fusion also transformed the Irish movement for national independence into one pregnant with revolutionary possibilities ... a new vigorous element which scorned the idea of *begging* for freedom in London, but which has resolutely set itself the task of working out its own emancipation on Irish soil.[119]

Perhaps Paul was being over-optimistic, although he goes on to warn that, 'it may be that the petty-bourgeois groups in the Sinn Féin movement will yield to the imperialists, rather that lead to the revolutionary demands of the Irish workers', so he was under no illusions that, from a Marxist point of view, it could all end unsatisfactorily. Nevertheless, at least his overall analysis appreciated that Sinn Féin had a dynamic and a dynamism which gave it a potential for changing things for the better. More importantly perhaps, he gave good socialist reasons why British workers should stand on their side of the barricades.

Comprehensions

There is no doubt that it was difficult for British socialists to comprehend the politics of Sinn Féin, or for that matter the IRA. A century later this remains an issue of dispute among many historians, so it may indeed be too much to expect contemporaries to acquire a thorough understanding. For the record, those involved in the Irish national struggle, for instance through the Volunteers/IRA, tended to be young and lower-middle to working class.[120] The more pertinent issue is how much that should really have mattered, specifically for British socialists. On one occasion, Sylvia Pankhurst offered this perspective:

As Communists we stand for the self-determination of peoples and for the breaking up of Empires. In so far as the Irish Sinn Féiners weaken the power of the British Capitalist government, we recognise that they are doing our work.'[121]

Pankhurst was not alone in echoing Marx and Connolly. The *Call* also spoke of a 'common subjection' which 'must unite British Labour and the Irish people.'[122] In the same newspaper Fred Willis went further when elaborating on the international implications of the Irish struggle: 'British Imperialist Capitalism knows full well that its existence, let alone dominance, is bound up with the integrity, let alone dominance of the British Empire'. Accordingly, if it was possible to 'loosen the bond' of British imperialism in Ireland, 'it slackens everywhere.'[123] Or, as he amplified a year later:

This Irish struggle for self-determination strikes a blow at the foundations of capitalism as embodied in British Imperialism ... the British Empire has become one of the strongest bulwarks of that capitalism we are out to destroy. So that, paradoxically as it may appear, every blow struck for Irish nationality is a blow struck also for that internationalism which is the very breath of our movement.[124]

These arguments and that of Pankhurst, just quoted, had a socialist logic to them which, Paul aside, many others cited here often did not. What is noteworthy is that the Pankhurst article was written just after she had returned from Russia, where she had been attending the Second Congress of the Third International. The second Fred Willis article is similarly timed. Both, of course, reflected the 'line' as laid down by Radek, Lenin and others at the Second Congress. For example, Radek's words, in the course of discussing Ireland, were that, 'British capital, based on a strong bourgeoisie, cannot be overthrown only in London, Sheffield, Glasgow and Manchester. It must also be beaten in the colonies. These are the Achilles heel.'[125]

As we have seen, the CPGB became more vocal on Ireland following the Second Congress. What now seems likely is that Willis and Pankhurst were heavily influenced by the theoretical explanations on imperialism expressed there. It is the case that, as has already been noted, Willis had made the same argument in an earlier article; however, also pertinent is that in the second article he talked of the 'vast difference between the nationalism of a dominant nation and that of an oppressed nationality', a classical, but then contemporary, Leninist argument.[126] Therefore it seems safe to assume that on this latter occasion he and Pankhurst had taken to heart the discussion on socialism and nationalism held at the Second Congress.

More generally, such socialists were uncertain or expressed contradictory opinions on the relationship between Irish nationalism and socialism. A further Fred Willis article, appearing this time in the first issue of the CPGB's theoretical journal, *Communist Review*, dated May 1921, is another example of this, and is as good a summary as any of the type of vacillating conclusions which characterised this discussion. He argues that for the communist, Irish national independence 'has no charms', although 'understands well enough the demands of an oppressed people for self-determination'. For him, 'the appeals of Irish patriotism ... sound hollow in his ears, strangely like those of any other crude patriotism – including his own British brand.' To this, he counter-poses 'the struggle of Irish peasants and workers against English or Irish landlords and capitalists', which is 'the real fight.' But then he acknowledges that 'any weakening of British imperialism ... weakens world capitalism. From this point of view the struggle of the Irish people, however national or patriotic it may be, is a blow struck for workers everywhere.' Which is just as well because in Ireland, 'for the time being, the class struggle is smothered by the urgency of the fight against foreign oppression.' But not for ever, for the article ends with a poetic, if unsubstantiated, piece of revolutionary optimism: 'The loom of history is weaving a fabric in Ireland in which the warp may be nationalism but in which the woof is decidedly of a class-war nature.' Or, if in doubt, hope for the best.

Two final examples well-illustrate the type of opposing and vacillating views which were evident during this discussion. The first was expressed in July 1919:

I urged that Ireland alone could never gain her own freedom, that her Republic depended on the revolt and success of British labour and that therefore the Irish workers ought not to antagonise the soldiers of occupation in Ireland, but should try and win them over to the Irish point of view; further that ... Irish labour should support British labour in the campaign against intervention in Russia, and should be prepared to play its part in the world wide establishment of Bolshevism.[127]

This speech was delivered in Dublin by the Scottish socialist John Maclean and is an example of the Irish being instructed to forget their own national struggle for the wider interests as they happen to be perceived by British socialists. Yet Maclean was well answered a year later. The irony is, the answer came from Maclean himself:

> The Irish situation, obviously, is the most revolutionary that has ever arisen in British history, but unfortunately lads who fancy themselves the only revolutionaries are too stupid or too obsessed with some crochet to see with sufficient clarity the tight corner the Irish are placing the British in. The Irish Sinn Féiners, who make no profession of socialism or communism, are doing more to help Russia and the revolution than all the professed marxian Bolsheviks in Britain.[128]

At least in these two quotations there is an appearance of genuine debate, a thought process in operation, starting with one position and ending up with another. And, yes, here, in the second quote, Maclean does seek to explain why British socialists should have reacted to the Irish revolution with enthusiasm, rather than the political hesitancy and ideological confusion which were the more common characteristics.

8

Ulster

In January 1907, the Labour Party conference was held in Belfast. On its second evening, Keir Hardie, the first Labour MP and the party's father figure, gave a speech to both delegates and his Belfast audience. This was not part of the conference itself, but at a public rally. Accordingly, it was not recorded in the conference minutes, but was reported in the local press. Here is an edited extract, as quoted in the *Northern Whig* of 26 January:

> We are going to make the glens of and hills of Scotland, Ireland and Wales resound with mirth, joy and happiness. We want the Irishman with his warm heart and generous impulse, the Saxon with his common sense and his practical way of looking at things, and the Scotsman with his caution and grip, and the Welshman who was much akin to the Irishmen all bounded together in one great common movement, together with the Frenchman, the Russian, the Spaniard, the Italian and the men and women of all nations. That was the work in which the Labour Party is engaged, godlike work, and putting life on a higher level. In such a work I am sure the people of Belfast and the North of Ireland will join.

These were noble words, and that the vision behind them of international comradeship was so tragically shattered seven years later does not lesson that nobility. But even here, in specifying as he did Belfast and the North of Ireland, there is a suggestion that Hardie is not simply including a local reference to indicate he remembered where he was speaking. Rather, that as far as that part of the world was concerned he was hinting that his sentiments had a particular aspirational relevance.

1885–1916

The emergence of the Ulster question in modern British/Irish politics can be located in the Irish results of the 1885 general election. Although the historical narrative which helped shape the question goes back to the seventeenth century Ulster Plantation, it was the success in the British and Irish 1885 general election of the Irish Home Rule Party under the leadership of Parnell which gave it its modern character. That election in Ireland saw Home Rule candidates winning 85 seats and the Conservatives 18; even in Ulster, the Home Rule movement was successful in 17 out of 33 seats. Nevertheless, the parliamentary eclipse of the Unionists in the south and west of the country, and their relative success in northeast Ulster, ensured that it was there where opposition to Home Rule would be concentrated. Popular feeling against Home Rule in parts of Belfast was exhibited by anti-Catholic rioting in June and, intermittently, from July to September 1886. By the end of the summer 32 people had been killed.

The defeat of the Home Rule Bill by the House of Commons in June 1886 and of another one by the Lords in 1893 meant that the issue of opposition to Irish Home Rule within northeast Ulster went into abeyance for 20 years. That opposition had been clearly demonstrated from 1885 to 1886, although, it can be added, not in the terms in which the 'Ulster question' was to be asked from 1912 to 1921: the possibility of Ulster's separation from the rest of Ireland. No parliamentary attempt was made to exclude Ulster or part of Ulster from the jurisdiction of an Irish parliament in these earlier years, nor did such a suggestion form any part of Unionist propaganda. The first parliamentary appearance of this proposal was in June 1912 with an amendment to the Liberal government's Home Rule Bill, introduced in parliament two months earlier. The amendment was to exclude the four eastern counties of Antrim, Down, Armagh and Londonderry from the jurisdiction of a Home Rule parliament. It came from Liberal back-bencher T. Agar Robert, but was opposed by the government. On its behalf Lloyd George denied that there was any support within the four counties for this proposal and that, in reality, the amendment sought to wreck Home Rule for Ireland as a whole by bestowing on Ulster 'the right to veto autonomy to the rest of Ireland'. As such, said Lloyd George, 'it was an intolerable demand'.[1]

The Irish Unionists' attitude was expressed by their leader, Sir Edward Carson. 'We do not accept this amendment as a compromise', he declared, 'there is no compromise possible.' Yet he voted for the amendment, explaining why by repeating one of his own remarks made to a public meeting in Ulster: 'if Ulster succeeds, Home Rule is dead'.[2] Carson was being consistent in placing his support for Ulster Unionism in the context of his opposition to Home Rule in its entirety. For him, as F. S. L. Lyons has said, 'the maintenance of the Union was, as he called it, "the guiding star of my political life" ... in his strategy the aim of Ulster resistance should not be to secure some special status for the north, rather to make Home Rule impossible for any part of Ireland.'³ Lyons also says that this strategy was not one necessarily shared by those in Ulster, but even there within the Unionist leadership the eventual solution of partition was always a second choice. As the official handbook to the Constitution of Northern Ireland, published by the Northern Ireland government in 1928, puts it the Ulster Unionist Party 'would have preferred that the Act of Union should remain unaltered; but at a time of political crisis they accepted a local constitution as the only means whereby the close connection of Ulster with Great Britain under the Act of Union could be maintained.'⁴

So not only Carson and the southern Irish Unionists but also those in the north saw Ulster as a weapon in a grander political strategy of defeating Home Rule completely. This may explain why Asquith, on behalf of the Liberal government in a speech in the House of Commons on 3 July 1912, maintained that 'the claim of Ulster in this matter is ... but a claim on behalf of a minority, and a comparatively small minority, of the population of Ireland to veto the wishes and frustrate aspirations, of the great mass of the Irish people.' A few weeks earlier Asquith was also saying, 'Ireland is a nation, not two nations',⁵ and this remark also reflects a common view, certainly one held within the British labour movement, as will be shown shortly. Regardless of such ruminations, the Ulster crisis of 1912 to 1914 was no ordinary affair, as we have seen. To elaborate further, there was the Unionist demonstration in Belfast on 9 April 1912 at which the Conservative leader, Andrew Bonar Law, pledged support for Ulster resistance to Home Rule; two days later, the Home Rule bill was introduced in the House of Commons; and soon after that, in July 1912, Protestant shipyard workers in Belfast expelled Catholics working there. Unionist feeling was manifested in September when over 200,000 signed the Ulster Covenant, pledging to use 'all means necessary to defeat the present conspiracy to set up a home rule parliament in Ireland'. The formation of the paramilitary UVF in January 1913 confirmed this intent, as did the announcement in September by Carson that in the event of the Home Rule bill coming into effect a provisional Ulster government would be established. A series of meetings between prime minister Asquith, Bonar Law and Carson followed and in February 1914 Redmond accepted a government proposal that any Ulster county could opt out of Home Rule for three years. Carson and the Ulster Unionists declined this compromise and continued their military-style preparations. The government went ahead with an Amending Bill to its Home Rule proposals, allowing for the temporary opt-out option, a proposal which was itself subject to a proposed amendment from the House of Lords in July to provide for the permanent exclusion of Ulster; a solution that was also put forward at the Buckingham Palace Conference of 21 July. The outbreak of war halted these deliberations and produced a further, temporary compromise: the Government of Ireland Act on the statute book, suspended until the end of war and with the proviso that it would not come into operation until parliament had had an opportunity of making special provision for Ulster, or part thereof, by special amending legislation.

These events laid the groundwork for the partition settlement of 1921. The Ulster Unionists remained determined and consistent in their opposition to Home Rule, with the sectarian attacks on Catholics in the Belfast shipyards and elsewhere in 1920 being the most dramatic illustration of such attitudes. For its part the post-war government of Lloyd George published, in December 1919, its plans for two new Irish parliaments, one for the six northeast counties. The loss of the other three Ulster counties (Donegal, Monaghan, Cavan) was accepted by the Ulster Unionist Council in February 1920, and the same month saw the introduction of the Government of Ireland Bill in the House of Commons, which was finally passed in December. In February 1921, Carson resigned as Unionist leader, citing his age and ill-health, giving way to James Craig who led the Ulster Unionists into a successful general election for the new Northern Ireland parliament in May. This parliament was officially opened by George V on 22 June. The Ulster Unionists accepted the partition of Ireland without enthusiasm, in line with their general attitude of seeing this as second best. This point has been stressed here a number of times because, when considering the degree to which the labour and socialist movement in Britain discussed, was prepared for and understood the dynamics behind the division of Ireland, it is only fair to preface any such evaluation with a recognition that the partition of Ireland was not even promoted by the Ulster Unionists themselves as the desired solution. Neither was it the official policy of the pre-war Conservative Opposition, and, although there were definite moves in the direction of partition by the Asquith government just before the outbreak of the war, it was not until December 1919 that it was officially endorsed by the government. Accordingly, if those directly concerned saw the partition settlement creep up on them, then it would be hardly surprising if the British left was similarly taken by surprise.

Socialists and Ulster before 1916

Necessarily brief and selective as the above outline of the Ulster controversy is, two further points can be emphasised. First, that the opposition to Home Rule in northeast Ulster, while generally restricted to those of the Protestant community, was an all-class alliance. Second, it was a mass movement. Both of these facts could be expected to produce head-scratching by progressive British observers. Home Rule was generally supported, not just by the socialist and labour movement in Britain but also by the Liberals, as a progressive, timely and democratic reform. As an important measure of reform, it was perhaps not surprising that it ran into the opposition of the Conservatives, a majority of the House of Lords and sections of the British Army. However, the events of 1912 to 1921, in Belfast especially, showed clearly that a majority of the working class there was also strongly opposed to the measure. For socialists, the dichotomy of a progressive reform stimulating the passionate and at times violent opposition of the majority of the working class in the industrial capital of the country affected by it raised theoretical problems which merited attention, discussion and explanation.

Such a debate had surfaced as early as September 1905 when, in a by-election in North Belfast, William Walker stood as a candidate for the Labour Representation Committee, and Ramsay MacDonald, as LRC secretary, acted as his agent. During the by-election Walker, a former president of the Irish Trades Union Congress and a former and future executive member of the LRC, stated his own Unionist beliefs. He also made a number of religiously sectarian comments, complaining in an election leaflet of his Unionist opponent, 'it is not Protestantism that Sir Daniel Dixon, defends.'[6] He also gave positive replies to a questionnaire saying he would 'resist' the opening of the offices of Lord Chancellor of England and Lord Lieutenant of Ireland to Catholics, 'contend against' the opening of diplomatic relations with the Vatican, and 'resist every attack upon the legislative enactments provided by our forefathers as necessary safeguards against the encroachment of the Papacy.'[7] In the course of the election and subsequently, MacDonald defended Walker's right to his Unionism because the LRC had no official position on Home Rule. However, he also said, 'I was never more sick of an election than that at North Belfast, and when the religious replies coming at the back of it knocked everything out of me.'[8] At least the whole affair gave MacDonald a first-hand knowledge of Belfast politics, and the controversy Walker's statement attracted within the LRC and the ILP, of which Walker was also a member, gave others some access to that knowledge.

There were similar opportunities to gain a greater understanding of Belfast's political terrain, and the theoretical issues involved for socialists. These included the holding of the Labour Party conference in Belfast in 1907, the debate, at times rather heated, between 1900 and 1912 over whether Irish labour should form its own party or be part of the British Labour Party, and the debate between William Walker and James Connolly in *Forward* in 1911 on the same issue and the more general one of Unionism and labour.[9] Connolly's writings in general, but particularly those on partition, provided another source, especially as many were first published in *Forward* and as such were comparatively easily available to British socialists.[10] The topicality of and interest in those writings could be expected to have increased after Connolly's participation in the Easter Rising and his subsequent execution. This is particularly the case with regard to his views on the partition issue as it has been argued that it was the fear of partition which was one reason why Connolly was in favour of desperate measures in 1916.[11] Connolly also had first-hand experience of Belfast politics and its working class as a union organiser there from 1911 to 1913. This experience informed his interpretation of working class divisions in northeast Ulster and their political consequences. This book will not examine or evaluate these in detail, but it is relevant to summarise them, if for no other reason than to see if they were reproduced within British socialism after Connolly's death. Two quotations from Connolly can be offered as representative. The first was written in *Forward* in August 1913:

If the North-East Corner of Ireland is therefore, the home of a people whose minds are saturated with conceptions of political activity fit only for the atmosphere of the seventeenth century, if the sublime ideas of an all-embracing democracy equally as insistent upon its duties as upon its rights have as yet found poor lodgement here, the fault lies not with this generation of toilers, but with the pastors and masters who deceived it and enslaved it in the past – and deceived it in order that they might enslave it. But as no good can come of blaming it, so also no good, but infinite evil, can come of truckling to it. Let the truth be told, however ugly. Here the Orange working class are slaves in spirit because they have been reared up among a people whose conditions of servitude are more slavish than their own. At one time in the industrial world of Great Britain and Ireland the skilled labourer looked down with contempt upon the unskilled and bitterly resented his attempt to get his children taught any of the skilled trades; the feeling of the Orangemen of Ireland towards the Catholics is but a glorified representation on a big stage of the same passions inspired by the same unworthy motives.[12]

His views on partition were summed up in a paragraph written for the *Irish Worker* in March 1914:

Such a scheme ... the betrayal of the national democracy of industrial Ulster, would mean a carnival of reaction both North and South, would set back the wheels of progress, would destroy the oncoming unity of the Irish labour movement and paralyse all advanced movements whilst it endured. To it Labour should give the bitterest opposition, against it Labour in Ulster should fight even to the death, if necessary, as our fathers fought before us.[13]

These quotations suggest that whatever the merits of Connolly's analysis it was an attempt to look at the issue through socialist eyes. His explanation of the labour aristocracy of northeast Ulster was a materialist one; his reason for opposing partition was based on his fear of a permanently divided working class. This analysis did not go uncontested. The Connolly/Walker debate has already been cited. In this dispute Walker's views have been summarised by the not unsympathetic Henry Patterson as ones which, 'studiously avoided earlier socialist positions on

Ireland.' Walker, says Patterson, 'contented himself with the assertion that Connolly was parochial and blinkered', and that 'Irish nationalism was a narrow and backward looking creed with no place in the strategy of the Irish working class.'[14] Patterson also says that it was not Walker's, but 'Connolly's diagnosis of the Ulster crisis' which, 'became accepted in the Irish labour movement outside Belfast, and by the majority of socialists in Britain',[15] and, at least before the Great War, there is some evidence to support this. For example, on behalf of the Labour Party, Ramsay MacDonald told the House of Commons in March 1913:

> So far as the Labour Party is concerned, we are quite immovable. The first question is: is Ulster to deny the rights of the rest of Ireland to self-government? We say, 'No, emphatically not.' Arising out of that, and a somewhat narrower question is this: is Ulster going to deny the right of Ireland to act as united nationality. We say, 'No, emphatically not.'[16]

MacDonald went on to say that if the parliamentary Irish Nationalists and the Ulster Unionists agreed to allow the temporary exclusion of Ulster from the jurisdiction of a Home Rule parliament Labour, while having 'our opinions about their wisdom or lack of it', would not 'prevent ... an agreement', but the general principle of opposition to permanently dividing Ireland remained. An explanation of why the prospect of such a division had arisen was offered by the PLP in a Commons debate in June 1913. The speaker was James O'Grady, who was another Labour MP who knew Belfast personally, having been a union organiser there for 15 years. For him, 'It is a known fact that during the last ten years in particular the growth of the labour movement in the town of Belfast had done more to bring Catholic and Protestant together to vote upon pure economic issues in political concerns than any other movement that has taken place.' It was this, said O'Grady, that produced 'these honourable members from Ulster' coming together, 'to seek to rend the movement by dividing these men into Protestant and Catholic.'[17] The optimism apparent in O'Grady's remarks concerning working class unity in Belfast, his reliance on what could be interpreted as a conspiracy theory to explain why that unity was threatened and MacDonald's general opposition to partition and his willingness to compromise on the issue were sentiments and opinions which were to re-surface from

1916 onwards. By then the issue had changed slightly. The rise of Sinn Féin and the support for a nationalism which went beyond Home Rule was always liable to increase the opposition to separation within Ulster. The relevant question here is, would it also produce a greater sympathy from those in Britain who, while ridiculing an 'Ulster' separate from a Home Rule parliament, may not so easily dismiss the right of 'Ulster' to opt out of an Ireland seeking a more definitive and final break from everything British?

Partition

George Boyce has argued that 'by the end of the war, the Ulster Unionist case for special treatment was generally accepted in Great Britain',[18] and as evidence he cites the Labour Party's policy of making provision for the rights of minorities in Ireland. Of course this policy was not officially adopted by Labour, through conference decision, until the special conference of December 1920, but it is true, as already described, that similar sentiments had been voiced before then by party leaders. A further example is in April 1919 when J. R. Clynes called for 'a united Ireland governed by the collective will of the people of Ireland, under conditions which would give the amplest and fullest safeguards to those who claim to represent Ulster's interest and rights.'[19] When the second reading of the Government of Ireland Bill was held in March 1920, Clynes repeated this view, saying, 'there should be adequate protection for the Ulster people from any sense of danger to their life, their property or their faith.'[20] At the same time he was strongly against the scheme of partition outlined in the bill, criticising it for being 'founded on a religious basis' which 'recognised neither the historic unity of the province of Ulster, nor of Ireland as a whole'.[21] This was also the position adopted by William Adamson when the third reading of the bill was held in November 1920: opposing partition, but promoting an Irish constitution which 'affords protection to the minority'.[22] Such remarks, and the policy officially adopted at the December 1920 conference, appear to confirm that Labour did endorse 'special treatment for Ulster', or at least for the Protestant minority in Ireland. Even the *Call* in 1917, while strenuously opposing any concession on partition argued:

Objecting as we do to the minority overriding the majority, we on the same grounds do not advocate the steamrolling of a minority ... A minority should have its representation, should be entitled to its voice being heard, its views being considered. This has never been denied to Ulster.[23]

This was not developed in subsequent issues of *Call* or its successor the *Communist*. These few sentences may therefore be assessed as bland guidelines, rather than definite or practical proposals. Certainly, the *Call's* general attitude to partition, as stated in June 1916, was unambiguous:

No sound argument can be advanced for the exclusion of Ulster. To speak of the difference of race is simply to argue for the disintegration of the United Kingdom, and is an example of nationalism gone mad. The fear that religious persecution of Protestants will occur under Home Rule is a bogey created by people for political purposes. The setting up of a free Irish Parliament would be the best possible way of destroying religious and sectarian intolerance. Finally, the absurdity of regarding Ulster as a homogeneous political unit will be recognised when it is remembered that the Nationalist population in that province nearly equals the Unionist.[24]

The arguments employed here will be examined shortly. What is stressed now is the forthright opposition to any partition scheme. It was not an exceptional opinion. Ramsay MacDonald's similar view in March 1913 has already been quoted, and, a couple of weeks after the above *Call* article, George Lansbury's *Herald* was reminding its readers, 'we have always stood out against the complete separation of the six Ulster counties from any scheme of Home Rule.' That was re-affirmed with the argument that such a settlement would be 'on the old lines of political, social and religious ascendancy.'[25]

Labour Leader was more ambiguous, and increasingly so as time went on. The substantial article 'Ireland A Nation', signed by E. D. Morel in May 1917, opposed partition but proposed a series of measures with which 'Ulster should be given a political power comparable to the economic power it wields at present.' What followed was a rare example of detailing of the type of minority safeguards which were called for in general terms within the labour movement both before and after this article appeared.

They included proportional representation in an Irish parliament, 'to secure minority representation', and a guaranteed Protestant majority in an Irish senate or upper house which would have the 'power of veto over any act of the Irish Parliament discriminating unjustly against the economic interests or religious beliefs of N.E. Ulster.' There were also the suggestions that 'N.E. Ulster could be given the right of appeal to the Judicial Committee of the Privy Council' and 'Ulster through her Parliamentary representatives might be even permitted the right of vetoing any particular appointment to an administrative post of which the activities were confined or largely confined to N.E. Ulster.'[26] Morel added that such proposals would 'concede to the prejudice of the powerful Ulster minority' but he did not say what should happen if Irish nationalists were unwilling to offer such concessions. This indeed was an obvious difficulty with the general 'safeguards for minorities' proposal: what if, in either a Home Rule or an independent parliament, no such safeguards were offered? Would this give legitimacy to any attempt of northeast Ulster to opt out? The manner in which *Labour Leader*'s position evolved, when no such concessions were forthcoming from nationalists, suggested, consciously or not, that it did. For while Snowden was still insisting in his column in the newspaper in January 1920 that 'to have two Parliaments in a small country like Ireland' was both an 'affront to national dignity' and 'a practical impossibility';[27] 18 months on, an editorial maintained, 'Everybody now recognises that some special provision will have to be made for N.E. Ulster'.[28] More significantly, the same editorial added, 'the final result may not in appearance be very different from the present Act', which did by then legislate for partition. There was the proviso that 'the constitutional details should be left to be worked out by a free assembly of Irishmen', but three months later this did not prevent *Labour Leader* from suggesting what those details should be:

> The Republicans ought to induce Ulster to a settlement by affirming, first, the retention of all present powers of the Ulster Parliament; secondly, the enlargement of these powers, particularly in financial matters; thirdly, relief from imperial taxation ... in return for recognition of an all-Ireland parliament within the Empire.[29]

This was still not the settlement promoted by the government, but it was coming close. The dynamic was certainly in that direction. What were once safeguards for minorities, then became the right of a parliamentary veto over a whole range of matters, and had now become a separate parliament within a federal Ireland. Snowden's dismissal of two parliaments on grounds of principle and practice had by the summer of 1921 been well overtaken. The argument could be made that it was also overtaken by events, for by the time the federal Ireland solution was being proposed, the Northern Ireland parliament was already in existence. Other realities may also have informed *Labour Leader*'s evolution. The anti-Catholic sectarian violence in Belfast in the summer of 1920 brought the comment, 'we would vain hope that these appalling happenings ... are merely the temporary outburst of fanaticism, but there is, unfortunately, little ground for such hope as that.'[30] If the Unionists' 'fanaticism' was indeed assumed to be more deep-seated than a 'temporary outburst', then it is hardly surprising that those making this assumption felt it necessary to put forward solutions which could contain that extremism. *Labour Leader*'s evolution had its Scottish counterpart in *Forward*. In July 1917 it denounced partition as an attempt to 'make two Irelands stand where only one stood before',[31] but four years later it had decided that 'we must make allowances' for 'the objection of Sinn Féin' by 'Ulstermen'.[32]

Other British socialists had arrived earlier at such conclusions, in particular the *New Statesman*. Although in June 1916 it was saying that a divided Ireland would be 'a great misfortune',[33] by January 1918, while observing that Ireland was 'irrevocably opposed to schemes of partition, temporary or otherwise', it added, in parenthesis, 'more's the pity perhaps'.[34] Three months later it was still the journal's view that partition was not 'practical politics',[35] and even by July 1919 it argued that while partition was 'an obvious solution' it would be 'very unpopular' in Ireland.[36] On the other hand, these judgements were accompanied by one which said that 'to use British troops to coerce a British population', by which it meant the population of Ulster, was also 'not practical politics'.

This description of the Protestants of Ulster as 'British' was not one that was pulled out of the air. 'Ireland is not one nation but two', the same article maintained, and, 'Belfast is as British as Manchester.' Accordingly, 'the bitter opposition between North and South is real and is, in existing circumstances, irremovable.' By the time of the establishment of the Northern Ireland parliament, circumstances had allowed the *New Statesman* to consolidate its theoretical explanation for partition while no longer needing to question its practicality. The comment in July 1921 was:

> Partition is no longer a policy, but a fact; and the continued refusal of Sinn Féin to recognise that fact is the most serious of the remaining obstacles to settlement ... Ireland is not one nation but two; and so it will remain until the South had learned to come to terms with the North without outside help.[37]

The view that Ireland was two nations, not one, was asserted rather than explained in depth. Curiously, although this is a theoretical contention which was to re-emerge 50 years later and attract considerable support,[38] it was not one that was heard much in this period, either from the Unionists or their British supporters. But elsewhere than the *New Statesman*, other Fabians suggested additional arguments for partition. In Bernard Shaw's pamphlet, *Irish Nationalism and Labour Internationalism*, published by the Labour Party in 1920, he argued that it 'might easily become an abusive name for quite beneficial measures of de-centralization and local autonomy',[39] although he made this recommendation in the context of a possible federal Ireland. It is also the case that although Shaw's pamphlet was in the name of Labour, others in the party were saying the opposite on partition. J. R. Clynes, who wrote the introduction for the pamphlet, two months earlier told the Commons:

> My colleagues for whom I am speaking wish me to say that we oppose this scheme of self-government because it provides a form of partition founded on a religious basis and recognises neither the historic unity of the province of Ulster nor of Ireland as a whole.[40]

Thus, the Labour Party until the signing of the Treaty was, as with the Communist Party, opposed to the division of Ireland. However, in the political spectrum between these two parties there were moves being made towards partition by the ILP and Fabian Society. To return to a point made earlier, the evolution of both these organisations in that direction would seem to owe more to their perception of political practicality and reality than an increased sympathy for Unionists in response to the rise of Sinn Féin. What was definitely the case was that, overall, by mid-1921 there was no unanimity on the matter within the working class movement. Was this, it can now be asked, connected with the level of comprehension of the issue?

Explanations

An implication behind the positions of Shaw and the *New Statesman*, and behind *Labour Leader*'s consideration of some form of partition, was that this was practical politics, especially after the Northern Ireland parliament had been established. There was little socialist theory in these arguments, or political theory of any sort, apart from the under-developed 'two nations' contention. Nevertheless, there was little doubt that divisions did exist in Ireland on self-determination and that those divisions were acute among sections of the northern working class. Accordingly, it is appropriate to enquire into the extent of socialist explanations which were offered as to those divisions and into the more general arguments employed against partition. A number have already been noted. In particular there was James O'Grady's assertion that the divide and rule tactics of 'honourable members from Ulster' were responsible, a view also put forward in the *Call*'s article quoted above when it complained that religious sectarianism had been 'whipped up' by 'people for political purposes'. That same article made the further point that Ulster was not a homogeneous political unit. Both these arguments were employed elsewhere. When Philip Snowden maintained in January 1918 that 'the opposition of Belfast to Home Rule is at bottom economic', he elaborated: 'So long as the Belfast capitalists can keep the Home Rule question to the front they can prevent the workers from uniting on economic issues.'[41] *Workers' Dreadnought* was well to the left of Snowden, but it shared the opinion that 'Carson and his lieutenants are making use of the religious weapon to smash trade unionism in Belfast'.[42] Robert Smillie too, speaking at the 1919 TUC, made accusations concerning the use to which religion had been put, saying that 'the capitalist has induced his victims in the north of the island to keep their eyes steadily on their chances of going to heaven after death, and while their attention was engrossed in that way, he has exploited them to his heart's content.'[43] The fullest exposition of this argument was found in a long article written by T. A. Jackson in the *Communist* in November 1921, part of which read:

The plain truth of the matter is that the 'Die-Hard' element – the ultra-'Orange' party – [is] indignant at the prospect of losing their 'right' to act as dictators of the destiny of Ireland ... It is not a question of religion, Protestant or any other, for the Carsonite crowd care as much about religion as I do about the psychology of the ichthysaurus. The whole point of the 'Ulster' agitation is the determination of an inner political clique never to 'surrender' to anything in the nature of a successful rebellion of the 'lower orders', and, quite incidentally, to keep in the hands of the clique whatever pickings there are to be obtained from the political body of Ireland. The Ulster bourgeoisie are taking no risks. They know their own proletariat and with what difficulty it has so far been held in mental bondage.[44]

Jackson's later book, *Ireland Her Own*, was Marxist in method and strongly influenced by Connolly's writings,[45] and whether or not he was aware of Connolly's analysis of the Ulster question when he wrote the above, there are certain strong similarities in interpretation, even in phraseology. For example Connolly saw the Protestant working class as 'slaves in spirit' (see above); Jackson said they were held in 'mental bondage.' Connolly's influence is also suggested in an article by G. B. Clark in *Forward* in September 1917 which spoke of the Ulster Protestants' origins as a 'privileged class' displaying a 'dislike and contempt for the "mere Irish".'[46]

Another more practical objection to partition, and one already noted, was to point out that Ulster was not reducible to its Protestant community. It was, said *Forward* in October 1919 a 'specious argument ... that self-determination must be applied to the Orange counties' because of the presence within it of 'counties, towns and villages' with Catholic majorities.[47] Even *Labour Leader*, at the time it was moving towards endorsement of some form of partition, was noting that 'Ulster's whole case rests upon an alleged homogeneity of the population which does not exist'.[48] This point was also made by *Labour Leader*'s Irish correspondent, Patrick Thompson, three years earlier when he said that Unionists, 'are in a decided minority of the whole population' of Ulster, and a minority, 'that cannot anywhere, even in scattered patches of territory claim that it has an incontestable case for a government distinct from the surrounding people'.[49] Another example of use of this observation came after the Irish municipal election results in January 1920 in which, as *Workers'*

Dreadnought noted, in nine county Ulster 'we have the important fact brought out that the supporters of Unionism are in a minority.'[50] The obvious flaw in this argument was that by then the concept of a six county Ulster was being promoted, and within those boundaries Unionism did have a majority. However, it is debatable whether that invalidates the general objection made in the article that, 'Ulster's alleged opposition to Irish independence is used as the principle argument for maintaining the Union'.

As already noted this was indeed Carson's motivation in seizing on the Ulster issue, and the whole controversy of his role in the Ulster agitation was another recurring theme in the labour press. Even those such as Snowden who were usually moderate in their language seemed to lose control at the thought of Sir Edward. He was, said Snowden in July 1919, 'the embodiment of the stupidity, the arrogance and the hopelessness of Ulster Unionism', and an 'ignorant, irreconcilable, fanatical demagogue.'[51] Not only that, the previous year when Carson resigned from the War Cabinet, Snowden maintained, 'his presence has been an insult to the intelligence of the nation', and had illustrated 'his proved incapacity for any position of responsibility'.[52] There was more in the same vein from different sources. When Carson was appointed to the Cabinet, the *Call* complained that it was 'an outrage on all democratic feeling that the man who was prepared to lead an insurrection of Ulster against the Crown ... should be so honoured'.[53] This view was a reminder of the role Carson had played in the pre-war Ulster crisis, but for a communist newspaper to object to someone leading 'an insurrection against the Crown' does seem rather out of character. Similarly, when the same newspaper fumed against 'the traitor Carson' in April 1918,[54] just what, it can be wondered, were the Marxists objecting to Carson being a traitor against? The Crown? The bourgeois parliament?

Such language may be nothing more than journalist colouring, but those who sought to blame Carson for the Ulster resistance to Home Rule, who insisted as Snowden did, that 'Sir Edward Carson has been the stumbling block in the way of the settlement of the Irish question',[55] could be accused of scapegoat politics: avoiding the problems to socialist theory of an apparently reactionary working class in the northeast of Ireland by putting it all down to the presence and behaviour of one individual. There were those who pointed an accusing finger wider. It was, said *Workers' Dreadnought*, 'Downing Street, Dublin Castle and Carsonism' which were attempting to, 'invoke religious hatred, as a last resort, to maintain Imperial Capitalism in Ireland',[56] and this was another common theme. The charge was that the working class divisions derived from past and present actions of British governments and British capitalism in Ireland. The *New Statesman* expressed the opinion in January 1919 that, 'the greatest obstacle in the past has always been, not that Ulster stood in the way of settlement, but that British statesmen encouraged Ulster to stand in the way.'[57] *Labour Leader* maintained in 1917, 'the problem of dealing with Ulster is the problem of dealing with the irreconcilable section of English Toryism'.[58] The *Communist* insisted in 1920, 'for the present condition of things the British ruling class is clearly responsible.'[59] Again, such judgements were more asserted than argued through, but they did suggest a conclusion that if Britain left Ireland the problem would, in time, disappear. Such was the prediction of *Labour Leader* in July 1921 when it said that 'if England withdraws her support' for the Ulster Unionists, 'and makes it plain that she will insist on common decency and justice on their part', then 'their rancour will die down, slowly perhaps, but let us hope, surely.'[60]

Such optimism, in whatever circumstance it is expressed, is a common characteristic of socialists, and even as worker attacked worker in Belfast there were still those prepared to give reassurance. There was *Labour Leader* in June 1921:

> On, the surface, the present political partition of Ulster from the rest of Ireland may seem an unmitigated evil ... There is a grain of socialist hope, for the men in control of the Ulster legislature are of the capitalist class, and when the workers who sent them there see their representatives at work they may at last learn that their lives and welfare are more in jeopardy from an employer in Belfast than from a Pope who sits in Rome.[61]

The *New Statesman* had another reason for optimism when accepting the possibility of partition in June 1916: 'if Home Rule proves to be the blessing which Home Rulers believe it will be, the conversion of Ulster is only a matter of time.'[62] Such thinking was very far away from that of James Connolly's prediction of 'a carnival of reaction' as a consequence of partition, but Marxists too were not free from rosy predictions. The Second Congress of Communist International was informed by an Irish representative in July 1920 that 'religious antagonisms' in northeast Ulster were 'steadily declining', and that 'in many respects the problems of the Communists are here much easier, it being possible to rally the proletariat to their banner on the straight issue of the capitalists state versus the proletariat state', and that, 'the lack of any nationalist or Republican feeling on the part of the proletariat renders them hostile to the establishment of an Irish bourgeois Republic'.[63] As to the appeal of Orange ideology, even when it appeared to be dominant among Protestant workers there were those who promised a different reality was around the corner. The *Socialist* assured its readers in July 1919:

> People say that July 12, 1919, was one of the best Orange demonstrations ever seen. We feel confident that July 12, 1920, will be a farce by comparison, because by then, even the unthinking will be wondering wherein lies the gain for them and they will be struggling out of party and into class issues.[64]

But perhaps the most naive and optimistic of all comments is located in William Paul's CPGB pamphlet, already mentioned. This does have some echoes of Connolly with the analysis that, 'the propertied interests have used religion as a political factor in blinding the [Protestant] working class; and they have used it to create a psychology which finds expression in reaction, in violence towards opponents [and] a blind bigotry', but then comes the politics of fantasy:

> The peculiar psychology of Orangeism ... with its fierce and violent hatred against its enemies will be easily diverted against a capitalist class during a revolutionary crisis. It was Carson who taught them how to arm against the *status quo*. It was Carson who showed them how flimsy were the specious prate about 'law and order' and 'constitution' ... When the workers move against Capitalism, the revolutionary movement of Ulster will have good reason for thanking Carson for his magnificent work.[65]

Paul, it should be remembered was writing in the wake of anti-Catholic pogroms, inspired at least in part by Carson's 'magnificent work'. Equally naive, not to say silly, was the assurance of the *Communist* in October 1921 that, 'the class consciousness of the Ulster working class is developing', because 'the circulation of the *Communist* is six times as high in Belfast as it is in Dublin.'[66] Similarly, but five years before, an article by William Stewart in *Forward* promised the impending triumph if the ILP:

> When the I.L.P. apostles who are to follow me, reach Belfast, they will find receptive audiences. They will meet with no disturbances from Orange drums or rival sectarian zealots. For though the old dividing faiths are doubtless still in existence, they are not so strong in evidence as in former years. A new uniting faith is beginning to intervene, the socialist faith.[67]

Four years later such optimism was still apparent, but it was accompanied by an analysis of Orangeism which, in a quite remarkable passage by William Regan in his 'Catholic Socialist Notes' column seemed to overturn everything all on the left had ever said on the topic:

> Large numbers of Orangemen in the North of Ireland are joining the Socialist movement. This is not surprising ... the truth is that even in religious matters he [the Orangeman] is not really as bigoted as many advanced people who claim to be neutral in religion and superior in all such petty prejudices. The Twelfth of July is often but a great tribal gala day in which he shies missiles at the Pope in the same innocent way as other men upset dollies on a showground ... The Orangemen dreads Home Rule because he fears it will result in clerical rule, reaction, and inefficiency ... in the shipyards of the North he is an excellent Trade Unionist and in industrial matters displays a sense of class solidarity.[68]

While Paul wrote after the anti-Catholic pogrom, in Regan's case they were a few weeks away, an outbreak which was, to be fair, described very fully by *Forward*.[69] If those events didn't finally shatter Regan's illusions then one a few months later surely did when his newspaper reported how 'the Orange crowd' had burned down the ILP hall in Belfast.[70] Given Regan's sustained campaign against Sinn Féin, already described, the passage quoted above may not be that surprising, and its relevance will be assessed in the final chapter of this study, but it certainly testifies to a considerable degree of either prejudice or ignorance of Belfast's working class realities. When trying to deal with those realities there were those

who could only react with a rather patronizing variant of despair. *Workers'*
Dreadnought in October 1920 advised: 'Ireland should learn from East
London to settle her religious differences by walking over them to unity
against foreign imperialism.'[71]

In contrast to both the false analogy from *Workers' Dreadnought* and
the false optimism of *Forward* and Paul, the following, from J. R. Clynes
in March 1920 is much more sober and even reminiscent of Connolly's
prophesy of 'a carnival of reaction' partition promised: 'Two parliaments,
in the judgement of those for whom I speak, would inevitably create rival
and separate interests, delaying, rather than hastening the period ... when
there shall be one parliament speaking for Ireland.'[72]

This statement, by itself, does not prove that Clynes had a more
Connollyite view of partition than either *Forward*, for which Connolly
used to write, or *Workers' Dreadnought*, for which his daughter wrote. A
more accurate test would come with reactions to the Treaty and its partition
clauses. What can be assessed now is the degree to which the working
class movement was prepared for these developments. Conclusions on
this are informed by the statements and paragraphs reproduced above.
Not only are they representative, but the articles or speeches from
which they are extracted make up the vast bulk of writings or statements
from the sources quoted which appeared in these five and a half years.
They do not amount to a great deal either in quantity, consistency or
theoretical clarity. There was no Fabian pamphlet on the Ulster question,
there was no article in the ILP's more theoretical *Socialist Review*. The
only really substantial articles were those written by T. A. Jackson, one,
already quoted, in the *Communist* of 26 November 1921 and Connollyist,
consciously or not; and the other in the same newspaper on 3 December
1921, entitled 'The Red Hand', which was mainly historical, dealing with
the role Ulster Protestants in particular had played in progressive Irish
national movements in the eighteenth and nineteenth centuries. This too,
it could be, profited from Connolly's similar observations recorded in his
Labour and Irish History. What is perhaps most surprising, to return to an
issue poised at the start of this chapter, is that apart from Jackson there is
little evidence of a knowledge of Connolly's writings on northeast Ulster
and the working class divisions. For however these writings are assessed
overall, they were a thorough-going socialist and materialist explanation
of the subject. Given the fame which Connolly's execution bestowed on
him, and the role of martyr he subsequently acquired among some British

socialists, it is interesting that none of his writings on the Ulster question and partition were reproduced by the socialist press in Britain. Neither did William Walker's views appear to permeate through, or be taken up by any section of the labour and socialist movement, with the possible exception of the William Regan article quoted above. If there was next to no awareness of the views of Irish socialists on what was both a complex and important issue a rather narrow, insular world of British socialism is suggested. On the other hand, there was a willingness to blame British governments and Britain's general and historical role in Ireland for the subsequent divisions in the country. In this respect at least the British working class movement did not appear too affected by the national self-identification, not to say jingoism, engendered by the war: there is little evidence of sympathy with the proclaimed Britishness of the Protestants. The exception to this is, of course, the TUC's handling of the Catholic expulsions in the summer of 1920, already detailed.

More generally, while it is true that the question of Ulster and the subsequent partition of Ireland caught many in Britain by surprise, socialists did have the benefit of Connolly's warnings, the personal experiences of MacDonald and O'Grady and the particular relevance for a labour movement of a divided working class to merit their attention and aid their understanding. Perhaps it was that very division and the difficulties for socialist theory it produced which persuaded many to give less attention to the question than it deserved. The comparative lack of coverage of Ulster, the tendency to scapegoat Carson, the occasional rather crude relapse into conspiracy theories, and the deterministic optimism that 'class' questions and workers unity were just around the corner were all examples of a theoretical laziness which declined to confront reality. In itself this can go a long way towards explaining why positions could change in the manner they did within the ILP, and why positions long-held within the Labour Party of outright opposition to partition were, when the crunch came, susceptible to being overturned. The shallowness of their intellectual foundations always made that possible.

9
The Treaty

George Barnes had come a long way when he rose, 'in morning dress' so Hansard recorded, in the House of Commons on 14 December 1921, 'to play a small part in the proceedings of this day which I venture to predict will become memorable in our annals.' Born in 1859 in Dundee, he had trained as an engineer in London and Dundee, worked at his trade in Barrow and London, and became an active member of the Amalgamated Society of Engineers of which he became general secretary. He was a founder member of the ILP and successfully stood as a Labour candidate in a Glasgow constituency in the general election of 1906. He became chairman of the Labour Party, in effect its leader from February 1910 to February 1911. Barnes joined Lloyd George's coalition, on behalf of Labour in 1916, but when Labour left the coalition at the end of the war he refused to go with them, standing as a Labour Coalition candidate in 1918 in Glasgow Gorbals. He defeated the official Labour candidate, John Maclean. Thus, on that day in December 1921 he had enough experience behind him to appreciate the importance of the occasion, and indeed acknowledged as such, saying, 'We are called upon to-day to do our part towards ending an age-long controversy which has embittered and poisoned the political life and relations of two countries.' He was speaking on the proposals for peace which had just been agreed between his government and Irish negotiators. For him, the historical and political relevance was that, 'Irishmen have been misunderstood by us and we have been continually misunderstood by Irishmen. Ireland has remained an enigma, a weakness and a menace.' Despite which, he maintained, 'They are not only with us but they are of us, because their blood is commingled with our blood, and in these days they are part of the British stock and we to a large extent are part of them.'

He noted that the peace terms would 'leave Ulster free to remain out if she wishes to remain out, but free also to come in.' He claimed, 'this agreement is endorsed by all the political parties.' And indeed, that 'The Labour party, which has always stood for Home Rule for Ireland, has claimed it as its own.' When he also said that really the agreement reflected the manifesto on which he had stood on behalf of the Coalition in 1918, honourable Members were recorded as shouting, 'No'. So he quoted this manifesto's promise 'to explore every possible avenue of peace with Ireland on the basis of self-government, with two reservations only, those being the non-separation of Ireland and the non-coercion of Ulster.'

The peace agreement had indeed stuck by the Ulster pledge. Barnes then went on to deal with the 'separation' issue and recalled that Abraham Lincoln, during the American Civil War, had defeated attempts to separate his country. Barnes continued that the British/Irish peace meant 'Neither can there be separation between this country and Ireland. Let all of us banish it from our minds.'[1]

Negotiations and Terms

A truce in the War of Independence came into operation on 11 July, 1921. It followed a plea for peace from George V, when opening the Northern Ireland Parliament on 22 June, and a letter to de Valera from Lloyd George the following day asking him to come to a conference in London to discuss a settlement. On 14 July, the two had the first of four meetings. During these discussions, the initial negotiating position of the British was laid on the table. Lloyd George offered a dominion status, qualified by: a limitation on the size of the Irish army; no Irish navy; recruitment facilities in Ireland for the British forces; air and naval facilities in Ireland for the British; a contribution by Ireland to the British war debt; the preservation of free trade between the two islands; and recognition of the Northern Parliament. Dominion status involved Ireland staying within the British Empire/Commonwealth and Irish parliamentarians swearing an oath of allegiance to the British monarch. This offer was discussed and rejected by first the Irish Cabinet then the Dáil. In neither, writes Frank Pakenham, later Lord Longford, in what is still the fullest account of the negotiations, 'does a single voice seem to have been raised in favour of acceptance.'[2]

The Irish proposals, as they emerged over the next few weeks centred on the concept of 'external association' with the Commonwealth. By this, Ireland would not be a dominion or a member of the Commonwealth but 'associated' with it; there would be no allegiance to the Crown;

the Irish would not be British subjects but there would be 'reciprocal citizenship'. On the details of what the 'association' would entail, this would include 'matters of common concern', in particular defence, peace and war. On Ulster there was the offer of unspecified autonomy within a united Ireland.

Even before serious negotiations opened de Valera had made it clear that, as he told the Dáil in the debate on the rejection of Britain's initial terms, 'we are not Republican doctrinaires.'[3] The negotiations began in earnest in London on 11 October. De Valera, whom the Dáil had just elected President of the Irish Republic, declined to participate. His reasons have been much debated ever since but they probably included a proviso that before signing anything the Irish negotiators refer back to Dublin. Those negotiators were Arthur Griffith, Michael Collins, Robert Barton, E. J. Duggan and Gavan Duffy. Griffith was second only to de Valera in the Irish government and was Minister of Foreign Affairs in the Irish Cabinet. Collins, the head of the IRA, was Finance Minister. They constituted the leadership of the delegation, the more Republican minded members of the Irish Cabinet, Austin Stack and Cathal Brugha, like de Valera, refused to go. The British negotiating team was headed by Lloyd George and included Winston Churchill, Austen Chamberlain and Lord Birkenhead. The agreed basis for the discussions which followed was, 'with a view to ascertaining how the association of Ireland with the community of nations known as the British Empire may best be reconciled with Irish national aspirations.'

The negotiations lasted until 6 December 1921. It is not necessary to go into the details here; they were held in secret, so the full story behind them did not emerge for some time. There were hints and leaks at the time as to what was on offer from the British, but fully informed contemporary reaction to the final terms could only focus on their outcome, not on how that outcome had been achieved. There was, however, one significant exception to this, for when the Treaty was debated publicly in the Irish Dáil from 14 December it was soon reported that Lloyd George had threatened 'war within three days' if the Irish delegates did not immediately sign the treaty once the negotiations had come to a halt. After which the Irish, without reference to Dublin, signed. The Treaty was more like Lloyd George's original offer than de Valera's counter-position. It conferred dominion status on the Irish Free State, formally equivalent to that of Canada but with important and limiting differences:

Ireland's coastal defences were to be undertaken by the British until an alternative 'arrangement' was made; harbour facilities at three southern Irish ports were to be retained by the British navy and, 'in time of war or of strained relations with a Foreign Power' there would be 'such harbour and other facilities as the British government may require.' Also, the Irish army was, in proportion to the two states' populations, to be no larger than that of the Britain. The Irish negotiators agreed to an oath of allegiance to the Crown after some final concessions from the British on its wording. The oath began with swearing allegiance to the constitution of the Irish Free State after which came the promise to be 'faithful' to the Crown, 'in virtue of the common citizenship of Ireland with Great Britain and her adherence to and membership of the group of nations forming the British Commonwealth of Nations.' Agreement on the Ulster question was secured by giving the Northern Ireland parliament the right to reject inclusion in the Free State and by appointing a boundary commission 'to determine in accordance with the wishes of the inhabitants so far as may be compatible with economic and geographic conditions, the boundaries between Northern Ireland and the rest of Ireland.' There was also a reaffirmation of the establishment of Council of Ireland, as legislated for in the Government of Ireland Act 1920. Ireland was to have fiscal autonomy and both the southern and northern parliaments were prohibited from passing laws which discriminated on the basis of religion.[4] The Treaty was denounced by de Valera, but his cabinet voted four to three in favour. The debate in the Dáil, which lasted until 7 January 1922 produced a 64 to 57 vote in favour. The Dáil also elected Arthur Griffith the new president of the 'Free State'.

The key debates in the Cabinet and in the Dáil centred on the oath of allegiance to the Crown and the assumed continued British presence in the Free State that this entailed. The Ulster issue did not feature highly, mainly because, as historian Joseph Lee has put it, 'de Valera, like Griffith and Collins, assumed that the Boundary Commission would so emasculate Northern Ireland that the rump would be forced into a united Ireland for economic self-preservation'.[5] That assumption stemmed from an unofficial assurance in this vein that was given to the Irish by Lloyd George. In the event, in December 1925 the Boundary Commission broke up in disagreement and the British and Irish Free State governments agreed that the border would stay where it was. The Council of Ireland never met. In the meantime, a civil war had been fought in the south over the treaty with the anti-Treaty forces, led by de Valera, finally accepting defeat in May 1923. He was to be voted into office in a general election nine years later. Thus, the Treaty did not end the Anglo-Irish controversy; it merely recreated it in new forms, as well as creating deep divisions within the southern Irish population. Again, a detailed historical judgement on the Treaty is not necessary here, although a summing-up by the major historian of the negotiations is relevant. Pakenham wrote in 1935:

> The aspirations of Ireland were not satisfied by the Treaty. The pro-Treaty Party might argue that they ought to have been satisfied. The fact remains – they were not. Ireland ... continued to be denied what a large part of the population persisted in regarding as essential to independence, and what certainly no independent nation, England for example, would dream of surrendering except under overwhelming force.[6]

The opinion of Lloyd George, although it was no doubt influenced by self-aggrandisement, was that 6 December 1921 was 'the greatest day in the history of the British Empire.'[7]

Reactions in Britain

Lloyd George told the House of Commons on 14 December, 'No agreement ever arrived at between two peoples has been received with so enthusiastic and so universal a welcome.' If there was an element of exaggeration in this claim, there was certainly little evidence at the time of dissenting voices in opinion-makers in British society. The only significant newspaper criticism came from the right, with the *Morning Post* refusing to join in what it called, 'the finely orchestrated chorus which greets the alleged settlement in Ireland', and complaining that it represented, 'an abandonment and betrayal of British powers and British friends in Ireland.'[8] A more typical reaction was that of *The Times*, which said that 'reason has prevailed' and foresaw 'the close of an age of discontent and distrust, and the beginning of a new era of happiness and mutual understanding.'[9] In evaluating such reactions it is important to bear in mind that just before the signing of the Treaty, press reports were pessimistic about the chance of agreement. On 5 December the *Daily Telegraph* reported that the 'outlook' was 'very grave'; the *Daily Chronicle* also spoke of the 'Grave Irish Outlook'; the *Daily Herald* reported a 'Dark Outlook'; and the *Daily Express* even had the headline, 'Irish Conference Fails'. Thus, when peace broke out, literally overnight, it would not be surprising if an enormous sense of collective relief produced over-optimism. Certainly, there was no suggestion in the immediate British reactions that there would be bitter opposition to the Treaty among many in the 'Irish Free State'. And yet, it can be wondered, why should there not have been? For the *Daily Herald* of 6 December when reporting with some accuracy what was on offer from the British declared, 'The Irish people will never agree to these terms. They stand for freedom and friendship; the British government stands for forced allegiance and truckling to the Ulster capitalists.'

Included in the Irish people were the Irish in Britain, and before examining the reaction of the *Daily Herald* and other organisations and individuals within the labour movement to the Treaty, or Articles of Agreement as it was formally called, it is useful to note the views of those of the Irish in Britain who had been campaigning strongly against British policy in Ireland. A comparative context will thereby be set for an analysis of labour movement reactions. The major newspaper of the Irish in Britain, the *Catholic Herald*, under the editorship of the former and future Labour Party candidate Charles Diamond welcomed the Treaty. 'The uppermost feeling in our minds must be one of gladness and satisfaction that we have lived to see this day', was an editorial comment. It was acknowledged that 'It may be said that Ireland has not got what she wanted' but 'if the Republic has not come, nor unity, that latter can only be a matter of time.'[10] A contrasting opinion was expressed in *Irish Exile*, the recently established newspaper of the ISDL. Its front page comment came in the form of a letter from Art O'Brien, secretary of the ISDL. This was headlined with a quotation from Charles Parnell, 'No man has the right to fix the boundary of the march of a nation', with the sub-title, 'The Treaty Agreement Between Great Britain and Ireland. A Word of Counsel to the Irish in Britain.' O'Brien warned, 'Be not misled into rejoicing and thanksgiving' and he continued:

> If, under the threat or renewed and intensified warfare and as an alternative to seeing their country ravished ... five Irishmen have been compelled to sign their names to the document ... that is not the cause

for us to rejoice ... The document ... is but another milestone on the long road of struggle to Irish freedom. It is not the goal ... The English people have cause to rejoice ... they have won another round.[11]

A fierce polemical battle between Diamond and O'Brien ensued, both in the pages of their respective newspapers and within the ISDL itself, with O'Brien's anti-Treaty position eventually emerging victorious at the annual conference of the ISDL in July 1922. In short, Irish people in Britain, as in their homeland, were divided over the Treaty, but the official position of the largest Irish organisation in Britain was at first critical of and then opposed. Thus, from very early on an alternative view to the chorus of praise within Britain which greeted the Treaty was available for those who wanted to listen.

Labour's Welcome

First reactions to the signing of the Treaty from the Labour Party were in interviews with J. R. Clynes and Arthur Henderson in the *Daily Herald* the day after the Treaty was signed. Clynes indicated support, but was cautious. 'It has been clear from the beginning of the negotiations that the settlement would finally have to be signed on the basis of concessions from both sides', he said. He went on to argue that the issues involved 'could not be considered on any rigid lines of logic or even on the basis of absolute reason', and that 'the mutual interests of the two countries and the special position of the minority in the North of Ireland all required a measure of give and take.' He concluded, 'Even if the settlement cannot be viewed as perfect, the settlement which will suffice is that accepted by the vast majority of Irish opinion.'[12] Henderson was much more enthusiastic. 'The whole of the British Labour movement will welcome the news of the settlement, not only with joy but with great satisfaction', he said. He also claimed that Labour Party policy, 'step by step', had 'been put into operation' by the government, 'until it reached the terminating point when an agreement was reached.' There was similar wording in the statement agreed by the NEC of the Labour Party and the General Council of the TUC the day after the Treaty was signed. Again there was the expression of 'the deepest satisfaction' concerning the outcome of the negotiations and the claim that it was Labour Party policy which had now been adopted:

The Labour Movement has constantly striven for an Irish settlement in harmony with the aspirations of the Irish people, and the Labour Party's Commission, which visited Ireland during the dark days of open strife, laid down the procedure which was, step by step, adopted, and which culminated in the present agreement. They therefore view with special satisfaction the successful termination of the negotiations.[13]

These sentiments were echoed in most of the comments from other prominent Labour Party figures. Ramsay MacDonald said he was 'glad of any settlement with which the representatives of the Irish people concur' and that 'the agreement has removed a crushing load from the minds of the nation, vindicated the policy of the Labour Party, and condemns all that has happened up to a few weeks ago.'[14] Another who claimed credit for the Labour Party was R. J. Davies, MP: 'British Labour will emerge from this terrible conflict with clean hands', he said, while adding, 'every sane person hopes that at long last we shall see a final settlement of the Irish problem.' Labour MP Jack Mills foresaw that 'there will be die-hards on both sides', but 'in spite of them it is a great step towards Irish freedom.' The left wing Labour MP Neil Maclean was more critical. He pointed out that 'the terms of settlement do not give the Republican form of government which many of the Irish people desire', but added, 'with that exception, however, they have become masters of their own house.' The most detailed comment on behalf of the Labour Party came in the course of the debate in the House of Commons on the Treaty. Clynes and Henderson spoke for the party. By then, Clynes had dropped his initial caution and declared the Treaty 'a victory for enduring national spirit over every obstacle and every form of force which that spirit has had to encounter for centuries.' He repeated the by now familiar claim that the Treaty terms 'travel on the lines advocated by Labour' and that accordingly, 'on the whole history of this Irish problem, and especially in relation to the stage which has now been reached, the conscience of the Labour Party is clear.' He went on to describe the Treaty as an 'instrument of a lasting and beneficent settlement' and an 'act of justice'. In summing up the party attitude he declared: 'I say, therefore, that the Labour Party rejoices with the rest of those who, either in this House or in the country welcome this Agreement. We are eager to approve it, and are convinced that it has the support of the vast majority of the Irish people.'[15]

Clynes spoke on the first day of the debate in parliament. By then, de Valera's opposition to the Treaty had been announced and explained, but by the third day of the Commons debate when Henderson spoke, the debate in Dáil had begun to display just how deep the divisions in Ireland were. Indeed, Henderson acknowledged as much when he spoke of 'the splendid courage and sincerity of those Irish plenipotentiaries who, knowing the risk they were taking – and they must have known the risk – were prepared to add their signatures to the Treaty.' It was also the appearance of divisions in Ireland which Henderson had in mind when he told the Commons, 'If it ever was incumbent upon the House to rise above the ordinary standard of party politics ... it is at a time like the present', because, he said, 'we all must recognise ... issues hanging in the balance which ... affect the vital interests of our people at home and of the British commonwealth of nations.' Thus, although the Labour Party, he explained, 'could have raised objections to this or that provision of the Treaty', for him 'any sort of criticism at this moment would not only be unhelpful but unfriendly.'

This was a 'don't rock the boat' philosophy: the need for the parties in Britain to preserve a united front on the Treaty in face of significant opposition to it in Ireland; and to say nothing critical of it which might encourage that opposition. As Henderson said, Britain's, 'vital interests' were at stake. At the end of his speech he recalled that, during the debate in the Commons on 31 October 1921, already detailed here, he had said that Labour would judge the outcome of the negotiations then underway on three counts: whether it 'satisfied the majority of the Irish people'; whether there was 'some form of protection' for the Protestant minority in Ireland; and 'from the standpoint of the security of our own country.' He now concluded that 'we can safely examine the Treaty from the standpoints of Nos. 2 and 3', but 'We have yet to find out ... if the Treaty is to secure the approval of the majority of the Irish people.' Nevertheless, Labour did not wait for that judgement to be given. It voted with the government and for the treaty as 'an honourable peace', said Henderson, which began 'a new era of friendship and mutual confidence between the British and Irish peoples.'[16]

The Labour Party's decision to support the Treaty, before being certain it fulfilled the first condition Henderson himself had listed, does not necessarily mean the settlement fell outside the wider boundaries of Labour's Irish policy. In fact, as has been shown, there were repeated claims from the party leadership that in agreeing to the Treaty's terms the government had adopted Labour's recommended basis for a settlement. Indeed, on 8 December Ramsay MacDonald, speaking on behalf of the party claimed that in signing the Treaty Lloyd George 'threw off the uniform of the "Black-and-Tans" and appeared in the civil garb of the Labour Party.'[17] How far was such claims sustainable? To recapitulate, Labour's policy, as recommended by the Special Commission and as accepted at the December 1920 conference was self-determination with the conditions Henderson re-iterated in October 1921 on the defence issue and on safeguards for minorities. Of course, many argued that 'self-determination' with conditions was not self-determination at all, and it does appear incontestable that in supporting the Treaty without knowing whether it had the support of the majority of the Irish people, Labour was abandoning even the pretence of the self-determination doctrine. To have strictly adhered to it, even in the modified form as outlined in Henderson's speech of October 1921, the party would have had to withhold its judgement on the Treaty until the attitude of the majority of the Irish had become clear. This would have meant, for instance, abstaining on the vote in parliament. Instead, there was a contrary impulse, when Henderson in his speech on the Treaty complained that the debate had gone on for too long and said that the vote should have been taken earlier. This would have ensured, he said, that 'they could have our decision before they came to a decision on the other side',[18] meaning in the Dáil. This occurred anyway, but it is surely a questionable version of the principle of self-determination to say Labour wanted the British parliament to vote for its support before the decision of the Irish parliament had been made. And while it may have been too much to expect Labour to adopt an abstentionist position, this was exactly the attitude of the ILPTUC. Given that the leadership of British Labour had attempted to make a principle out of its previous consultation with its Irish counterpart, it was notably inconsistent to drop this principle at the crucial moment. Not only did British Labour not follow Irish Labour's lead on the Treaty, there is no indication that any consultation was sought or occurred.

As for the two conditions on self-determination previously laid down by the party, on defence and the minority issue, the problem is that Labour never detailed these. So it is difficult to be precise in determining whether the Treaty's formulations on these issues squared, in practice, with Labour's general policy outlines. However, on defence, there is no doubt that the restrictions imposed on the Irish, specifically on the size of its army and on naval facilities for Britain, did tally with Labour's general insistence that Ireland should not become a 'military or naval menace' to Britain. It is not possible to make the same judgement in respect of Ulster. If anything, the reverse was the case. At no point did the Labour Party endorse partition, temporary or otherwise, and on some occasions this had been its major criticism of the government's proposals. For instance, Arthur Henderson had written in *Widnes Weekly*, in April 1920:

> The Labour Party is opposed to the government's method of dealing with the claim of the Irish people ... The broad ground of objection to the government bill is that it denies the Unity of Ireland. It sets up two Parliaments for the Irish, one for the Nationalists, one for Ulster ... it is a scheme of partition which violates the principle of national unity.[19]

This, of course, was written before the Boundary Commission proposal, a scheme which, as explained, encouraged both supporters and opponents of the Treaty in Ireland to believe that partition would be temporary. Furthermore, in accepting partition the Irish signatories to the Treaty had, it could be argued, relieved the Labour Party of the need to honour its opposition to such a scheme. Finally, it certainly was the case that partition did provide for the protection of the religious minority in Ireland, or at least that portion of it living in northeast Ulster. Nevertheless at no time had the party said that this was what they meant when they advocated such protection. The opposite is the case and endorsement of partition only became party policy after the Treaty was signed.

All in all, it is difficult to sustain Labour's claim that the Treaty represented the practical implementation of its own policy, with the proviso that the lack of details of that policy did allow somewhat elastic interpretations of it to be made. Perhaps Labour's rush to endorse the Treaty also stemmed from a wish to see the whole Irish business settled, and consequently the party declined to look too closely at how it was, and if it was being settled. For left-wing critics of the Labour Party the whole affair left a bad taste in the mouth. 'The Labour Party, which has sat on the fence throughout the struggle', commented *Workers' Dreadnought*, 'never openly committing itself to one definite proposal, now unctuously claims credit for the expected settlement.'[20]

In time, such claims faded, at least as far as J. R. Clynes was concerned. Sixteen years later, in his memoirs, he did not repeat the enthusiastic endorsement he had given the Treaty in the House of Commons. 'By the summer of 1921', he recorded 'the Cabinet was forced to recognise that Ireland could never be conquered. Two parliaments, one for Belfast and one for Dublin were forced on the country, to the dissatisfaction of everybody concerned.'

It may be too easy a jibe to point out that at the time this 'everybody' did not include the Labour Party, so perhaps it is best to value the benefit of hindsight and to conclude with Clynes' more historical judgement, 'the position today finds the Irish question still unsettled.'[21]

The Others

When the collapse of the Treaty negotiations seemed imminent the advice of the *Daily Herald* to the Labour Party was to be resolute. On 2 December 1921, foreseeing the possible outbreak of renewed military conflict, there was the editorial comment that 'Labour should at once be busy getting together its local councils of action to stop the Irish war as it stopped the Russian.' Then, four days later, predicting a possible general election if the negotiations broke down, came the advice, 'Let Labour make ready to carry its doctrine of "self-determination and no more war" to the polls.'[22] Obviously, it would have been problematic for Labour to follow this recommendation as it did not itself endorse the 'doctrine' of self-determination, at least insofar as the *Daily Herald* had enunciated it in the same article:

> The Irish have a clear simple, indefeasible right to self-determination, and that means choosing, not what form of government we think good for them (or convenient for ourselves), but what form of government they desire. If they desire a Republic, that is their business and not ours. We are perfectly at liberty, if we choose, to think it unwise of them. But we have no earthly right to murder them to prevent them being wise or unwise.

Given this approach, and the fact that, as already noted, the *Daily Herald* had predicted and justified Irish rejection of the Treaty terms, it is appropriate to start with this newspaper in looking at how the rest of the working class movement reacted to the settlement. Its first editorial comment began:

> Ireland has many and bitter wrongs both ancient and recent, to forgive, but its plenipotentiaries have shown a magnificent spirit in consenting to rise above the sort of resentment which darkens so much of the rest of the world, and we hope and believe all will imitate them in their magnanimity.[23]

The previous day the *Herald* had accused the government of 'truckling' to the Ulster capitalist, now it said that Ulster 'is given all that it could ever, without absolute insanity, have demanded', so presumably this 'truckling' had been maintained, even though the newspaper went on to 'confidently predict' that the northern state would not opt out of a united Ireland 'for long'. The editorial then said that 'on the details of the settlement ... we do not propose to comment' but that 'what matters is the great hope for the future that the settlement gives.' By 10 December, when the dissension in Ireland over the Treaty had become evident, the future was looking not quite so hopeful. The *Daily Herald* of that day asked, 'What are to make of the divisions in the Dáil Cabinet?', and gave as an answer, 'we cannot see that it reflects any discredit upon anybody concerned.' Specifically, the editorial said that both the plenipotentiaries and de Valera were acting 'honestly'. It added 'for our part we should like to see a plebiscite on the question, whatever the Dáil decides', but that with or without such a course of action, 'We do not presume to advise the Irish people what decision they shall take.'

This abstentionist position lasted just four days. The next editorial comment was, 'We earnestly hope that the Irish Parliament will ratify the treaty' as it was 'a constructive compromise on which may be weaved the solid fabric of Irish peace and liberty.'[24] Unlike other labour movement newspapers the *Daily Herald* came out every 24 hours. It did not have a week to reflect and decide an attitude. In this context the varying opinions the newspaper expressed in just over a week have mitigating circumstances. There was criticism of the government when it seemed as if the negotiations were about to break down, there was praise for the

Irish when they did not. This was followed by defending the right of the Irish to reject the terms and then a hope that they would not. Put this way, the range of opinions, while stretching from opposition to support for the Treaty, with the former stated before the terms were made public, is not as illogical as it seems at first glance. However the inconsistency which is glaring is the promise not to 'presume' to tell the Irish what to do and then, four days later, making just such a presumption.

Another supporter of the Treaty was *Labour Leader*, and there at least there was no inconsistency. To recap, even in August when the terms on offer were more restrictive on self-determination than those in the Treaty that newspaper had urged acceptance with the headline 'Ireland's Offer and Ireland's Answer: Will Sinn Féin Release Us to Look After Our Own Business'. The headline when the Treaty was signed was 'Triumph for Peace Negotiations', with the newspaper's editor, B. R. Carter writing of 'the hour of triumph for an honourable compromise.'[25] Two weeks later, in an initialled article, Carter was writing again. The entire front page was given over to 'Why The Treaty Should Be Ratified. An Open Letter To An Irish Patriot.' This was in reply to someone with the pseudonym 'M' who apparently had written 'in terms of bitter reproach of those in the Labour Party in this country who ... entreated you to enter in the proposed new relationship with the British Commonwealth of Nations.' The letter from 'M' was not published but, reported Carter, 'the most stinging words are reserved for those amongst us who stood for the fullest power of "self-determination" in Irish affairs, and who counsel you ... to ratify these "articles of association".' Carter claimed that 'the vast bulk of the Labour movement in this country' supported the Treaty. He suggested that the oath of allegiance was not important and that 'there may come a day ... when both the Irish and the English will laugh at such a thing as "allegiance" to Empires and Kings.' On partition, there was not the assurance given by others that this would be temporary but rather that 'Ulster is another lock-like reality of politics. It cannot be wished away.' Carter ended with a reminder of Lloyd George's threats of war if the Irish did not sign. 'Consider well and wisely' the 'almost certain result of ... repudiation' of the Treaty, he said. 'Almighty God, as ever, would be on the side of the big battalions.'[26]

It is worth recalling that the official ILP position, as decided at its 1921 conference was not, to use Carter's phraseology 'self-determination in Irish affairs', but rather 'self-determination without qualification

... even if it means granting recognition of the independent Republic'. Nevertheless it would wrong to accuse the editor of speaking only for himself. R. C. Wallhead, the ILP chairman, reacted to the Treaty with the comment, 'It seems very probable that the age-long tale of oppression and tragedy in Ireland is ending ... The ILP greets the Irish Free State.'[27] The 1922 ILP conference repeated this sentiment. Held in April that year a resolution was passed which 'hails the Irish Free State', although this time there was the proviso, 'while reiterating its belief in the right of the Irish people to freely determine for themselves their form of political State without regard to the exigencies of British politics.'[28] Again, it appears that the use of hindsight, even if this time of only a few months duration, qualified the initial enthusiasm.

Over-optimism was also a characteristic of the first comment from the *New Statesman*:

It is unnecessary to say much about the Irish settlement, for it seems to be a real settlement, leaving no loose ends on doubtful issues that need to be debated ... the present agreement is certainly a stable and final agreement ... Ulster may stand out for a year, but if the government of the Irish Free State knows its business and can suppress the violence, Ulster will not pay the British income tax more than once again.[29]

Leaving aside the misjudgement on Ulster, which was a general one, what is striking about such comments is the apparent total lack of awareness of the degree of opposition there would be within the 'Irish Free State' to the terms of the Treaty. All those within the British working class movement who endorsed the Treaty displayed an ignorance of this. The excuse could be offered that everyone in Britain who commented on the Treaty was similarly guilty, but the same cannot be said of those on the left who did criticise the Treaty. Here too, however, there were confusions. One of the most curious was in the response of *Workers' Dreadnought*, for initially this was no response whatsoever. The issue dated 17 December, eleven days after the Treaty was signed, said nothing on the terms of the Treaty, even an acknowledgement that it had been signed. Instead there was a critical analysis of Sinn Féin, which it now described as 'at present dominated by the small middle class', so perhaps this was coded attack on the signatories of the Treaty. Clarification came the following week, although even then there seemed to be a lack of decisiveness. The article began by saying that the Treaty 'is not what the Irish desire' because 'their wish is set upon an Irish Republic', but then it was hailed as victory for the Irish, 'a triumph, won by their brave determined fight', and proof that those 'who are willing to stake their all will overcome the strongest and most powerful oppressors'. A successful outcome to the Irish struggle was implied, but the article then maintained 'de Valera is right; this Agreement will not satisfy the Irish.' It continued with an attack on Arthur Griffith saying he had 'ceased to be a Sinn Féiner and has become merely a Home Ruler.' This suggested that the Treaty was a Home Rule solution, which would make it even more difficult to interpret as an Irish victory; equally confusing was the placing of the mantle of political purity on Sinn Féin which only the previous week had been described as middle class. There then followed a look to the future. 'The movement for an Irish Republic will not be quenched' was the first prediction. The second was:

> Even should the Downing Street Agreement be ratified by the Dáil ... the Irish people may not look for peaceful times, for the Irish employers of labour have announced that all wages agreements are to terminate at the end of the year ... Ireland may begin 1922 with a general strike ... We desire to see the Nationalist struggle ended in order that the class consciousness of the worker may develop.

Whether or not this meant that *Workers' Dreadnought* would have been quite happy for the Treaty to signal the end of the 'nationalist struggle' is not clear, but given the general state of confusion into which the newspaper appears to have been thrown by its signing, it is not surprising it looked with visible relief to the wages struggles to come. As to the Ulster issue, *Workers' Dreadnought* did not share the general opinion that this was virtually settled and that a united Ireland was around the corner. However it did not really know what to make of that either:

> The fighting elements of the Belfast populace seem in no mood to accept peace with Southern Ireland, and even if peace is made it will be some time before the turbulence there dies away. The situation is a peculiar one.[30]

By the following week *Workers' Dreadnought* had finally arrived at a more straightforward attitude. The Treaty had now become 'a sad, humiliating compromise of the stand for a completely independent Irish Republic' and if it was ratified it would only be because the Irish were 'faced with a stronger Power which threatens a war of extermination.' However, there was still the economic struggle to look forward to, with a reminder of the termination of the wages agreements and the hopeful questioning, 'shall we see a general strike in Ireland? Shall we see an Irish Commune?'[31]

The CPGB had a less optimistic view of the future. Indeed, in a curious incident it even decided the best course of action was to personally and privately advise the opponents of the Treaty on the best way to avoid disaster. The story of this is in the autobiography of Willie Gallagher, who in 1921 was a member of the executive of the party. According to Gallagher, just before the Treaty was signed he learnt the contents of it from a journalist, and following an urgent discussion at the CPGB headquarters he was sent to Dublin to warn the government there of what was about to occur. With Tom Johnson, of the Irish Labour Party he then went to see Cathal Brugha, the Minister for Defence in the Irish Cabinet. With Brugha, says Gallagher, were Constance Markievicz, a Minister without Portfolio in the government, and 'young officers'. He also says that when he told them that a treaty 'involving partition' had been drawn up and was about to be signed Brugha and the rest 'simply refused to belief me.' Gallagher continues:

> I suggested that they should arrest Griffith and Collins as soon as they landed, and then issue a call to the people of Ireland to prepare for whatever eventuates. But this would call for a declaration of policy. I asked the Defence Minister to give consideration to a document I had prepared, setting out a programme for his government to follow in order to make life better and brighter for the workers and small farmers.[32]

On the face of it this is rather an improbable tale. However, there were precedents. William O'Brien of the ILPTUC was later to recall that when the negotiations between the British and Irish seemed on the verge of collapse Cathal Brugha, then the Irish government's Minister for Defence, had asked his advice on possible help in Britain should hostilities resume. Apparently, he was considering assassinations in the House of Commons. First Brugha asked him if he thought British unemployment activists would lend a hand, to which O'Brien replied that 'it was my opinion that the unemployed would not do the things he had in mind.' Then Brugha asked about British communists, and although O'Brien said 'he did not think they would do anything either' he did arrange a meeting with the CPGB and Brugha. At this were Gallagher and Arthur MacManus.[33] There is no account of what happened at that meeting, but that it took place encourages the belief that the subsequent one referred to by Gallagher also did, as personal ties had already been made. So accepting the Treaty meeting has a factual basis what is to be made of it? The Communist Party had, in public, made somewhat of a virtue of its refusal to tell the Irish working class how to conduct its struggle, believing this smacked of imperialistic attitudes. And yet here was Gallagher arriving in Dublin, not only advising the arrest of Collins and Griffith, but even producing a social and economic programme on which the anti-Treatyites were recommended to campaign. It is hardly surprising that, according to Gallagher, 'this was too much for Catha Brugha'[34] who then asked Gallagher and Johnson to leave.

At least this story showed the CPGB did not share the illusions in the Treaty of others on the left. Indeed its public comments on the Treaty were the most critical. There was 'little to rejoice at and little of a settlement', was the first comment in the *Communist*, in an article by T. A. Jackson. It was the British, he said, who 'have gained much and lost little' and he attacked the non-recognition of the Republic and the right of 'an arbitrarily created area ... to contract out of the Irish Free State.' Nor did Jackson subscribe to the *Workers' Dreadnought* optimism about class struggles around the corner. The possibility of the emergence of a 'mass party ... in an avowedly proletarian or Communist form' depended 'upon many things.' He said that if the leader of the 1913 lock-out struggle, James Larkin, had been in Ireland such a party would come, but 'If, on the other hand, de Valera goes into opposition at the head of a Republican party it will not.'[35] It was a remarkably accurate prophesy, written by someone who, incidentally, had been just recently taken on as a journalist for the *Communist* after being asked by the editor if he could 'write articles about anything but Ireland', with Jackson assuring him that he could.[36] The definitive position of the CPGB came in a statement from the party executive which appeared as an advertisement in the *Daily Herald* on 23 December and in the *Communist* itself on 31 December. This included:

> The Communist Party alone regards the Treaty as dishonourable and inadequate – as a 'settlement' which leaves unsettled the vital fact of Ireland's right to independence and makes clear only the determination of British Imperialism never to admit that right ... It does not acknowledge Ireland's rights: it enforces and legalises Britain's usurped authority. It does not set Ireland free ... Only from fear of barbarous repression has any section of Irishmen been willing to accept it – even temporarily. Only under the 'monstrous iniquity' of a threat of instant war from the lips of Britain's Prime Minister were some of the plenipotentiaries induced to sign. To uphold this as a final satisfaction of Irish National rights is a fraud and a crime which should brand British Imperialist politicians with infamy as long as the world lasts ... The Communist Party ... prepares itself and calls upon the toiling masses to prepare themselves for unflinching support for those Irish Republicans who, refusing to be associated with this Treaty, persevere with the struggle for the ideas of Pearse and Connolly.

This statement was significant not just because it placed the CPGB on the other side of the barricades to the Labour Party, the TUC, the ILP and the *New Statesmen*, but also because, as with Jackson's first article it also displayed an awareness that the national struggle was far from settled. Leaving the emotive language aside, these two articles were in many ways the CPGB's finest theoretic hour on Ireland, showing both perception and realism. The same cannot be said of the reactions to the Treaty of the rest of the British labour movement.

10

Conclusions

Afterwards

Afterwards, in 1937, J. H. Thomas wrote:

> Geographically, England, and Ireland should be together; politically there is nothing that anyone who believes in liberty, freedom and democracy cannot obtain within the four corners of the statue of Westminster. I still look forward to the Irish Free State taking its part in and being a loyal member of the British Commonwealth of Nations.[1]

Also in 1937, J. R. Clynes wrote:

> I worked with the Labour Party to secure for Ireland a full measure of self-government ... subject to the principle we were always required to support – that there should be no separation of the two countries. Ireland, of course, is not the property of England and the Irish Members passionately declared that they should be considered a being herself ... But such consideration required reciprocal recognition of a general British interest, which inevitably interwove with Irish interests, and this fact many of the headstrong men of Ireland could not be made to admit.[2]

Afterwards, towards the end of his days, George Bernard Shaw objected to a proposed plaque in Dublin proclaiming his Irish identity. He said, 'all my political services have been given to the British labour movement and to international socialism.'[3]

Afterwards, in 1931, Hannah Sheehy Skeffington, wife of the 1916 pacifist martyr Francis and a formidable agitator in her own right, wrote to Sylvia Pankhurst:

I know of no English rebel who understands the Irish situation and the international one so well. The comments and sympathy of English comrades drive me mad at times, as they show such a blind spot where we are concerned, in fact our friends are the worst. Your paper, *Dreadnought* was always fine.'[4]

Afterwards, Ramsey MacDonald became the first Labour Prime Minister and then in 1931 led a Conservative dominated coalition. J. H. Thomas and Philip Snowden joined him; all were expelled from the Labour Party. Arthur Henderson opposed MacDonald, and for a short time was leader of the Labour Party. In 1934, he won a Nobel Peace Prize for his work for disarmament. George Lansbury was leader of the Labour Party from 1932–35, until his pacifism was rejected by his party in the face of the growth of fascism in Europe. Oswald Mosley of the Peace With Ireland Council left the Conservatives and successfully stood as an Independent in the 1922 general election, and then in 1924 joined the Labour Party, which he left in 1932 to form his own fascist party.

Afterwards, Art O'Brien was jailed for Republican activities in Britain, but eventually was Irish Minister to France and Belgium. Labour MP James O'Grady, who had walked the streets of Dublin with his hotel maid carrying his luggage in 1918 when recruiting to the British Army, became Britain's Governor of Tasmania and then of the Falkland Islands.

Hesitant Comrades

In November 1918, the International Committee of the ILPTUC issued 'An Open Letter to the Workers of Great Britain', which was published in the *Herald*. The second paragraph made clear where the Irish were coming from: 'We approach you in the spirit of fraternity, believing that the wrong you do to Ireland by your inaction and acquiescence in tyranny is due to your ignorance of the true relationship that exists between England and Ireland'. The letter went on to explain that 'a new generation has arisen' in Ireland, one that was no longer content with Home Rule and demanded instead that Ireland should have 'the right to determine her own form of government, to choose her own sovereignty, to make her own laws without limit or hindrance by any external authority.' They likened the reluctance of British workers to endorse these principles to 'liberal slave owners', saying, 'Is it to be said of you that you are willing to concede anything to Ireland except the one thing she demands – freedom'. In particular the ILPTUC ridiculed the attempts by 'your leaders' to restrict Ireland's sovereignty on the issues of defence and Ulster. They complained of 'your hesitancy'; a hesitancy which, as the letter as a whole spelt out, included both an unwillingness to endorse unconditional Irish self-determination and to act in support of this.[5]

This book has attempted to explore the validity of these accusations, and to test them not just from Easter 1916 to November 1918 when the open letter appeared, but up to December 1921, after which a new chapter in British/Irish relations began. What has emerged is indeed an examination of 'hesitancy'; a hesitancy by most of the British labour movement to devote time, energy and intellectual endeavour to explore what was happening in Ireland in those years; a hesitancy to give the Irish majority what they wanted; a hesitancy to relate what was happening in Ireland to their own values; and, most of all, a hesitancy to decisively change the course of British/Irish history.

Elaboration on these themes follows, but first there is another important observation which contributes to more rounded evaluation. What is important to acknowledge, indeed highlight, is that the leadership of the entire labour movement of Britain disassociated themselves from the British side in the Irish War of Independence. This was not their war. They were fiercely critical not just of the British government for conducting the war, but also of the actions of the British security forces in pursuing it. Some of the phrases quoted earlier bear repeating. Commenting on Bloody Sunday, the *Labour Leader* talked of the government employing 'methods of terrorism'. In October 1920 the *Daily Herald* railed against British forces' 'slaughter of innocent Irish children', and in November 1920 of a British 'reign of terror'. In October 1920 *Labour Leader* spoke of 'British tyranny'. The report of the Labour Party's Commission on Ireland described British 'terrorism' and its 'reign of terror'; it said of one wing of the British security forces – the Auxiliaries – that they were 'undisciplined and uncontrollable'. The *New Statesman* of September 1920 concluded, 'The likeness between Ireland under the English in 1920 and Belgium under the Germans in 1914 is becoming more odious every day.' Arthur Henderson, speaking on behalf of the Labour Party in the House of Commons in October 1920, talked of 'the lack of discipline in the armed forces of the Crown, resulting in the death of innocent citizens' and 'a policy of military terrorism.'

These were harsh criticisms, but, as we have seen, they were also being made by Asquith's Liberals, the Peace With Ireland Council, individual Conservatives, sections of the women's movement and the Irish in Britain. This is why they are just a starting point of any more general evaluation of the British labour movement and the Irish revolution. As a guide to this, and of more than passing significance, there are available the contemporary judgements of the Irish themselves, in particular the Irish in Britain and the organised working class in Ireland. Here is what the *Catholic Herald*, the popular newspaper among the Irish in Britain and edited by Labour parliamentary candidate Charles Diamond, said in August 1920:

> Labour is willing to use direct action and all kind of extreme measures about the affairs of any other country in the world; but it allows Ireland to be trampled on by brute force and every semblance of liberty destroyed and neither direct or indirect action is even contemplated. On this matter many Labour leaders seem to be just on the same path as the old Tory and Liberal coercionists.[6]

That criticism was a familiar one among the Irish in Britain. On this occasion it was made before the Labour's Irish campaign of early 1921, but it is similar in tone to that adopted in 1922 by P. J. Kelly, the president of the Irish Self-Determination League:

> The Irish population in this country, belonging as they do to the working class, are predisposed to the Labour Party. So far as Ireland is concerned, we have found that party, with few outstanding exceptions, to be devoid of principle, especially on the question of the self-determination of peoples, lacking in courage in great causes, and as imperialistic as either [the Conservatives and Liberals].[7]

As for the opinion of the British labour movement's Irish counterpart, as early as the Leeds Convention in 1917 William O'Brien of the ITUCLP, addressing the delegates, said:

> In Ireland you have a small nationality at your door which is demanding the right of its own life … I gather from reading some of the capitalist papers that revolution is popular nowadays. Twelve months ago you

had a revolution in Ireland. The papers and politicians that acclaimed the revolution in Russia did not acclaim the revolution in Ireland whose leaders were taken out and shot like dogs.[8]

This accusation of doubled standards did not, it appear, have much effect. Because in 1920 the ILPTUC sent this similar message:

Irish Labour congratulates the British workers on the formation of the Council of Action and its success in rallying the democratic forces in opposition to Winston Churchill's projected war on the Russian Workers Republic. The same evil influence is responsible for the regime of the jack-boot now operating without restraint in Ireland ... We solemnly ask British Labour – Do you intend that the war upon Ireland will continue ... we ask you, the British workers, to speak and act as resolutely and defiantly respecting the use of British military power in Ireland as you have done ... for the war on Russia.[9]

There is an impression of a sense of hopelessness in all of this. There were others who made similar points. The playwright Sean O'Casey, once a member of the Irish Citizen Army, offered the view in June 1919 that the Labour Party 'seem to be hiding their light under a bushel when Ireland is mentioned'.[10] A despairing *Catholic Herald* in March 1920 said, 'Ireland is in the throes of a national agony, a victim of merciless militarism, and British Labour remains quiescent and inactive', and added, like a plea from the heart, that the labour movement 'must get a move on.'[11]

To examine why such critics believed Labour did not 'get a move on' it is again useful to look at the Irish critics' own explanations. For the *Catholic Herald*, the 1920 Labour Party conference at Scarborough revealed the answer. This was when the conference, against the wishes of the party leadership, adopted the full self-determination position. Charles Diamond's editorial ran:

Whatever may be the cowering and shiverings of some Labour leaders ... the great bulk of the Labour movement in England is sound on the Irish question. At Scarborough it has shown the courage, sincerity and depth of its sentiment by an unequivocal recognition of Irish self-determination ... The rank and file of Labour ... clearly recognises it knows what self-determination means, and they are prepared to see its application made unreservedly in Ireland. They lead their 'leaders'. The Labour leaders distort and trim and whittle down in regards to Ireland ... Such Labour leaders are either devoid of principle or they stifle it.[12]

These comments insist that the leadership's Irish policies did not reflect those of the rank and file and the views of the working class. *Catholic Herald*'s view, in January 1920, was that not just on Ireland but on India and Egypt as well, 'The vast majority of the workers are sound on these questions', and that 'If they had honourable and fearless leaders, they would have made their power felt on these matters long ago.'[13] On occasions the newspaper even identified the leaders in question. J. H. Thomas was denounced as a 'fervid imperialist' over Ireland[14] while J. R. Clynes was 'one of the rottenest Labour oracles on the subject of Ireland ... a man out to pose as a "statesman" and to run with the hair and hunt with the hounds, all the time keeping an eye on a job, the future and a salary ... the miserable dodger'.[15]

The Scarborough pro-self-determination vote suggests there was something in the *Catholic Herald*'s view, at least for the last six months of 1920, that it was this leadership and not the rank and file which was at fault in failing to take the Irish issue forward. So too does the ILP's conference vote on the same lines. So too do the calls for action from the local councils of action and elsewhere for strikes in support of the Irish. But those who were the special targets of Charles Diamond's wrath would, of course, have none of this. Indeed it was in a book published in 1920 that Thomas made one of his more intemperate remarks on this issue. After saying 'the Irish are a peculiar race', he continued: 'It is unquestionable that the British people, or at least a large majority of them, not having any personal knowledge of Ireland or the Irish, look upon them as hopeless and violent imbeciles.'[16]

It was such remarks that made Thomas one of the favourite targets for the left, and indeed the Irish left. Tom Johnson of the ILPTUC, and not exactly a Republican firebrand himself, was reported in the summer of 1921 as saying that Thomas, 'has persistently tried to prevent the British Labour Party declaring for genuine self-determination ... While he professes a kind of friendship for Ireland and Ireland's claim, he really is the most persistent opponent of Irish freedom in the British Labour movement.'[17]

There is more than an element of truth in these remarks, nevertheless it would be intellectually lazy to place all the blame for what the Irish saw as the failures of British working class on Ireland on the head of one or two individuals. An alternative explanation was to blame the British people in entirety. We have already seen examples of this, but one more example can be quoted. This is from *Labour Leader* of 23 December 1920 which complained, 'The public in Great Britain has been singularly apathetic about the disgraceful doings of the government in Ireland'. But, in the very same issue of the paper, there was a letter from Frank Kenyon who was secretary of the ILP in Failsworth near Manchester. He wrote 'to enter a protest against the inactivity' of the ILP's leadership body, the NAC, on Ireland, saying 'We in the branches get no intimation that a combined effort on the part of the I.L.P. (such as was done during the Russia crisis) is going to be made to end the state of affair in Ireland.' And he went on to compare the ILP unfavourably with Asquith's Liberals' efforts on Ireland. Or considers what *Labour Leader*'s sister paper, *Forward*, said in October 1920 after reporting on the activities of the Black and Tans: 'Is it too late to ask for action among the workers of Britain or are they so besotted in the hypocrisies of their masters that from the Irish people can expect nothing but cant?'[18] But compare this with the following, which appeared in the same newspaper just two months earlier in response to calls from Sinn Féin for strike action in Britain over Ireland: 'Isn't it the very essence of Sinn Féin policy that the English should not interfere in Irish affairs? ... So why do they ask the British people to determine the course of events in Ireland?'[19]

Running these two quotations together allows the discussion on leadership and rank and file to be taken further, a leadership including not just Labour Party and TUC leaders but also those who sought to replace or offer an alternative to them. For it is obvious that a *Forward* readership which had read disparaging remarks about calls for action on Ireland one month would be unlikely to respond to similar calls two months later. Moreover, leadership involves more than calls for action, it also comprises ideological leadership. In this instance it includes the explanations of the 1916 Rising; the clarity with which the issues of socialism and nationalism were relayed to the working class by its leaders and the left press; the extent of their coverage on Ireland; and the attention paid to the Ulster question. The neglect or discomfort shown in respect of all these matters, evidenced in this book, not just by the leadership of the working class but also by those who offered themselves as alternatives, meant that any potential the working class as a whole may have had to intervene decisively into the Irish crisis went uncultivated.

What was the reason for this? There were, at times, local contexts. For example, Tom Gallagher's informative study of the Glasgow Irish has observed that the Labour Party/ILP in Glasgow while 'vocal in its criticism of British policy in Ireland ... had to be careful not to alienate protestant skilled workers who identified with their strongly unionist counterparts in Belfast'.[20] Gallagher tends to stress the criticism of British policy by the Glasgow ILP. For instance, he cites John Wheatley sharing a May Day platform in 1919 with Countess Markievicz of Sinn Féin.[21] In fact, although Gallagher does not say so, Markievicz's presence on the platform was subsequently criticised by *Forward*,[22] which actually validates his more general observation concerning the restraining influence of the presence of the Protestant community in Glasgow. But it is also the case that the ILP's disassociation from Markievicz fits in with its general political scepticism of the Irish rebels. As with James Sexton's opposition to the ISDL inspired Liverpool dock strike in support of Irish political prisoners, both concerns about splitting that city's working class and personal political antagonism to those prisoners informed Sexton's opposition to the strike. So local circumstances did matter, but they mattered most when they coalesced with an existing political motivation.

Overall, the more general context of the period is more important: both the Great War and the fact that following it socialists and trade unionists had many other issues competing for attention; even if it is worth repeating the contemporary judgement of G. D. H. Cole that the labour movement should have taken up the Irish issue rather than 'frittering away its strength on minor troubles'. There was also the context that the pacifism of individuals and organisations such as the ILP always made solidarity with the IRA unlikely, although there is no evidence that Republicans demanded such explicit endorsement. But as well as such influences and whatever the precise contextual moment in time there were more important, deeper doubts. As far as the Labour Party/ILP is concerned the following, written by Ramsay MacDonald in 1909 is instructive:

Had there been no Irish Party, the history of Labour politics would have been altogether different from what it is. And yet it is necessary that the Labour Party should clearly understand the gulf that separates its tactics from that of the Irish, and not be misled by the many false analogies which it is usual to draw from the method of that Party. The Irish Party acts upon the assumption that it is in an alien Parliament; it is there by the coercion of the constitution, it wants to force its demands upon a hostile people ... its leaders come to us ... asking that their people be let go ... But that is not a description of the Labour Party. It desires to gain possession of what the Irish Party desires to be rid of; it is not trying to get the country to let it go, but is endeavouring to persuade the country to give it confidence; it is not at war but at peace with the nation; what it would destroy, were it to injure Parliament, would not be an alien power but its own heritage.[23]

MacDonald is referring here to the gulf between Labour and the Nationalist Party. The gulf was even greater between Labour and Sinn Féin from 1916 to 1921 when the Republicans rejected any association with the British parliament and were prepared to defend such a rejection by physical force. That ideology, strategy and tactics were opposed to the very core belief of British social democracy, as stated above by MacDonald, a belief that the reforming capacity and the evolutionary character of the British state could provide a cure-all for society's ills. The majority of Irish, in the years of this study, rejected this and by so doing challenged Labour's political philosophy. It would not be surprising if Labour, for its part, found it difficult to express comradeship with the Irish national struggle.

Another restraining ideological influence was highlighted by the Irish Transport and General Workers' Union in February 1920 when its newspaper complained that the PLP's Commission of Inquiry report did not endorse self-determination. For the ITGWU it was Labour's 'fatal obsession with the responsibility of Empire that has been responsible for the miserable failure of this report'.[24] Certainly, at this time, there was no threat to the stability of that empire, 'so direct and serious as the Irish movement of Sinn Féiner', to quote from one article from the Bolshevik press in 1920.[25] But for the Labour Party, a belief in the worthiness of the Empire had become an article of faith to the extent loyalty to it was placed above loyalty to the socialist goal of Irish self-determination. This was evident most definitively at the end of the day when Henderson said that the Anglo-Irish Treaty should be accepted because of the 'vital interests of our people at home and of the British commonwealth'. With such an ideological commitment it was always unlikely that the leadership of the British Labour Party would rush to embrace the cause of Irish separation, or organise on its behalf.

This was all the more so because of that leadership's suspicion of, or hostility to, the non-parliamentary methods of the Irish. Yet for those further to the left, the tactics adopted by the Irish from 1919 to 1921 were the essence of revolutionary struggle – general strikes, organs of dual power, a willingness to take up arms if necessary, the overthrow of the existing state control. The problem for those in Britain whose own political culture did not rule out such methodology was that in Ireland they were being used in the course of what was a nationalist struggle and not one for workers' power. Communists found it difficult to relate that nationalism to their own politics, so they too, like their Labour counterparts looked forward to a different reality. The *Communist Review* said in May 1921:

> But events move rapidly in these days and the growth of Communism among the organised workers of Britain, together with the difficulties inevitably created within capitalism by its collapse into anarchy will force the British and Irish worker to join hands ... the duty of the Communist Party is to assist this development ... It is no easy task.[26]

Those last two phrases sum up the attitudes the communists showed. Agitation on Ireland was a 'duty', but duties are usually carried out without enthusiasm, if indeed they carried out at all. This particular one was 'no easy task', so it is hardly surprising that it was not undertaken with the diligence demanded by the Irish, or indeed by their international comrades in the Third International. The complaints from the latter were summed up in a speech by Lenin to the Second Congress of the Third International in August 1920, when he complained, 'There are two hundred thousand British soldiers who are applying ferocious terror methods to suppress the Irish. The British Socialists are not conducting any revolutionary propaganda among these soldiers.'[27] By 'Socialists', Lenin meant those who stated their loyalty to the Third International. That they were reluctant to do as Lenin demanded and make Ireland a priority stemmed from their own theoretical uncertainty, from their gloomy assessment of the state of consciousness on Ireland among the British working class and from the attraction of other, less complicated, issues. There were exceptions. Most notable was T. A. Jackson whose writing on socialism and nationalism, Ulster and the Treaty can be singled out, both for their perception and for their application of traditional Marxist methodology; and Sylvia Pankhurst, who, despite her occasional doubts put support for the Irish revolution before other considerations.

But overall, it is apparent that the militancy of the British working class and its left wing in the immediate post-war years described by many historians did not encompass Ireland, at least to the extent the Irish wanted, Yes, they did have allies. They were present, for example in the Carpenters Union and its attempt to stand up to anti-Catholic sectarianism and the TUC's capitulation to it; and in ASLEF's strike call over the British state murders in Cork. But there were always those such as J. H. Thomas who, without much difficulty it must be admitted, ensured that any such enthusiasm was quenched. And, after all, as the collective leadership and rank and file of British trade unionism were unwilling to strike in support of the miners on Black Friday, then they were hardly likely to down tools over Ireland. For the Labour Party in particular there were too many difficulties and too many dilemmas. These were summed up in the following comment from *Forward* after the party's Scarborough conference which backed unconditional self-determination:

> Does the Labour Party ... now support a declaration from Ireland in favour of a free and independent Republic, with an Army and Navy of its own, the control of foreign policy? If the Labour Party endorsed such a policy, it might as well march into the wilderness ... If it rejected that policy, it would be deep in conflict with the force predominant in Ireland just now ... I should imagine even some of the most ambitious Labour leaders are not sorry that for the present the solution to the Irish Question is in other hands than theirs. [28]

The last sentence is a fitting final comment on the Labour Party and Ireland in these years. Except to add that Labour's support for Lloyd George during the Treaty negotiations and their outcome suggests that had the 'solution' to the 'Irish Question' been in Labour's hands in late 1921 the result would have been little different than as it turned out.

More generally, to return to an occasion raised at the start of this book, there was in this period no repetition of the set-piece demonstration of Bloody Sunday in Trafalgar Square in 1887 when the tens of thousands of London Irish and the British left march marched together in a common cause. Well, perhaps there was at least one echo. That was at the requiem mass and funeral procession of Irish hunger striker, IRA volunteer and elected member of the British House of Commons Terence MacSwiney in London in October 1920. The mass was attended by Arthur Henderson, Clynes, Thomas and, the Labour Party mayors of London borough, including future prime minister Clement Atlee That collective presence, was, it seems likely, more a consequence of public opinion than personal grief. That opinion was witnessed by the *Daily Herald*:

> The vast throng of marchers, Irish residents in England, first woman of Cumann na mBan, of all classes, but one spirit ... After them were members, hundreds after hundreds, of the Irish Self-determination League. Each of the 27 London branches had their banner ... Thousands of ordinary men and women, most of them very poor ... And the English crowd that poured out of the sordid streets of South London were quiet too. Sight-seeing perhaps, but not in a sight-seeing mood, moved by death, moved by heroism, and moved by the spectacle of those many marchers. And nowhere a sneer or a laugh; for these were the Commons of England and not the House of Commons.[29]

Therein is an appropriate symbolism with which to conclude. The 'Commons of England' were on this occasion and on others as well willing to take to if not the streets then at least the pavements to express their sympathy with the Irish national revolution. They were respectful, they were 'moved'. Nevertheless, the *Daily Herald* reporting is correct. They were more sightseers than active allies. They were hesitant comrades.

Notes

Prologue

1. *Pall Mall Gazette*, 14 November 1887.
2. Hill, Christopher, *The World Turned Upside Down*, Penguin, London, 1972, p. 236.
3. Collins, Henry, 'The London Corresponding Society', in John Saville (ed.) *Democracy and the Labour Movement*, Lawrence and Wishart, London, 1959, p. 187.
4. For a more detailed survey see Bell, Geoffrey, *The British in Ireland*, Pluto Press, London, 1984, pp. 14–22.
5. For greater detail see Stevenson, John, *Popular disturbances in England*, Longmans, New York, 1979; Jackson, J. A., *The Irish in Britain*, RKP, London, 1964; Winer, Robert, *Bloody Foreigners*, Abacus, London, 2004.
6. Kapp, Yvonne, *Eleanor Marx. Volume II: The Crowded Years 1884–1898*, Virago, London, 1979, pp. 198–99.
7. Bell, Geoffrey, *Troublesome Business*, Pluto Press, London, 1982, pp. 92–93.
8. *Justice*, 23 February 1884.

1. Easter 1916

1. House of Commons debates, 3 May 1916.
2. Ibid., 24 November 1920.
3. For an analysis of the reasons for Irish enlistment see, Jeffery, Keith, *Ireland and the Great War*, Cambridge University Press, Cambridge, 2011.
4. Miliband, Ralph, *Parliamentary Socialism*, Merlin Press, London, 1972, p. 39.
5. For more details see Wrigley, Chris, *Arthur Henderson*, GPC Press, Cardiff, 1990.
6. Miliband, *Parliamentary Socialism*, p. 121.
7. Cole, G. D. H., *A History of the Labour Party from 1914*, Routledge and Kegan Paul, London, 1946. Cole says that although the ILP's membership in 1914 on the basis of its affiliation fees to the Labour Party was 3,000, its actual membership was 'considerably greater'.
8. McBriar, A. M., *Fabian Socialism and English Politics*, Cambridge University Press, London, 1966, p. 141.

9. Ibid., p. 344–45.

10. Kendall, Walter, *The Revolutionary Movement in Britain, 1900–21*, Weidenfeld and Nicolson, London, 1969, p. 312. These figures should be treated with caution as, Kendall says, the majority in 1914 were 'merely card-carrying members'.

11. Smith, Joan, 'Labour Tradition in Glasgow and Liverpool', *History Workshop*, Spring 1984, Issue 17, p. 34.

12. Levenson, Samuel, *James Connolly*, Martin, Brian and O'Keefe, London, 1973, p. 59.

13. Pelling, Henry, *The British Communist Party*, A & C Black, London, 1978, p. 16.

14. Lansbury, George, *My Life*, Constable, London, 1928, pp. 27–28.

15. Ibid., p. 64.

16. Ibid., p. 66.

17. Stubbs, Barry, *The British Labour Party and Ireland, 1900–1951*, M.Phil., London School of Economics, 1976 (unpublished), p. 15.

18. Bell, *Troublesome Business*, p. 23.

19. Ibid., p. 24.

20. Ibid., p. 23.

21. Ibid., p. 39.

22. Ibid., p. 25.

23. Howell, David, *British Workers and the Independent Labour Party, 1886–1906*, MUP, Manchester, 1983, p. 142.

24. Ibid., p. 386 and p. 214.

25. Smith, 'Labour Tradition in Glasgow and Liverpool', p. 42.

26. Bell, *Troublesome Business*, pp. 6–7.

27. Kendall, *The Revolutionary Movement in Britain, 1900–21*, p. 373.

28. Challinor, Raymond, *The Origins of British Bolshevism*, Croom Helm, London, 1977, p. 158.

29. For details of these events see Stewart, A. T. Q., *The Ulster Crisis*, Faber and Faber, London, 1969; Dangerfield, George, *The Damnable Question*, Quartet, London, 1979.

30. Boyce, D. George, 'Ireland and British Politics', 1900–1939 in Chris Wrigley (ed.), *A Companion to Early Twentieth Century Britain*, Blackwell, Chichester, 2009, p. 104.

31. Townshend, Charles, *Easter 1916*, Allen Lane, London, 2005, p. 61.

32. Lenin, V. I., *On Britain*, Progress Publishers, Moscow, 1973, pp. 172–73.

33. Levenson, *James Connolly*, p. 242.

34. Boyce, D. G., *Englishmen and Irish Troubles*, Jonathon Cape, London, 1972, pp. 62–63.

35. *Herald*, 29 April 1916.

36. *Labour Leader*, 17 April 1916.
37. Ibid., 4 May 1916.
38. *Socialist Review*, Vol. 13, No. 78, August/September 1916.
39. *Call*, 5 May 1916.
40. Ibid., 18 May 1916.
41. *Women's Dreadnought*, 6 May 1916.
42. Ibid.
43. Ibid.
44. *Labour Leader*, 11 May 1916.
45. *New Statesman*, 29 April 1916.
46. Ibid., 6 May 1916.
47. Bell, *Troublesome Business*, p. 34.
48. *Socialist Review*, Vol. 13, No. 78, August/September 1916.
49. *Call*, 22 June 1916.
50. *Herald*, 13 May 1916.
51. Thorne, Will, *My Life Battles*, George Newnes, London, 1925 and 1998, pp. 120–21.
52. House of Commons debates, 3 May 1916.
53. Ibid., 8 May 1916.
54. This is discussed in Bell, *Troublesome Business*, p. 33.
55. Wrigley, Chris, *Arthur Henderson*, p. 134.
56. *Forward*, 6 May 1916.
57. Ibid., 13 May 1916.
58. Boyce, *Englishmen and Irish Troubles*, p. 32.
59. Dangerfield, *The Damnable Question*, p. 211.
60. Lee, J. J., *Ireland, 1912–1985*, Cambridge University Press, Cambridge, 1989, pp. 28–36.
61. For example, see Yeates, Padraig, *A City in Wartime, Dublin 1914–18*, Gill and Macmillan, Dublin, 2011, pp. 115–118.
62. Beckett, J. C., *The Making of Modern Ireland 1603–1923*, Faber & Faber, London, 1966, p. 441.
63. Dangerfield, *The Damnable Question*, p. 212.
64. Ibid.
65. Levenson, *James Connolly*, p. 327.
66. Ibid., pp. 326–27.
67. *Catholic Herald*, 6 May 1916.
68. Ibid., 13 May 1916.
69. Levenson, *James Connolly*, p. 38.
70. Ellis, P. Beresford (ed.), *James Connolly: Selected Writings*, Penguin, London, 1973, p. 35.
71. Levenson, *James Connolly*, p. 238.

72. Lenin, *On Britain*, pp. 257–58.
73. *Labour Leader*, 27 April 1916.
74. *Herald*, 29 April 1916.
75. *Forward*, 20 May 1916.
76. *New Statesman*, 6 May 1916.
77. *Herald*, 27 June 1916.
78. Berresford Ellis, *James Connolly*, pp. 274–75.
79. Pearse, P. H., *Ghosts*. In *The Best of Pearse*, Mercier, Cork, 1965, p. 13.
80. *Forward*, 13 May 1916.
81. *Call*, 4 May 1916.
82. Bell, *Troublesome Business*, p. 82.
83. This is covered in Gallagher, Tom, *Glasgow, the Uneasy Peace*, Manchester University Press, Manchester, 1987.
84. *Communist Review*, May 1924, Vol. 5, No. 1.
85. White, Captain J. R., *Misfit: An Autobiography*, Jonathan Cape, London 1930, p. 345.
86. *Forward*, 20 May 1916.

2. Interesting Times

1. Wilson, Trevor, (ed.), *The Political Diaries of C.P. Scott, 1911–1928*, Collins, London, 1970, p. 77.
2. Hattersley, Roy, *David Lloyd George*, Little Brown, London, 2010, p. 14.
3. Lyons, F. S. L., *Ireland Since the Famine*, Fontana, London, 1973, p. 381.
4. Quoted in Hattersley, *David Lloyd George*, p. 395.
5. Cronin, Sean, *Irish Nationalism*, Pluto Press, London, 1983, p. 121.
6. *Labour Leader*, 2 March 1917.
7. Townshend, Charles, *The Republic*, Allen Lane, London, 2013, pp. 9–10.
8. Ibid., p. 13.
9. Dangerfield, *The Damnable Question*, p. 288–90.
10. *The Times*, 17 January 1919.
11. *Herald*, 4 January 1919.
12. Ibid., 11 January 1919.
13. Coogan, Tim Pat, *Ireland Since the Rising*, Pall Mall Press, London, 1966, p. 25.
14. *Herald*, 1 February 1919.
15. Beckett, *The Making of Modern Ireland 1603–1923*, p. 246.
16. Macardle, Dorothy, *The Irish Republic*, Gollancz, London, 1938, p. 344.
17. Foster, R. F., *Modern Ireland*, Penguin, London, 1989, p. 198.
18. *New Statesman*, 24 September 1920.
19. Foster, *Modern Ireland*, p. 498.

20. *Daily Herald*, 26 October 1920.
21. *Labour Leader*, 28 November 1920.
22. Macardle, *The Irish Republic*, p. 434.
23. English, Richard, *Irish Freedom*, Pan, London, 2006, p. 287.
24. Kostick, Conor, *Revolution on Ireland*, Pluto Press, London, 1996, p. 32. Also see: O'Connor, Emmet, *Syndicalism in Ireland 1917–1923*, Cork University Press, Cork, 1988.
25. *New Statesman*, 13 April 1918.
26. *Labour Leader*, 14 October 1920.
27. Ibid., 28 October 1920.
28. *Daily Herald*, 23 November 1920.
29. *Herald*, 27 March 1919.
30. *Daily Herald*, 26 October 1920.
31. Ibid., 23 November 1920.
32. These and following: Labour Party, *Report of the Labour Commission on Ireland*, Labour Party, London, 1921.
33. N. A. CAB 23 September 19527: 5 February 1919.
34. *Workers' Dreadnought*, 28 June 1919.
35. Butler, David, and Freeman, Jennie, *British Political Facts 1900*–1960, Macmillan, London, 1963.
36. Ibid., p. 233.
37. Ibid., pp. 226–27.
38. Ibid., pp. 122–23.
39. Ibid., p. 98.
40. Kendall, *The Revolutionary Movement in Britain, 1900–21*, p. 293.
41. Quoted in Wrigley, Chris, 'The State and the Challenge of Labour in Britain', in Chris Wrigley (ed.), *Challenge of Labour, Central And Western Europe 1917–1920*, Routledge, London, 1993, p. 264.
42. Miliband, *Parliamentary Socialism*, p. 56.
43. David Howell, *A Lost Left*, Manchester University Press, Manchester 1986, p. 187.
44. Macfarlane, L. J., *The British Communist Party: Its Origin and Development Until 1929*, MacGibbon and Key, London, 1966, p. 27.
45. Worley, Matthew, *Labour Inside the Gates: A History of the British Labour Party Between the Wars*, I. B. Taurus, London, 2005, p. 12.
46. This is covered in Wrigley, C. J., *David Lloyd George and the British Labour Movement*, Harvester, Hassocks, 1976.
47. Coates, David, *The Labour Party and the Struggle for Socialism*, Cambridge University Press, Cambridge, p. 13.
48. Howell, *A Lost Left*, p. 189.
49. Ibid., p. 190.

50. See Rothstein, Andrew, *The Soldiers' Strikes of 1919*, Journeyman Press, London, 1985.

51. Quoted in Deacon, Alan, 'Concession and Coercion: The Politics of Unemployed Insurance in the Twenties', in Biggs, Asa, and Saville, John (eds), *Essays in Labour History 1918–39*, Croom Helm, London, 1977, p. 11.

52. Wrigley, *The Challenge of Labour*, p. 273.

53. Quoted in Crosby, Travis L., *The Unknown Lloyd George*, I. B. Taurus, London, 2014, p. 268.

54. Ibid., p. 269.

55. Taylor, A. J. P., *English History, 1914–1945*, Oxford University Press, London, 1965, p. 144.

56. Lenin, *On Britain*, p. 469.

57. Cole, *A History of the Labour Party from 1914*, p. 396.

58. Foot, Michael, *Aneurin Bevan: A Biography. Volume 1: 1897–1945*, Granada, London 1975, p. 42.

59. James Hinton, *The First Shop Stewards' Movement*, Allen and Unwin, London, 1973, p. 13.

60. Deacon, 'Concession and Coercion', in *Essays in Labour History*, p. 12.

61. Ibid., p. 12.

62. Ibid., p. 13.

63. Kendall, *The Revolutionary Movement in Britain, 1900–21*, p. 187.

64. Ibid., pp. 194–95.

65. Somerville, Henry, 'The Political Impotence of British Labour', *Studies*, March 1921, Vol. X.

66. Hobsbawm, E. J., *Revolutionaries*, Quartet, London, 1977, p. 14.

67. N.A. CAB. 24/96, C. P. 462.

68. Wrigley, *The Challenge of Labour*, p. 263.

69. Thompson, Willie, *The Good Old Cause*, Pluto Press, London, 1992, p. 7.

70. Howell, *A Lost Left*, p. 212.

71. Chesterton, G. K., *What Are Reprisals?*, Peace With Ireland Council, London (undated but probably 1921).

72. *Irish Exile*, Vol. 1, No. 1, March 1921.

73. Boyce, *Englishmen and Irish Troubles*, p. 81.

74. Berkeley, George F., *My Experiences With the Peace With Ireland Movement*, Bureau of Military History, Statement of Witness, document no. W. S. 994.

75. Ibid., p. 29.

76. Ibid., p. 38.

77. Ibid., p. 37.

78. Ibid., p. 69.

79. Boyce, *Englishmen and Irish Troubles*, p. 77.
80. Curtis, Liz, *The Cause of Ireland*, Beyond the Pale, Belfast 1994, p. 372.
81. Berkeley, *My Experiences With the Peace With Ireland Movement*, p. 37.
82. Boyce, *Englishmen and Irish Troubles*, p. 81.
83. *Irish Exile*, Vol. 1, No. 2, April 1921.
84. *Irish Exile*, Vol. 1, No. 6, August 1921.
85. See Fitzpatrick, David, 'A Curious Middle Place', in Roger Swift and Sheridan Gilley (eds), *The Irish in Britain*, Pinter Press, London, 1989, p. 44.
86. See, for example, *Catholic Herald*, 7 February 1920.
87. N.L.I., Art O'Brien Papers, MS 8432, Irish Self-Determination League, report of the Third Annual Conference, 1 April 1921, p. 10.
88. N.L.I., Art O'Brien Papers, MS 8433, Minutes of the executive committee of the Irish Self-Determination League, 23 February 1920.
89. N.A. CAB 24/118, C.P. 2455.
90. N.L.I., Art O'Brien Papers, MS 8435, Executive Committee Minutes, 23 February 1920.
91. *Catholic Herald*, 11 March 1922.
92. N.L.I., Art O'Brien Papers, MS 8432, Irish Self-Determination League report of the Third Annual Conference, 1 April 1921, p. 10.
93. Boyce, *Englishmen and Irish Troubles*, p. 86.
94. N.A. CAB. 24/113, C.P. 1977.
95. Peter Hart, *The IRA at War*, Oxford University Press, Oxford, 2003, p. 165–67.
96. N.A. CAB 24/94, C.P. 256.
97. N.A. CAB 24/98, C.P. 620.
98. *Catholic Herald*, 14 February 1920.
99. N.A. CAB 24/100, C.P. 2222.
100. *Manchester Guardian*, 29 November 1920.
101. *Catholic Herald*, 1 May 1920.
102. *Irish Exile*, New Series, November 1921, Vol. 1, No. 9.
103. N.L.I. Art O'Brien Papers, MS 8432, Irish Self-Determination League report of the Third Annual Conference, 1 April 1921, p. 10.
104. *Catholic Herald*, 7 February 1920.
105. N.A. CAB 24/100 'C.P.' 840.
106. N.L.I. Art O'Brien Papers, MS 8435, Irish Self-Determination League, First Annual Delegate Conference, p. 6.
107. *Irish Exile*, April 1921, Vol. 1, No. 2.
108. *Catholic Herald*, 7 May 1921.
109. Harding, Keith, *The Irish Issue in the British Labour Movement*, D.Phil. thesis, University of Sussex, 1983, p. 241.

110. Hart, *The IRA at War*, p. 177.
111. See for instance, BMH testimonies of Michael O'Leary (W.S. 797), Patrick O'Donaghue (W.S. 847) Sorcha McDermott (W.S. 388) Joseph Good (W.S. 388) and William Daly (W.S. 291).
112. *Daily Herald*, 1 October 1920.
113. Ibid., 19 October 1920.

3. The Labour Party

1. Shirley Williams, 'Forward', E Sylvia Pankhurst, *The Home Front*, 1932, The Cresset Library edition, London, 1987, p. xiv.
2. *The Call*, 17 January 1918.
3. Bell, *Troublesome Business*, p. 35.
4. Labour Party Conference Annual Report, January 1918, p. 12.
5. Benn, Hilary, 'James O'Grady', in Alan Haworth and Dianne Hayte (eds), *Men Who Made Labour*, Routledge, London, 2007, p. 138.
6. Labour Party Conference Annual Report, June 1918, p. 69.
7. Ibid., p. 69.
8. Ibid., p. 70.
9. *Labour Leader*, 17 June 1920.
10. Ibid., 24 June 1920.
11. Labour Party Annual Conference Report, 1920, p. 160.
12. Ibid., p. 121.
13. Ibid., p. 161.
14. Ibid., p. 162.
15. Bell, *Troublesome Business*, p. 63.
16. *Labour Leader*, 6 January 1921.
17. Bell, *Troublesome Business*, p. 65.
18. Labour Party National Executive Committee (NEC) Minutes, 6 March 1917.
19. *Call*, 17 January 1918.
20. Labour Party NEC Minutes, 13 February 1918.
21. Labour Party Annual Conference Report, June 1918, p. 15.
22. Labour Party NEC Minutes, 10 April 1918.
23. Ibid., 29 April 1918.
24. Labour Party Annual Conference Report, June 1918, p. 15.
25. Labour Party NEC Minutes, 29 April 1918.
26. Labour Party Annual Conference Report, June 1918, p. 16.
27. Labour Party NEC Minutes, 8 May 1918.
28. Labour Party Annual Conference Report, June 1918, p. 16.
29. Labour Party NEC minutes, 8 May 1918.

30. Ibid., Policy and Programme Sub-Committee, 24 July 1918.
31. Labour Party NEC Minutes, 9 October 1918.
32. Bell, *Troublesome Business*, p. 40.
33. Labour Party NEC Minutes, 9 July 1919.
34. Reported in *Workers' Dreadnought*, 3 January 1920.
35. Labour Party NEC minutes, 10 February 1920.
36. *Forward*, 3 April 1920.
37. *Labour Leader*, 15 April 1920.
37. *Socialist Review*, No. 94, July/September 1920.
38. *The Times* 7 October 1920.
39. *New Statesman*, 20 November 1920.
40. *Workers' Dreadnought*, 27 November 1920.
41. *New Statesman*, 20 November 1920.
42. Labour Party NEC minutes, 18 August 1920.
43. *Watchword of Labour*, 3 October 1920.
44. House of Commons debates, 20 October 1920.
45. Minutes of International Sub-Committee of the Labour Party NEC, TUC and PLP, 10 November 1920.
46. *Irish Times*, 17 November 1920.
47. See Chapter 10.
48. *Watchword of Labour*, 27 November 1920.
49. Labour Party NEC Minutes, 18 November 1920.
50. Mitchel, Arthur, *Labour in Irish Politics, 1890–1930*, Irish University Press, Dublin, 1974, p. 74.
51. Harding, *The Irish Issue in the British Labour Movement*, p. 284.
52. Labour Party NEC Minutes, 18 June 1921 and 24 June 1921.
53. Labour Party NEC Minutes, 12 July 1921.
54. *Daily Herald*, 7 September 1921.
55. TUC Parliamentary Committee Minutes, 6 September 1921.
56. McCarrick, Billy, *The British Labour Party, British Politics and Ireland 1886–1924*, Ph.D thesis, University of Ulster, 1992, pp. 173–74.
57. Miliband, *Parliamentary Socialism*, 1972, p. 64.
58. *Labour Leader*, 16 May 1918.
59. *Call*, 1 January 1920.
60. House of Commons debates, 15 September 1914.
61. House of Commons debates, 18 October 1916.
62. Ibid.
63. House of Commons debates, 21 May 1917. The Labour speaker was G. J. Wardle.
64. House of Commons debates, 23 October 1917.
65. Ibid.

66. Kendle, John, *Ireland and the Federal Solution*, McGill-Queens University Press, Kingston and Montreal, 1989, p. 204.
67. Bell, *Troublesome Business*, p. 38.
68. Sexton, James, *Sir James Sexton, Agitator*, Faber and Faber, London, 1936, p. 8.
69. Ibid., p. 81.
70. Bell, *Troublesome Business*, p. 44.
71. Parliamentary Labour Party, *Parliamentary Labour Party Commission of Inquiry into the Present Conditions in Ireland*, Labour Party, London, 1920.
72. Ibid.
73. Bell, *Troublesome Business*, p. 38.
74. *Watchword of Labour*, 28 February 1920.
75. *Daily Herald*, 26 February 1920.
76. Bell, *Troublesome Business*, p. 57.
77. Ibid., p. 61.
78. House of Commons debates, 21 October 1920.
79. Ibid.
80. Ibid.
81. Ibid.
82. House of Commons debates, 11 November 1920.
83. Ibid.
84. *Daily Herald*, 2 September 1921.
85. House of Commons debates, 21 October 1921.
86. Ibid., col., 1462.
87. Jenkins, Roy, *Asquith*, Collins, London, 1964, 1988 edition, p. 489.

4. The Trades Union Congress

1. J. H. Thomas, *My Story*, Hutchinson, London, 1937, p. 36.
2. Ibid., p. 32.
3. Ibid., p. 81.
4. Ibid.
5. Mackenzie, Norman, & Mackenzie, Jean (eds), *The Diaries of Beatrice Webb*, Virago, London, 1984, p. 327.
6. TUC Annual Congress Report, 1916, p. 58.
7. Ibid., pp. 404–05.
8. TUC Annual Conference Report, 1918, p. 291.
9. Minutes of the Parliamentary Committee of the TUC, 29 August 1916.
10. See: Moran, Bill, 'Jim Larkin and the British Labour Movement', *Saotha*, Vol. 4, 1978.
11. Minutes of the Parliamentary Committee of the TUC, 27 August 1918.

12. TUC Conference Report, 1918, pp. 290–91.
13. This and the following quotations from Tillet: ibid., p. 291.
14. Ibid., p. 293.
15. Minutes of the Parliamentary Committee of the TUC, 2 November 1918.
16. TUC Conference Report, 1919, p. 391.
17. Ibid.
18. *Labour Leader*, 25 September 1919.
19. Ibid., 14 August 1919.
20. Miliband, *Parliamentary Socialism*, pp. 74–75.
21. Minutes of the Parliamentary Committee of the TUC, 29 December 1919.
22. Minutes of the Parliamentary Committee of the TUC, 21 April 1920.
23. Quoted in: Townshend, Charles, 'The Irish Railway Strike of 1920: Industrial Action and Civil Resistance in the Struggle for Independence', *Irish Historical Studies*, 1979, xxi, p. 266.
24. Ibid., p. 268.
25. Minutes of the Parliamentary Committee of the TUC, 16 June 1920.
26. Ibid.
27. TUC Conference Report, 1920, p. 88.
28. Ibid., p. 115.
29. *Daily Herald*, 14 July 1920.
30. This and wording of the resolution, *Daily Herald*, 14 July 1920.
31. TUC Conference Report, 1920, p. 88.
32. *Daily Herald*, 14 July 1920.
33. *New Statesman*, 17 July 1920.
34. Somerville, 'The Political Impotence of British Labour', pp. 8–9.
35. *Daily Herald*, 14 July 1920.
36. Ibid., 26 July 1920.
37. Ibid., 27 July 1920.
38. NA, CAB. 24/118, 'C.P.' 2455.
39. TUC Conference Report, 1920, p. 64.
40. Minutes of the Parliamentary Committee of the TUC 17 November 1920.
41. Somerville, 'The Political Impotence of British Labour', p. 8.
42. Farrell, Michael, *Northern Ireland, The Orange State*, Pluto Press, London, 1981, pp. 27–28.
43. Ibid., p. 29.
44. *Journal* (of the Amalgamated Society of Carpenters, Cabinetmakers and Joiners), July 1920.
45. Ibid.
46. *Journal*, August 1920.
47. Patterson, Henry, *Class Conflict and Sectarianism*, Blackstock, Belfast, 1980, p. 130.
48. Ibid., p. 136.

49. Quoted in: Farrell, *Northern Ireland, The Orange State*, p. 31.
50. Patterson, *Class Conflict*, p. 137.
51. Ibid., p. 137.
52. *Journal*, October 1920.
53. TUC Conference Report, 1921, p. 268.
54. TUC Conference Report, 1920, p. 382.
55. Ibid., p. 382.
56. Ibid., p. 384.
57. TUC Conference Report, 1921, p. 113.
58. *Journal*, October 1920.
59. TUC Conference Report, 1921, p. 113.
60. Ibid., p. 113.
61. Minutes of the Meeting of the Executives of Trade Unions Concerned in Belfast Dispute, 26 January 1921. TUC. Library, 941.5, HD 6669.
62. *Journal*, October 1920.
63. Ibid., December 1920.
64. Ibid., November 1920.
65. Minutes of the Parliamentary Committee of the TUC, 21 September 1920.
66. Ibid., 18 October 1920.
67. TUC Conference Report, 1921, p. 277.
68. Ibid., pp. 110–11.
69. Ibid., p. 111.
70. Ibid., p. 111.
71. Ibid., p. 111.
72. Farrell, *Northern Ireland*, pp. 33–34.
73. TUC Conference Report, 1921, p. 113.
74. Ibid., p. 115.
75. Ibid., p. 115.
76. Ibid., p. 116.
77. Ibid., p. 116.
78. Minutes of the Meeting of the Executives of Trade Unions Concerned in Belfast Dispute, 26/1/21, T.U.C. Library, 941.5, HD 6669.
79. Ibid.
80. Minutes of the Parliamentary Committee of the TUC, 21/6/21.
81. Minutes of the General Council of the TUC, 7/12/21.
82. TUC. Conference Report, 1921, pp. 268–69.
83. Ibid.

5. Alternatives

1. Koss, Stephen, *The Rise and Fall of the Political Press in Britain. Volume 2: The Twentieth Century*, Hamish Hamilton, London, 1984, p. 249.

2. Minutes of the National Administrative Council (NAC) of the Independent Labour Party, 21–24 April, 1916.

3. *Labour Leader*, 6 July 1916.

4. Ibid., 12 October 1916.

5. Ibid., 26 October 1916.

6. Ibid., 28 December 1916.

7. Ibid., 1 March 1917.

8. Ibid., 29 March 1917.

9. Ibid., 26 April 1917.

10. Ibid., 3 May 1917.

11. For further details, see Chapter 8.

12. Thompson, Laurence, *The Enthusiasts – A Biography of John and Katherine Bruce Glasier*, Victor Gollancz, London, 1971, p. 32.

13. Ibid., p. 106.

14. *Labour Leader*, 17 May 1917.

15. See Chapter 1.

16. *Labour Leader*, 31 May 1917.

17. Ibid., 19 July 1917.

18. Ibid., 13 September 1917.

19. Ibid., 14 February 1918.

20. Ibid., 2 May 1918.

21. Ibid., 23 May 1918.

22. Ibid., 7 July 1918.

23. Ibid., 1 August 1918.

24. Ibid., 12 September 1918.

25. Ibid., 5 December 1918.

26. For example: ibid., 11 April 1918.

27. *Socialist Review*, Vol. 13, No. 86, July–September, 1918.

28. Minutes of NAC of the ILP, 10–11 October, 1918.

29. *Labour Leader*, 17 April 1919.

30. Ibid., 3 July 1919.

31. Ibid., 10 July 1919.

32. Ibid., 18 September 1919.

33. Ibid., 29 September 1919.

34. Ibid., 24 December 1919.

35. Independent Labour Party, *Conference Report*, 1919, p. 75.

36. *Labour Leader*, 29 January 1920.

37. Ibid., 5 February 1920.

38. Ibid., 19 February 1920.

39. Ibid., 11 March 1920.

40. Ibid., 6 May 1920.

41. Independent Labour Party, *Conference Report*, 1920, p. 96.
42. *Labour Leader*, 17 June 1920.
43. *Socialist Review*, Vol. 13, No. 94, July–September, 1920.
44. Ibid., No. 95, October–December, 1920.
45. Ibid., 13 January 1921.
46. Ibid., 21 July 1921.
47. For further details and discussion of ILP's position on Ulster, see Chapter 8.
48. Independent Labour Party, *Conference Report*, 1921, p. 141.
49. *Labour Leader*, 28 October 1920.
50. Ibid., 18 August 1921.
51. Ibid., 25 August 1921.
52. *Forward*, 1 March 1919.
53. Ibid., 3 May 1916.
54. Ibid., 20 May 1916.
55. Ibid., 22 July 1916.
56. Ibid., 4 November 1916.
57. Ibid., 1 September 1917.
58. Ibid., 1 December 1917.
59. Ibid., 10 August 1918, 24 August 1918.
60. Ibid., 8 June 1918.
61. Ibid., 26 September 1921.
62. Ibid., 10 January 1920.
63. Ibid., 3 April 1920, 7 August 1920.
64. Ibid., 6 November 1920.
65. Ibid., 20 August 1921.
66. For Wheatley's position see Ian S. Wood, 'John Wheatley, the Irish and the Labour Movement in Scotland', *Innis Review*, Vol. 31, 1980.
67. *Forward*, 27 August 1921.
68. Klugmann, James, *History of the Communist Party of Great Britain. Volume 1: Formation and Early Years 1919–24*, Lawrence and Wishart, London, 196), p. 38.
69. *Call*, 1 June 1916.
70. Ibid., 22 June 1916.
71. Ibid., 13 July 1916.
72. Ibid., 27 July 1916.
73. Ibid., 2 August 1917.
74. Ibid., 30 August 1917.
75. Ibid., 1 November 1917.
76. Ibid., 10 January 1918.
77. Ibid., 17 January 1918.

78. Ibid., 7 March 1918.
79. Ibid., 21 March 1918.
80. Ibid., 4 July 1918.
81. Ibid., 22 May 1919.
82. Ibid., 9 January 1919.
83. Issues of 9 January 1919, 13 February 1919, 6 March 1919, 22 May 1919, 21 August 1919, 18 September 1919, 25 September 1919, 16 October 1919, 13 November 1919, 11 December 1919.
84. Issues of 6 March 1919, 8 September 1919, 16 October 1919, 11 December 1918.
85. *Call*, 13 February 1919.
86. Ibid., 22 May 1919, 21 August 1919, 18 September 1919, 11/21/19.
87. Ibid., 6 March 1919.
88. Ibid., 1 January 1920.
89. Ibid., 11 March 1920.
90. *Communist*, 23 September 1920.
91. Ibid., 7 October 1920.
92. *Call*, 20 May 1920.
93. *Communist*, 30 September 1920, 25 November 1920.
94. *Call*, 10 June 1920.
95. Ibid., 25 March 1920.
96. *Communist*, 18 September 1920.
97. Ibid., 2 December 1920.
98. *Call*, 3 June 1920.
99. *Communist*, 5 August 1920.
100. Ibid., 28 October 1920.
101. Ibid., 25 November 1920.
102. Ibid., 5 March 1921.
103. Ibid., 26 March 1921, 2 April 1921, 16 April 1921.
104. Ibid., 16 April 1921.
105. Ibid., 13 January 1921.
106. Ibid., 15 October 1921.
107. Paul, William, *The Irish Crisis*, Communist Party of Great Britain, London, 1921, reprinted by and Cork Workers' Club, Cork, 1976, pp. 11–12.
108. *Communist*, 9 September 1920.
109. The Second Congress of the Communist International, *Minutes of the Proceedings*, Vol. One, New Park, London 1977, pp. 127–28.
110. Ibid., pp. 145–47.
111. Report of the Sixth Annual Conference of the British Socialist Party, 1917, pp. 4–5.
112. Report of the Seventh Annual Conference of the British Socialist Party, 1918, pp. 10–11.

113. Report of the Ninth Annual Conference of the British Socialist Party, 1919, p. 31.
114. Ibid., pp. 31–32.
115. Communist Party of Great Britain, Communist Unity Convention, 31 July to 1 August 1920, Official Report, pp. 21–22.
116. Ibid., p.60.
117. Challinor, *The Origins of British Bolshevism*, p. 268.
118. Winslow, Barbara and Pankhurst, Sylvia, *Sexual Politics and Political Activism*, UCL Press, London, 1996, pp. 123–24.
119. McBriar, *Fabian Socialism and English Politics*, pp. 344–45.
120. See, for example: Hobsbawm, E. J., *Labouring Men*, Weidenfeld & Nicolson, London, 1964, pp. 250–72.
121. Fabian Tract, No. 99, *Local Government in Ireland*, London, 1900, p. 13.
122. Shaw, Bernard (ed.), *Fabianism and the Empire*, The Fabian Society, London, 1900.
123. Quoted in Bell, *Troublesome Business*, p. 6.
124. Ibid.
125. *Workers' Dreadnought*, 6 December 1919.
126. *Fabian News*, December 1916.
127. In a letter to the *Daily News*; see Chapter 1.
128. Inglis, Brian, *Roger Casement*, Coronet Books, London, 1974, pp. 340–46, 433–37.
129. Shaw, Bernard, *How to Settle the Irish Question?*, The Talbot Press, London and Dublin, 1917, p. 9.
130. Shaw, Bernard, *Irish Nationalism and Labour Internationalism*, Labour Party, London, 1920, p. 13. For more discussion on the pamphlet, see: Bell, *The British in Ireland*, pp. 51–52.
131. Quoted in: Gibbs, A. M., 'Bernard Shaw's Other Island', in Oliver MacDonagh, W. F. Mandle and Pauric Travers (eds.), *Irish Culture and Nationalism 1750–1950*, Macmillan, London. 1983, p. 114.
132. Ibid., pp. 122–25.
133. McCarron, Margaret Patricia, *Fabianism in the Political Life of Britain 1919–1923*, Catholic University of America, Washington, 1952, p. 165.
134. Ibid.
135. Clynes, J. R., *Memoirs 1869–1924*, Hutchinson, London, 1937, p. 311.
136. The compilation and titles of lectures which follows is as advertised in the appropriate editions of *Fabian News*.
137. *Fabian News*, July, 1917.
138. *New Statesman*, 20 May 1916.
139. Ibid., 27 May 1916.
140. Ibid., 5 August 1916.
141. Ibid., 7 October 1916.

142. Ibid., 10 March 1917.
143. Ibid., 20 October 1917.
144. Ibid., 26 January 1918.
145. Ibid., 27 April 1918. For further discussion on the journal's attitude to partition, see Chapter 8.
146. Ibid., 18 May 1918.
147. Ibid., 13 April 1918.
148. Ibid., 11 May 1918.
149. Ibid., 25 January 1919.
150. Ibid., 5 July 1919.
151. Ibid., 31 January 1920.
152. Ibid., 17 April 1920.
153. Ibid., 25 September 1920.
154. Ibid., 2 October 1920.
155. Ibid., 20 November 1920, 18 December 1920, 1 January 1921.
156. Ibid., 18 December 1921.
157. Ibid., 5 July 1919.
158. Ibid., 10 June 1916.
159. Ibid., 15 July 1916.
160. Ibid., 21 October 1916.
161. Ibid., 13 April 1918.
162. Ibid., 1 September 1917.
163. Ibid., 5 July 1919.
164. Ibid., 17 July 1920.
165. Ibid., 24 July 1920.
166. Ibid., 4 September 1920.
167. Ibid., 11 September 1920.
168. Ibid., 25 September 1920.
169. Ibid., 2 October 1920.
170. Ibid., 16 October 1920, 23 October 1920.
171. Ibid., 20 November 1920.
172. Ibid., 27 November 1920.
173. Ibid., 8 December 1920.
174. Holroyd, Michael, *Bernard Shaw. Volume 2: 1898–1918. The Pursuit of Power*, Penguin, London, 1989, p. 320.
175. Ibid., p. 318.

6. Voices from Below

1. *The Times*, 30 October 1920.
2. *Workers' Dreadnought*, 9 October 1920.

3. *Call*, 6 May 1920.
4. Lenin, *On Britain*, p. 456.
5. N.A. CAB. 24/118, 'C.P.' 2455.
6. Bell, *British in Ireland*, p. 56.
7. House of Commons debates, 19 March 1921.
8. *Catholic Herald*, 22 January 1921.
9. *Labour Leader*, 30 September 1920.
10. Ibid., 23 December 1920.
11. *New Statesman*, 5 August 1916.
12. Ibid., 31 January 1920.
13. Ibid., 20 August 1921.
14. N.A. CAB. 24/116, 'C.P.' 2237.
15. Boyce, *Englishmen and Irish Troubles*, p. 46.
16. Berkeley, *My Experiences With the Peace With Ireland Movement*, p. 33.
17. *New Statesman*, 25 September 1920.
18. Berkeley, *My Experiences With the Peace With Ireland Movement*, pp. 131–33.
19. *Forward*, 9 March 1918.
20. Ibid., 2 February 1918.
21. *Labour Leader*, 25 September 1919.
22. Ibid., 1 April 1921.
23. Ibid., 15 April 1921.
24. Ibid., 22 April 1921.
25. Ibid., 6 December 1920.
26. Ibid., 30 December 1920.
27. Ibid., 20 January 1921.
28. Ibid., 25 August 1921.
29. *Forward*, 25 December 1920.
30. *Labour Leader*, 19 October 1916.
31. Ibid., 12 May 1918.
32. Ibid., 16 October 1918.
33. Ibid., 25 May 1919.
34. Ibid., 27 November 1919.
35. Ibid., 29 July 1920.
36. Ibid., 26 February 1920, 4 March 1920.
37. Ibid., 15 July 1920.
38. Ibid., 22 July 1920.
39. Ibid., 2 September 1920.
40. Ibid., 23 September 1920.
41. Ibid., 21 October 1920.
42. Ibid., 30 December 1920. I have been unable to trace this pamphlet.

43. Ibid., 17 February 1921.
44. Ibid., 24 February 1921.
45. Ibid., 10 March 1921.
46. Ibid., 24 March 1921.
47. Ibid., 29 April 1921.
48. Ibid., 20 May 1921.
49. Ibid., 7 July 1921.
50. Ibid., 1 September 1921.
51. Ibid., 2 December 1920.
52. Council of Action, *Report of Special Conference of Labour on the Russian Polish War*, London, 1920, p. 3.
53. Lenin, *On Britain*, p. 469.
54. N.A. CAB.24/118, 'C.P.' 2455.
55. See: White, Stephen, 'Labour's Council of Action 1920', *Journal of Contemporary Studies*, Vol. 9, No. 4, 1974.
56. Ibid., p. 102.
57. Labour Party Archives (LPA), CA/GEN/595.
58. LPA CA/GEN/596.
59. LPA. CA/GEN/1013.
60. LPA. CA/GEN file.
61. White, *Misfit*, p. 106.
62. Ibid., p. 106.
63. L.P.A. CA/GEN/755.
64. LPA CA/GEN/1756.
65. Quoted in: White, *Misfit*, p. 111.
66. Ibid., p. 116.
67. L.P.A. CA/GEN 1015.
68. *Watchword of Labour*, 28 August 1920.
69. Labour Party Annual Conference Report, 1921, p. 24.
70. Hamilton, Mary Agnes, *Arthur Henderson: A Biography*, London and Toronto, William Heinemann, 1938, p. 207.
71. N.A. CAB. 24/118, 'C.P.' 2474.
72. N.A. CAB. 24/118, 'C.P.' 2475.
73. N.A. CAB. 24/118, 'C.P.' 2493.
74. N.A. CAB. 24/120, 'C.P.' 2603.
75. N.A. CAB. 24/120, 'C.P.' 2667.
76. *Daily Herald*, 18 January 1921.
77. Ibid., 21 January 1921.
78. Ibid., 22 January 1921.
79. Ibid., 26 January 1921.

80. Ibid., 28 January 1921.
81. Ibid., 3 February 1921.
82. Ibid., 4 February 1921.
83. Ibid., 7 February 1921.
84. Ibid., 8 February 1921.
85. Ibid., 10 February 1921.
86. Ibid., 11 February 1921.
87. Ibid., 16 February 1921.
88. For example, *Daily Herald* reports of meetings in Bath, Worcester, Nottingham (25 January 1921), Burnley, Norwich (26 January 1921), Southport (3 February 1921), Wolverhampton (7 February 1921), Ashton-Under-Lyne and Wellingborough (8 February 1921).
89. Thomson, Sir Basil, *The Scene Changes*, Collins, London, 1939, p. 393.
90. Cole, *A History of the Labour Party*, p. 109.
91. Boyce, *Englishmen and Irish Troubles*, p. 80.
92. *New Statesman*, 12 March 1921.
93. Labour Party NEC minutes, 22 April 1921.
94. Labour Party Conference Agenda, 1919, 1920 and 1921.
95. *Daily Herald*, 26 January 1921, and *Forward*, 29 January 1921.
96. BMH, W.S. 797, Michael O'Leary.
97. *Liverpool Echo*, 30 April 1920.
98. Belcham, John, *Irish Catholic and Scouse*, Liverpool University Press, Liverpool, 2007, pp. 264–67.
99. *New Statesman*, 19 August 1919 and 26 August 1916.
100. *Catholic Herald*, 3 January 1920.
101. Art O'Brien Papers, National Library of Ireland, MS 8429, 8430; Irish Self-Determination of Great Britain, *Report of the Third Annual Conference*, 1922, p. 9.
102. *Catholic Herald*, 1 May 1920.
103. The most sustained and detailed account of which is in the classic: Denvir, John, *The Irish in Britain from the Earliest Times to the Fall of Parnell*, Kegan Paul, London, 1892.
104. Boyce, *Englishmen and Irish Troubles*, p. 69.
105. *Daily Herald*, 11 February 1921.
106. *Labour Leader*, 17 February 1921.
107. *Daily Herald*, 14 February 1921.
108. *The Times*, 12 February 1921.
109. Ibid., 12 February 1921.
110. Ibid., 18 February 1921.
111. All comments, *The Times*, 18 February 1921.

112. White, *Misfit*, p. 105.

113. ILPTUC. *Conference Report 1921*, p. 26.

7. Socialism and Nationalism

1. *Labour Leader*, 28 March 1920.

2. Hobsbawm, E. J., *The Age of Empire*, Cardinal, London, 1989, p. 142.

3. Hobsbawm, E. J., *Nations and Nationalism Since 1780*, Cambridge University Press, Cambridge, 1992, p. 108.

4. Hobsbawm, *Age of Empire*, p. 144.

5. For further detail and discussion, see: Hobsbawm, *Age of Empire*, pp. 142–64.

6. Joll, James, *The Second International*, Routledge and Kegan, London, revised edition 1977, p. 114.

7. Ibid., p. 125.

8. Clark, Charles, *Sleepwalkers*, Penguin, London 2012, p. 245.

9. For details of this debate see: Lowy, Michael, 'Marxists and the National Question' in *New Left Review 96*, March/April 1976.

10. Joll, *Second International*, p. 182.

11. Lowy, *New Left Review 96*, p. 92.

12. Ibid., p. 86.

13. Lenin, V. I., *On the National Question and Colonial Questions*, Progress Publishers, Moscow, 1977 edn, p. 6.

14. Ibid., pp. 7–8.

15. Ramsay MacDonald, James, 'Labour and the Empire', 1907, as reproduced in: Dowe, Robert E., *Society and the Victorians, No. 22*, Harvester University Press, Sussex, 1974, p. 49.

16. Ibid., p. 108.

17. Ibid., pp. 73–78.

18. Ibid., p. 102.

19. Alfred Cobban, *The Nation State and National Self-Determination*, Collins, London, 1969, p. 50.

20. Ibid., p. 53.

21. Bell, *British in Ireland*, p. 37.

22. *Labour Leader*, 30 August 1917.

23. Labour Party, *Labour and the New Social Order*, Labour Party, 1918, p. 22.

24. Cobban, *Nation State*, pp. 61–62.

25. McCardle, Dorothy, *The Irish Republic*, Gollancz, London, 1937, pp. 310–11.

26. *Call*, 7 June 1917.

27. Ibid., 10 January 1918.

28. Ibid., 24 April 1918.

29. *Labour Leader*, 18 January 1917, 22 February 1917.

30. Bell, *British in Ireland*, p. 36.

31. Marx, Karl and Engels, Friedrich, *On Ireland*, Progress Publishers, Moscow, 1971. For summaries and discussion, see Jackson, *Irish in Britain*; Clarkson, J. D., *Labour and Nationalism in Ireland*, AMS Reprint, New York, 1925; Woodis, Jack, 'Ireland – Common Cause of British and Irish People', *Marxism Today, July 1973*; Cummins, Ian, *Marx, Engels and National Movements*, Croom Helm, London, 1980.

32. Marx, Karl and Engels, Friedrich, *Selected Correspondence*, Progress Publishers, Moscow, 1965, p. 237.

33. Ibid., pp. 196–97.

34. Ibid., p. 280.

35. Cummins, *Marx, Engels*, p. 113.

36. Ibid., p. 115.

37. See, for example: Berresford Ellis (ed.), *James Connolly*; Ransom, Bernard, *Connolly's Marxism*, Pluto Press, London, 1980; Anderson, W. K., *James Connolly and the Irish Left*, Irish Academic Press, Dublin, 1994; Newsinger, John, 'Irish Labour in a Time of Revolution', *Socialist History*, Vol. 22, 2002.

38. Berresford Ellis (ed.), *James Connolly*, p. 145.

39. Quoted in: Dudley Edwards, Owen and Pyle, Fergus, 1916, *The Easter Rising*, MacGibbon and Kee, London, 1968, p. 129.

40. Irish Labour Party and Trades Union Congress, *Irish Labour and its International Relations*, 1919 – as reprinted by the Cork Workers' Club, Cork, (no date), p. 31.

41. Ibid., p. 47.

42. Ibid.

43. See also: O'Conner, Emmet, *Reds and the Green, Ireland, Russia and the Communist Internationals*, UCD, Dublin, 2004, pp. 27–28.

44. Irish Labour Party and Trades Union Congress, *Irish Labour*, p. 53.

45. *The Second Congress of the Communist International, Minutes of the Proceedings: Volume 1*, New Park Publications, London, 1977, p. 317.

46. For more on this, see: O'Conner, Emmet, *Syndicalism in Ireland 1917–1923*, Cork University Press, Cork, 1988.

47. Bertil Hessel (introduction), *Theses Resolutions and Manifestos of the First Four Congresses of the Third International*, Ink Links, London, 1980, p. 76.

48. Lenin, V. I., *On National Liberation and Social Emancipation*, Progress, Moscow, 1986, pp. 136–37.

49. Second Congress of the Communist International, *Minutes*, Vol. One, p. 128.

50. *Communist*, 16 April 1921.
51. *Workers' Dreadnought*, 28 February 1920.
52. *Socialist*, 13 February 1919.
53. Ibid., 20 March 1918.
54. Ibid., 15 May 1919.
55. Ibid., 3 April 1919.
56. *Communist*, 15 October 1921.
57. Cummins, *Marx, Engels*, p. 112.
58. Bell, *British in Ireland*, pp. 224–26.
59. Quoted and discussed in Anderson, *James Connolly*, p. 47.
60. Letter and comment, *Labour Leader*, 18 January 1917.
61. Ibid., 8 March 1920.
62. Minutes of the NAC of the ILP, 5 February 1918, London School of Economics, M 897: 7.
63. *Labour Leader*, 7 June 1917.
64. Ibid., 21 June 1917.
65. Ibid., 12 July 1917.
66. For further details of McLoughlin, see: McGuire, Charlie, 'An Irish Revolutionary in Britain: S McLoughlin and the British Socialist Movement', *Irish Studies Review*, Vol. 16, No. 2, May 2008.
67. Ibid., quoting: *Socialist*, 27 May 1920.
68. *Call*, 30 May 1918.
69. *Workers' Dreadnought*, 28 February 1920.
70. *Forward*, 15 July 1916.
71. *Socialist Review*, No. 99, October–December 1921.
72. *Call*, 1 August 1918.
73. Ibid., 1 January 1920.
74. *Communist*, 2 April 1921.
75. *Workers' Dreadnought*, 3 January 1920.
76. *Plebs*, January 1922.
77. *Workers' Dreadnought*, 13 November 1920.
78. *Plebs*, December 1921.
79. *Communist*, 25 November 1920.
80. *Call*, 6 March 1918.
81. *Forward*, 25 June 1916.
82. Ibid., 1 December 1917.
83. *Communist*, 16 April 1921.
84. *Labour Leader*, 11 October 1917.
85. Ibid., 26 February 1920.
86. *Forward*, 5 April 1919.
87. 84., *Labour Leader*, 16 May 1918.

88. Shaw, Bernard, *Irish Nationalism and Labour Internationalism*, Labour Party, London, 1920, p. 5.
89. *Workers' Dreadnought*, 17 May 1919.
90. Ibid., 24 May 1919.
91. Ibid., 20 December 1919.
92. Ibid., 10 January 1920.
93. Ibid., 20 October 1920.
94. *Forward*, 6 April 1918.
95. Ibid., 5 February 1921.
96. *Labour Leader*, 22 May 1919.
97. *New Statesman*, 1 September 1917.
98. Larkin, Emmet, *James Larkin*, NEL, London, 1968, p. 57.
99. *Call*, 22 January 1920.
100. *Communist*, 25 November 1920.
101. *Workers' Dreadnought*, 14 August 1920.
102. Ibid., 20 October 1920.
103. *New Statesman*, 8 February 1919.
104. *Labour Leader*, 11 July 1918.
105. Ibid., 23 May 1918.
106. *Socialist Review*, No. 95, Oct/Dec, 1920.
107. Ibid., No. 96, Jan./March 1921.
108. *Workers' Dreadnought*, 10 May 1920.
109. N.A. CAB. 24/122, 'C.P' 2859.
110. *New Statesman*, 18 January 1919.
111. Ibid., 2 July 1921.
112. Report of the Seventh Annual Conference Report of the British Socialist Party, 1918, p. 11.
113. *Forward*, 4 November 1916.
114. Ibid., 2 December 1916.
115. Ibid., 30.12/16.
116. Ibid., 20 January 1917.
117. Ibid., 3 July 1920.
118. *Forward*, 15 January 1921.
119. Paul, William, *The Irish Crisis*, (CPGB, London 1921), Cork Workers' Club, Cork, (no date), p. 9.
120. Townshend, *The Republic*, p. 43.
121. *Workers' Dreadnought*, 9 October 1920.
122. *Call*, 11 December 1919.
123. Ibid., 21 August 1919.
124. *Communist*, 23 September 1920.

125. Second Congress of the Communist International, *Minutes*, Vol. One, p. 128.
126. See, for instance, Lenin, *On the National and Colonial Questions*, pp. 1–19, in the course of which Lenin cites Marx's writings on Ireland.
127. Maclean, John, *In the Rapids of Revolution*, Allison and Busby, London, 1978, pp. 161–62.
128. Ibid., p. 178.

8. Ulster

1. Gwynn, Denis, *The History of Partition*, Browne and Nolan, Dublin, 1950, p. 437.
2. Ibid., p. 43.
3. Lyons, *Ireland Since the Famine*, p. 300.
4. Gwynn, *History of Partition*, p. 17.
5. Lyons, *Ireland Since the Famine*, p. 304.
6. Bell, *British in Ireland*, p. 17.
7. Ibid., p. 17. See also: Patterson, Henry, *Class Conflict and Sectarianism*, Blackstaff, Belfast, 1980.
8. Bell, *British in Ireland*, p. 19.
9. This debate is reproduced in: The Cork Workers' Club, *The Connolly/ Walker Controversy: On Socialist Unity in Ireland*, No. 9 in The Cork Workers' Club Historical Reprints series, Cork, 1974.
10. For example, of the six articles reproduced in Berresford Ellis (ed.), *James Connolly*, dealing with partition, four were first published in *Forward*, as were 17 of the 32 published in Cork Workers' Club, *Ireland Upon the Dissecting Table: Connolly on Ulster and Partition*, Cork Workers' Club, Cork, 1972.
11. Connolly's participation in the Rising is controversial. See, for example: Greaves, Desmond, *The Life and Times of James Connolly*, Lawrence and Wishart, London, 1973. Howell, David, *A Lost Left*, MUP, Manchester, 1986; Ransom, *Connolly's Marxism*; Morgan, Austen, *James Connolly*, MUP, Manchester, 1988; Newsinger, 'Irish Labour...', *Socialist History*.
12. Berresford Ellis, *James Connolly*, pp. 265–66.
13. Ibid., p. 275.
14. Patterson, *Class Conflict*, p. 80.
15. Ibid., p. 84.
16. House of Commons debates, 9 March 1914.
17. House of Commons debates, 10 June 1913.
18. Boyce, *Englishmen and Irish Troubles*, p.103.
19. House of Commons debates, 24 March 1919.

20. House of Commons debates, 29 March 1920.
21. House of Commons debates, 29 November 1920.
22. House of Commons debates, 11 November 1920.
23. *Call*, 15 March 1917.
24. Ibid., 1 June 1916.
25. *Herald*, 26 June 1916.
26. *Labour Leader*, 3 May 1917.
27. Ibid., 1 January 1920.
28. Ibid., 21 July 1920.
29. Ibid., 20 October 1921.
30. Ibid., 2 September 1920.
31. *Forward*, 29 July 1916.
32. Ibid., 3 July 1920.
33. *New Statesman*, 10 June 1916.
34. Ibid., 26 January 1920.
35. Ibid., 27 April 1918.
36. Ibid., 5 July 1919.
37. Ibid., 2 July 1921.
38. There is now a vast amount of literature on this. It began with: Irish Communist Organisation, *The Economics of Partition*, Irish Communist Organisation, Dublin, 1969 (subsequently, the ICO became the BICO – British and Irish Communist Organisation). Then: Belinda Probert, *Beyond Orange and Green*, Zed, London, 1978; Geoffrey Bell, *The Protestants of Ulster*, Pluto Press, London, 1976; Austen Morgan and Bob Purdie *Ireland, Divided Nation, Divided Class*, Ink Links, London, 1980.
39. Shaw, Bernard, *Irish Nationalism and Labour Internationalism*, Labour Party, London 1920, p. 10.
40. House of Commons debates, 29 March 1920.
41. *Labour Leader*, 31 January 1918.
42. *Workers' Dreadnought*, 2 October 1920.
43. TUC Conference Report, 1919, p. 392.
44. *Communist*, 26 November 1920.
45. Jackson, T.A., *Ireland Her Own*, Lawrence and Wishart, London, 1946.
46. *Forward*, 1 September 1917.
47. Ibid., 18 October 1920.
48. *Labour Leader*, 17 November 1921.
49. Ibid., 12 December 1918.
50. *Workers' Dreadnought*, 24 January 1920.
51. *Labour Leader*, 17 July 1919.
52. Ibid., 24 January 1918.
53. *Call*, 15 March 1917.

54. Ibid., 24 August 1918.
55. *Labour Leader*, 19 August 1920.
56. *Workers' Dreadnought*, 14 August 1920.
57. *New Statesman*, 25 January 1919.
58. *Labour Leader*, 3 May 1917.
59. *Communist*, 2 September 1920.
60. *Labour Leader*, 21 July 1921.
61. Ibid., 21 July 1921.
62. *New Statesman*, 10 June 1921.
63. Second Congress of the Communist International, *Minutes*, Vol. One, p. 177.
64. *Socialist*, 24 July 1919.
65. Paul, *Irish Crisis*, pp. 4–5.
66. *Communist*, 1 October 1921.
67. *Forward*, 23 December 1916.
68. Ibid., 8 May 1920.
69. Ibid., 7 August 1920.
70. Ibid., 11 September 1920.
71. *Workers' Dreadnought*, 2 October 1920.
72. House of Commons debates, 29 March 1920.

9. The Treaty

1. House of Commons debates, 14 December 1921.
2. Pakenham, Frank, (Lord Longford), *Peace by Ordeal: The Negotiations of the Anglo–Irish Treaty, 1921*, Sidgwick and Jackson, London, 1935, 1962, p. 77.
3. Lyons, *Ireland Since the Famine*, p. 429.
4. For the full text see Pakenham, *Peace by Ordeal*, pp. 288–93.
5. Lee, *Ireland*, p. 53.
6. Pakenham, *Peace by Ordeal*, p. 274.
7. Dangerfield, *The Damnable Question*, p. 341.
8. Pakenham, *Peace by Ordeal*, p. 260. He also quotes other, more favourable press reaction.
9. Ibid., p. 261.
10. *Catholic Herald*, 10 December 1921.
11. *Irish Exile*, December 1921.
12. This and the following, *Daily Herald*, 7 December 1921.
13. Minutes of the NEC of the Labour Party, 7 December 1921.
14. This and the following individual comments, *Labour Leader*, 15 December 1921.

15. House of Commons debates, 14 December 1921.
16. House of Commons debates, 16 December 1921.
17. *Daily Herald*, 9 December 1921.
18. House of Commons debates, 16 December 1921.
19. *Widnes Weekly*, 1 April 1920.
20. *Workers' Dreadnought*, 24 December 1921.
21. Clynes, J. R., *Memoirs, 1869–1924*, Hutchinson, London, 1937, p. 316.
22. *Daily Herald*, 6 December 1921.
23. Ibid., 7 December 1921.
24. Ibid., 14 December 1921.
25. *Labour Leader*, 8 April 1921.
26. Ibid., 22 December 1921.
27. *Labour Leader*, 15 December 1921.
28. Independent Labour Party, *Conference Report*, 1922, p. 85.
29. *New Statesman*, 10 December 1921.
30. *Workers' Dreadnought*, 24 December 1921.
31. Ibid., 31 December 1921.
32. William Gallagher, *Last Memoirs*, Lawrence and Wishart, London 1960, p. 172.
33. This account is from Thomas J. Morrissey, *William O'Brien, 1881–1968*, Four Courts Press, Dublin 2007, p. 200.
34. Gallagher, *Last Memoirs*, p. 172.
35. *Communist*, 17 December 1921.
36. T. A. Jackson, *Solo Trumpet*, Lawrence and Wishart, London, 1933, p. 163.

10. Conclusions

1. Thomas, *My Story*, pp. 187–88.
2. Clynes, *Memoirs*, p. 209.
3. Holroyd, *Bernard Shaw*, p. 39.
4. Winslow, Barbara, *Sylvia Pankhurst, Social Politics and Political Activism*, University College London Press, London, 1996, p. 103.
5. *Herald*, 16 November 1918.
6. *Catholic Herald*, 21 August 1920.
7. Irish Self-Determination League, Third Annual Conference Report, 1922, p. 4.
8. Morrissey, *William O'Brien*, p. 124.
9. *Watchword of Labour*, 28 August 1920.
10. Keohane, Leo, *Captain White*, Merrion Press, Dublin, 2014, p. 189.
11. *Catholic Herald*, 27 March 1920.

12. Ibid., 3 July 1920.
13. Ibid., 10 January 1920.
14. Ibid., 3 January 1920.
15. Ibid., 23 October 1920.
16. Thomas, J. H., *When Labour Rules*, Collins, London, 1920, p. 147.
17. *Irish Exile*, July 1921.
18. *Forward*, 2 October 1920.
19. Ibid., 18 August 1920.
20. Gallagher, Tom, *Glasgow, The Uneasy Peace*, Manchester University Press, Manchester, 1987, p. 88.
21. Ibid., p. 88.
22. *Forward*, 7 September 1919.
23. Quoted in Bealey, Frank, *The Social and Political Though of the Labour Party*, Weidenfeld and Nicolson, London, 1970, p. 69.
24. *Watchword of Labour*, 28 February 1919.
25. Quoted in, O'Conner, *Syndicalism in Ireland*, p. 41.
26. *Communist Review*, Vol. 1, No. 1, May, 1921.
27. Lenin, *On Britain*, p. 464.
28. *Forward*, 3 July 1920.
29. *Daily Herald*, 29 October 1920.

Bibliography

Manuscript Sources

British Trade Union Congress:
Minutes of the Parliamentary Committee Minutes of the General Council.
Minutes of the Meeting of the Executives of Trade Unions Concerned in Belfast Dispute.

National Archive:
Cabinet Papers: CAB.24/96-120.
Independent Labour Party:
Minutes of the National Administrative Council.

Labour Party:
National Executive Committee Minutes.

Art O'Brien Papers:
(National Library of Ireland) MS 8429–8435.

Academic Manuscripts:
Harding, Keith, *The Irish Issue in the British Labour Movement*, Ms, D.Phil. thesis, University of Sussex, 1983.
McCarrick, Billy, *The British Labour Party, British Politics and Ireland 1886–1924*, Ms, PhD thesis, University of Ulster, 1992.
Stubbs, Barry, *The British Labour Party and Ireland, 1900–1951*, M.Phil. thesis, London School of Economics, 1976.

Bureau of Military History

Berkeley, George F., *My Experiences With the Peace With Ireland Movement*, W.S. 994.
Daly, William, W.S. 291.
Good, Joseph, W.S. 388.
O'Leary, Michael, W.S. 797.
O'Donaghue, Patrick W.S. 847.
McDermott, Sorcha, W.S. 388.

Contemporary Newspapers and Periodicals

Catholic Herald
Communist

Communist Review
Daily Herald
Dreadnought
Fabian News
Forward
Herald
Irish Exile
Irish Times
Journal (of the Amalgamated Society of Carpenters, Cabinetmakers and Joiners)
Labour Leader
Manchester Guardian
New Statesman
Plebs
Socialist
Socialist Review
Studies
The Times
Watchword of Labour
Woman's Dreadnought
Workers' Dreadnought

Contemporary Printed Political Material

British Socialist Party: Annual Conference Reports.
British Trades Union Congress: Congress Reports.
Communist Party of Great Britain Communist Unity Convention: Official Report.
Council of Action Report: Special Conference of Labour on the Russian Polish War, 1920.
House of Commons: Parliamentary Debates.
Irish Labour Party and Trades Union Congress: Conference Reports.
Irish Self Determination League: Conference Reports.
Independent Labour Party: Annual Conference Reports.
Labour Party: Agendas of Annual Conference.
Labour Party: Annual Conference Reports.

Books, Pamphlets and Articles

Anderson, Perry, *Arguments Within English Marxism*, Verso, London, 1980.
Anderson, W. K., *James Connolly and the Irish Left*, Irish Academic Press, Dublin 1994.

Bealey, Frank, *The Social and Political Thought of the Labour Party*, Weidenfeld and Nicolson, London, 1970.

Beckett, J. C., *The Making of Modern Ireland*, Faber and Faber, London, 1966.

Bell, Geoffrey, *The British in Ireland*, Pluto Press, London, 1984.

Bell, Geoffrey, *Protestants of Ulster*, Pluto Press, London, 1976.

Bell, Geoffrey, *Troublesome Business*, Pluto Press, London, 1982.

Belcham, John, *Irish, Catholic and Scouse*, Liverpool University Press, Liverpool, 2007.

Benson, John, The Working Class in Britain 1850–1939, Longman, London, 1989.

Biggs, Asa and Saville, John (editors), *Essays in Labour History 1918–39*, Croom Helm, London, 1977.

Boyce, D. G., *Englishmen and Irish Troubles: British Public Opinion and the Making of Irish Policy, 1918–22*, Jonathan Cape, London, 1972.

Bullock, Alan, *The Life and Times of Ernest Bevin. Volume I: Trade Union Leader 1881–1940*, Heineman, London, 1960.

Butler, David and Freeman, Jennie, *British Political Facts 1900–1960*, Macmillan, London, 1963.

Challinor, Raymond, *The Origins of British Bolshevism*, Croom Helm, London, 1971.

Chesterton, G. K., *What Are Reprisals?*, Peace With Ireland Council, London, 1918.

Clark, Charles, *Sleepwalkers*, Penguin, London, 2012.

Clarkson, J. D., *Labour and Nationalism in Ireland*, 1925, AMS Reprint, New York, 1923.

Clynes, J. R., *Memoirs 1869–1924*, Hutchinson, London, 1937.

Coates, David, *The Labour Party and the Struggle for Socialism*, Cambridge University Press, Cambridge, 1975.

Cobban, Alfred, *The Nation State and National Self-Determination*, Collins, London, 1969.

Cole, G. D. H., *A History of the Labour Party from 1914*, Routledge and Kegan Paul, London, 1946.

Cole, G. D. H., and Postgate, Raymond, *The Common People*, University Paperbacks, Methuen, London, 1964.

Communist International, *The Second Congress of the Communist International: Minutes of the Proceedings: Volume 1*, New Park, London, 1977.

Coogan, Tim Pat, *Ireland Since the Rising*, Pall Mall Press, London, 1966.

Cork Workers' Club, *The Connolly/Walker Controversy*, Cork Workers' Club, Cork, 1974.

Cronin, Sean, *Irish Nationalism*, Pluto Press, London, 1983.

Crosby, Travis. L., *The Unknown Lloyd George*, I. B. Taurus, London, 2014.

Cummins, Ian, *Marx and the National Movements*, Croom Helm, London, 1980.

Curtis, Liz, *The Cause of Ireland*, Beyond the Pale, Belfast, 1994.

Dangerfield, George, *The Damnable Question*, Quartet, London, 1979.

Dangerfield, George, *The Strange Death of Liberal England*, Macgibbon and Kee, London, 1966.

Denvir, John, *The Irish in Britain from the Earliest Times to the Fall of Parnell*, Kegan Paul, London, 1892.

Dowse, Robert, *Left in the Centre*, Longman, London, 1966.

Ellis, Peter Berresford, *James Connolly Selected Writings*, Penguin, London, 1977.

English, Richard, *Irish Freedom*, Pan, London, 2006.

Fabian Society, *Fabian Tract No. 99, Local Government in Ireland*, Fabian Society, London, 1907.

Farrell, Michael, *Northern Ireland, The Orange State*, Pluto Press, London, 1981.

Foot, Michael, *Aneurin Bevan: A Biography. Volume 1: 1897–1945*, Granada, London, 1975.

Foster, R. F., *Modern Ireland*, Penguin, London, 1989.

Foster, R. F., *Vivid Faces*, Allen Lane, London, 2014.

Hywel, Francis, and Smith, David, *The Fed: A History of the South Wales Miners in the Twentieth Century*, Lawrence and Wishart, London 1980.

Gallagher, Tom, *Glasgow The Uneasy Peace*, Manchester University Press, Manchester, 1987.

Gallagher, William, *Last Memoirs*, Lawrence and Wishart, London, 1960.

Gibbs, A. M., 'Bernard Shaw's Other Island', in Oliver MacDonagh, W. F. Mandle and Pauric Travers (eds.), *Irish Culture and Nationalism 1750–1950*, MacMillan, London, 1983.

Mandle, W. F. & Travers, Pauric (eds.), *Irish Culture and Nationalism 1750–1950*, Macmillan, London, 1983.

Greaves, Desmond, *The Irish Transport and General Workers Union*, Gill and Macmillan, Dublin, 1982.

Greaves, Desmond, *The Life and Times of James Connolly*, Lawrence and Wishart, London, 1973.

Gwynn, Denis, *The History of Partition*, Browne and Nolan, Dublin, 1950.

Hamilton, Mary Agnes, *Arthur Henderson*, Heinemann, London, 1938.

Hart, Peter, *The IRA at War*, Oxford University Press, Oxford, 2003.

Hattersley, Roy, *David Lloyd George*, Little Brown, London, 2010.

Hayte, Dianne, *Men Who Made Labour*, Routledge, London, 2007.

Hessel, Bertil, 'Introduction', *Theses, Resolutions & Manifestos of the First Four Congresses of the Third International*, Ink Links, London, 1980.

Heyck, Thomas, *The Dimensions of English Radicalism: The Case of Ireland*, University of Ilinois, Illinois, 1974.

Hinton, James, *The First Shop Stewards Movement*, Allen and Unwin, London, 1973.

Hobsbawm, E. J., *The Age of Empire*, Cardinal, London, 1989.

Hobsbawm, E. J., *Labouring Men*, Weidenfeld and Nicolson, London, 1964.

Hobsbawm, E. J., *Nations and Nationalism Since 1780*, Cambridge University Press, Cambridge, 1991.

Hobsbawm, E. J., 'Problems of Communist History', *New Left Review*, No. 54, March/April 1969.

Hobsbawm, E. J., *Revolutionaries*, Quartet, London, 1977.

Holton, Bob, *British Syndicalism 1900–1914*, Pluto Press, London, 1976.

Holroyd, Michael, *Bernard Shaw. Volume 2: 1898–1918, The Pursuit of Power*, Penguin, London 1989.

Howell, David, *British Workers and the Independent Labour Party Party, 1888–1906*, Manchester University Press, Manchester, 1983.

Howell, David, *A Lost Left*, Manchester University Press, Manchester, 1986.

Inglis, Brian, *Roger Casement*, Coronet, London, 1974.

(British and) Irish Communist Organisation, *The Economics of Partition*, Dublin, 1969.

Irish Labour Party and Trades Union Congress, *Irish Labour and International Relations*, Cork Workers' Club, Cork, undated.

Jackson, J. A., *The Irish in Britain*, Routledge & Kegan Paul, London, 1964.

Jackson, T. A., *Ireland Her Own*, Lawrence and Wishart, London, 1946.

Jackson, T. A., *Solo Trumpet*, Lawrence and Wishart, London, 1933.

Jenkins, Roy, *Asquith*, Collins, London, 1964.

Joll, James, *The Second International*, Routledge, Kegan and Paul, London, 1977.

Jones, Barry and Keating, Michael, *Labour and the British State*, Clarendon Press, Oxford, 1985.

Kapp, Yvonne, *Eleanor Marx The Crowded Years*, Virago, London, 1979.

Kendall, Walter, *The Revolutionary Movement in Britain 1900–21*, Weidenfeld and Nicolson, London, 1969.

Kendle, John, *Ireland and the Federal Solution*, McGill-Queens University Press, Kingston and Montreal, 1989.

Keohane, Leo, *Captain White*, Merrion Press, Dublin, 2014.

Klugmann, James, *History of the Communist Party of Great Britain. Volume 1: Formation and Early Years 1919–24*, Lawrence and Wishart, London, 1969.

Koss, Stephen, *The Rise and Fall of the Political Press in Britain. Volume 2: The Twentieth Century*, Hamish Hamilton, London, 1984.

Kostick, Conor, *Revolution on Ireland*, Pluto Press, London, 1996.

Labour Party, *Labour and the New Social Order*, Labour Party, London, 1918.

Labour Party, *Report of the Labour Commission on Ireland*, Labour Party, London 1921.

Lansbury, George, *My Life*, Constable, London, 1926.

Larkin, Emmet, *James Larkin*, Nel Mentor, London, 1968.

Lee, J. J., *Ireland, 1912–85*, Cambridge University Press, Cambridge, 1989.

Lenin, V. I., *On Britain*, Progress Publishers, Moscow, 1973.

Lenin, V. I., *On National Liberation and Social Emancipation*, Progress Publishers, Moscow, 1986.

Lenin, V. I., *On the National Question and Colonial Questions*, Progress Publishers, Moscow, 1967.

Levenson, Samuel, *James Connolly*, Martin, Brian and O'Keefe, London, 1973.

Leventhal, F. M., *Arthur Henderson*, Manchester University Press, Manchester, 1989.

Lowy, Michael, 'Marxists and the National Question', *New Left Review*, 96, March/April 1976.

Lyons, F. S. L., *Ireland Since the Famine*, Fontana, London, 1973.

McBriar, A. M., *Fabian Socialism and Politics*, Cambridge University Press, London, 1966.

Macardle, Dorothy, *The Irish Republic*, Gollancz, London, 1937.

McCareron, Margaret Patricia, *Fabianism in the Political Life of Britain 1919–23*, Catholic University of America Press, Washington, 1952.

MacDonald, James Ramsay, *Labour and the Empire*, Labour Party, London, 1907.

Macfarlane, L. J., *The British Communist Party*, Macgibbon and Kee, London, 1966.

Mackenzie, Norman & Jeanne, (eds.) *The Diaries of Beatrice Webb*, Virago, London, 1987.

MacIntyre, Stuart, *A Proletarian Science: Marxism in Britain, 1917–33*, Cambridge University Press, Cambridge, 1980.

McKinley, Alan and Morris, R. J., *The ILP on Clydeside*, Manchester University Press, Manchester, 1991.

McLean, Lain, *The Legend of Red Clydeside*, John Donald, Edinburgh, 1982.

Maclean, John, *In the Rapids of Revolution*, Allison and Busby, London, 1978.

Maclean, John, *Ireland's Tragedy, Scotland's Disgrace* (pamphlet), June 1920 (Troops Out Movement reprint, undated).

McGuire, Charlie, 'An Irish Revolutionary in Britain: S McLoughlin and the British Socialist Movement', *Irish Studies Review*, Vol. 16, No. 2, May 2008.

Martin, David, and Rubinstein, David (eds), *Ideology and the Labour Movement*, Croom Helm, London, 1979.

Marx, Karl, and Engels, Frederick, *On Ireland*, Progress Publishers, Moscow, 1971.

Marx, Karl, and Engels, Frederick, *Selected Correspondence*, Progress Publishers, Moscow, 1965.

Miliband, Ralph, *Parliamentary Socialism*, Merlin, London, 1972.

Milton, Nan, *John Maclean*, Pluto Press, London, 1973.

Minkin, Lewis, *The Labour Party Conference*, Manchester University Press, Manchester, 1980.

Mitchel, Arthur, *Labour in Irish Politics, 1890–1930*, Irish University Press, Dublin, 1974.

Moore, Bill, *How We Stopped War Against Russia but Failed to Free Ireland*, Holberry Society, Sheffield, 1981.

Moran, Bill, 'Jim Larkin and the Brtish Labour Movement', *Saotha*, Vol. 4, 1978.

Morgan, Austen, *Labour and Partition*, Pluto Press, London, 1991.

Morrissey, Thomas J., *William O'Brien, 1881–1968*, Four Courts Press, Dublin, 2007.

Neal, Frank, *Sectarian Violence, The Liverpool Experience*, Manchester University Press, Manchester, 1988.

Newsinger, John, 'Irish Labour in Time of Revolution', *Socialist History*, No. 22, 2012.

O'Conner, Emmet, *Reds and the Green, Ireland, Russia and the Communist Internationals*, UCD, Dublin, 2004.

O'Connor, Emmet, *Syndicalism in Ireland 1917–1923*, Cork University Press, Cork, 1988.

Pakenham, Frank, *Peace By Ordeal*, NEL, London, 1962.

Pankhurst, E. Sylvia, *The Home Front*, 1932, Cresset 1987.

Pankhurst, Sylvia (and others), *Rebel Ireland*, Workers' Socialist Federation, London, 1919.

Patterson, Henry, *Class Conflict and Sectarianism*, Blackstaff, Belfast, 1980.

Paul, William, *The Irish Crisis 1921 – The C.P.G.B. Stand*, Cork Workers' Club, Cork, 1975.

Pelling, Henry, *The British Communist Party*, A. & C. Black, London, 1978.

Pelling, Henry, *Origins of the Labour Party*, Macmillan, London, 1954.

Ransom, Bernard, *Connolly's Marxism*, Pluto Press, London, 1980.

Rothstein, Andrew, *The Soldiers' Strike of 1919*, Journeyman Press, London, 1987.

Rothstein, T., *From Chartism to Labourism*, Martin Lawrence, London, 1929.

Saville, John (ed.), *Democracy and the Labour Movement*, Lawrence and Wishart, London, 1959.

Saville, John, *The Labour Movement in Britain*, Faber and Faber, London, 1988.

Sexton, James, *Sir James Sexton, Agitator*, Faber and Faber, London, 1936.

Shaw, Bernard (ed.), *Fabianism and the Empire*, Grant Richards, London, 1900.

Shaw, Bernard, *How To Settle the Irish Question*, Talbot Press (Dublin) and Constable (London), 1917.

Shaw, Bernard, *Irish Nationalism and Labour Internationalism*, Labour Party, London, 1920.

Smillie, Robert, *Life for Labour*, Mills and Boon, London, 1924.

Smith, Joan, 'Labour Tradition in Glasgow and Liverpool', *History Workshop*, Issue 17, September 1984.

Stevenson, John, *Popular Disturbances in England*, Longman, New York, 1979.

Somerville, Henry, 'The Political Impotence of British Labour', *Studies*, Vol. X, March 1921.

Stewart, A. T. Q., *The Ulster Crisis*, Faber and Faber, London, 1969.

Swift, Roger and Gilley, Sheridan (eds), *The Irish in Britain 1815–1939*, Pinter Press, London, 1989.

Sheridan, Roger and Gilley, *The Irish in the Victorian City*, Croom Helm, London, 1985.

Tanner, Duncan, *Political Change and the Labour Party*, Cambridge University Press, Cambridge, 1990.

Taylor, A. J. P., *English History 1914–45*, Oxford University Press, London, 1965.

Thomas, J. H., *My Story*, Hutchinson, London, 1937.

Thomas, J. H., *When Labour Rules*, Collins, London, 1920.

Thomson, Sir Basil, *The Scene Changes*, Collins, London, 1939.

Thompson, Willie, *The Good Old Cause*, Pluto Press, London, 1992.

Thorne, Will, *My Life Battles*, George Newnes, London, 1925, Lawrence and Wishart, 1998.

Thompson, Laurence, *The Enthusiasts – A Biography of John and Katherine Bruce Glacier*, Victor Gollancz, London, 1971.

Townshend, Charles, *Easter 1916*, Allen Lane, London, 2005.

Townshend, Charles, 'The Irish Railway Strike of 1920: Industrial Action and Civil Resistance in the Struggle for Independence', *Irish Historical Studies*, xxi, 1979.

Townshend, Charles, *The Republic*, Allen Lane, London, 2013.

White, Stephen, 'Labour's Council of Action 1920', *Journal of Contemporary Studies*, Vol. 9, No. 4, October 1974.

Wilson, Trevor, (ed.) *The Political Diaries of C. P Scott, 1911–28*, Collins, London, 1970.

Winslow, Barbara, *Sylvia Pankhurst, Social Politics and Political Activism*, University College London Press, London, 1996.

Wrigley, Chris, *Arthur Henderson*, GPC Books, Cardiff, 1990.

Wrigley, Chris (ed.), *A Companion to Early Twentieth Century Britain*, Blackwell, Chichester, 2009.

Wrigley, Chris (ed.), *Challenge of Labour, Central and Western Europe 1917–1920*, Routledge, London, 1993.

Wrigley, C. J., *David Lloyd George and the British Labour Movement*, Harvester, Hassocks, 1976.

Worley, Matthew, *Labour Inside the Gates*, I. B. Taurus, London, 2005.

Yeates, Padraig, *City in Wartime, Dublin 1914–18*, Gill and Macmillan, Dublin, 2011.

Index

Lightning Source UK Ltd.
Milton Keynes UK
UKHW011846210121
377477UK00001B/70